THE ENLARGEMENT OF THE HEART

Archimandrite Zacharias

THE ENLARGEMENT
OF THE HEART

"Be ye also enlarged" (*2 Corinthians 6:13*)
in the Theology of Saint Silouan the Athonite
and Elder Sophrony of Essex

edited by
Christopher Veniamin

MOUNT THABOR PUBLISHING
2006

THE ENLARGEMENT OF THE HEART:
"BE YE ALSO ENLARGED" (2 CORINTHIANS 6:13)
IN THE THEOLOGY OF SAINT SILOUAN THE ATHONITE
AND ELDER SOPHRONY OF ESSEX

Copyright © 2006 by The Stavropegic Monastery of St. John the Baptist, Essex, UK

Published by
Mount Thabor Publishing
PO Box 109
South Canaan, PA 18459 USA

www.thaborian.com

Printed in the United States of America

ISBN 0-9774983-2-8

Library of Congress Control Number: 2006930326

Contents

FOREWORD

The Enlargement of the Heart is an astoundingly majestic presentation of the nature and purpose of human existence in two of the most important figures in contemporary Orthodoxy: St. Silouan the Athonite (1866–1938) and his faithful disciple, Elder Sophrony of Essex (1896–1993). Himself a disciple of the Elder Sophrony, Archimandrite Zacharias bears witness to the golden thread of Tradition passing on from one generation to the next, inasmuch as his writings evince that inspiration which is born of the undistorted vision of Christ in glory. And as he demonstrates with seemingly effortless ease, it is in the clarity of this vision that the divine purpose in the creation of man is made manifest.

About the Author

A member of the Patriarchal Stavropegic Monastery of St. John the Baptist, England, founded by his spiritual father and mentor, and the official translator of Elder Sophrony's writings from Russian into Greek, the Very Reverend Dr. Zacharias Zacharou holds degrees in Theology from the Institute of St. Sergius in Paris, France, and the University of Thessalonica, Greece, also receiving the degree of Doctor of Theology from the latter institution for his work on the theology of Elder Sophrony, which was published in English as *Christ, Our Way and Our Life: A Presentation of*

the Theology of Archimandrite Sophrony, translated by Sister Magdalen
(South Canaan, PA: Saint Tikhon's Seminary Press, 2003).

About the Book

Father Zacharias' *The Enlargement of the Heart* consists of a series
of lectures delivered in Wichita, Kansas at the 2001 Clergy
Brotherhood Retreat of the Antiochian Orthodox Christian
Church, and an Appendix comprised of two lectures given at
a one-day Conference on Monasticism. The Retreat was held
under the direction of the Right Reverend Basil Essey, Bishop of
Wichita and the Diocese of Mid-America on February 6–9, and
the Conference was organized by his Chancellor, Schemamonk
Paul, at the Cathedral Church of St. George in Wichita on February
10. Each lecture is published here in full together with its *Asides*
and corresponding *Questions & Answers* (with the exception of
the first lecture, which had no session for *Questions & Answers*).

A Note on Biblical References

For purely practical reasons, the numbering of Old Testament
passages has been given according to the Massoretic (Hebrew) text,
followed by most English translations of the Bible. The Roman
numeral Lxx is used to draw the reader's attention to instances
where the Septuagint (Greek) text differs from the Massoretic.
New Testament quotations are occasionally corrected in favour
of a more literal translation of the original Greek.

C. V.

SAINT TIKHON'S ORTHODOX THEOLOGICAL SEMINARY
FEAST OF ST. SILOUAN THE ATHONITE
24 SEPTEMBER, 2006

SAINT SILOUAN THE ATHONITE
AND HIS DISCIPLE THE ELDER SOPHRONY

WHILE THE BLESSED ELDER and Founder of our monastery, Fr. Sophrony, was still with us, some of us, his monks, would eagerly seek out an opportunity – "in season, out of season" (2 Tim. 4:2) – to visit him and speak with him, in order to be edified by his word. Every contact with him was a source of inspiration, and new horizons in life would open up before us. The Elder lived in a little house at the edge of the monastic enclosure. In his last years he was considerably weakened by old age, and he would sleep in intervals in an armchair. It often happened that in our contact and our conversations with the people that visited us, a question or a problem would arise that solicited the Elder's attention. We would go to him seeking the appropriate answer. Occasionally, we would find him asleep, gently shake his armchair and wake him up. We then presented him with the question that had arisen. He would open his eyes and almost immediately the answer would flow from his mouth. It was a marvellous and wondrous event. His voice came from beyond, from heaven. The grace that was in his words would inform and irresistibly convince not only our own hearts but also the hearts of the people that had sought the will of God, and to whom we transmitted his words.

Aside: The great miracle that impressed me (living near Fr. Sophrony) more than anything else, was the word of God coming from his mouth, and the energy of grace with which it was loaded. We had seen so many miracles when he was praying for people, and none of us cared for that, because he himself did not pay attention to them. But we were all astonished – amazed – at the word proceeding from his mouth.

As I was saying last night to our Bishop, once he prayed for an ill person a second time and the person was not healed, but he was very happy, because, while he was reading the prayers the second time, he lifted up his stole from the sick man and he said to him: "Look! We are not wonderworkers, we are priests, and pray for the reconciliation of people with God." And somehow Fr. Sophrony was sad and did not want to pray any more. Then the man looked at him with a smile, and said: "Yes, I am not healed physically, but my soul is healed." Because he was a man who did not have faith, he doubted, and it was his wife and his mother-in-law who brought him almost by force to the monastery for Fr. Sophrony to read prayers for him. And I am telling you, the joy of Fr. Sophrony for that was much greater than when he was reading prayers, and miracles were happening in a very astonishing manner.

Once, a man who had his face deformed by a stroke was in bed and almost dying. Fr. Sophrony taking Fr. Kyrill, our Abbot, with him went and read prayers for him. And Fr. Kyrill came back in great awe saying to me, "You know, while *Pappous* – "Grandfather", as he called Fr. Sophrony – was reading the prayer, the face of the ill person was straightening up." And the prophecy of Ezekiel came to my mind about the dry bones coming up, forming a skeleton, nerves and flesh, and the spirit of life coming to them (Ezek. 37:1–14). And even for such healings he was not so happy as that time when the man said, "My soul is healed." *End of aside.*

Our Elder had one belief and one desire. He was totally convinced that the word of God, for our generation, was given to his Spiritual Father, St. Silouan. He fervently desired to make this word known if possible to all the people of the earth, for whom the saint himself had prayed that they may know God in the Holy Spirit. He wanted us also to participate in this fervent desire of his, thereby repaying as far as possible our sacred obligation to the saint. One day, during one of our conversations, he urged me to write down the thoughts that, from time to time, I had expressed to him concerning the significance of St. Silouan's words. Rather perplexed, for I was acutely aware of my own poverty and insignificance, I asked him, "But Father, what can I write?" His answer was to be my guiding star. In a decisive tone he said to me, "Repeat what I have said!" From that moment I understood a phenomenon which is frequently observed in the history of monasticism.

Every time that the word of God would be born in the heart of a holy monk, and by which word God would announce the deep judgments of His will to the people, then generations of monks from that same monastery would repeat the words of that holy monk. They would analyse his thought and enlarge upon his teachings. Thus, they would rekindle in the souls of their contemporaries the true faith, which was once for all delivered to the saints (cf. Jude 1:3). In this way, they would minister to the word of the saints, they would build the Body of the Church, and at the same time work out their own salvation. A characteristic example of this was at work for centuries in the Monastery of Studios, in Constantinople.

Consequently, the suggestion and the request of our Elder Sophrony to occupy ourselves with the word of his holy teacher, Silouan, is both meet and right according to tradition. The only stumbling block is my own unworthiness. The Elder himself, humbly and without doubt, believed that the direct and revelatory word of God came to St. Silouan; while Fr. Sophrony likened his own work to that of a postman delivering a letter that he has not written himself. He is merely transmitting the word of his Father, Silouan, whose word merits the closest attention and profound study, not just in an objective manner, but by personally living it.

With apostolic conviction, St. Silouan's word gives the answers to the urgent problems and impasses of his generation. It also defines with Christlike authority the sure criteria for determining the authentic knowledge of God in the Orthodox Church. For example, he says somewhere that the criterion for the presence of the Holy Spirit, the criterion of the truth, is the love for one's enemies.

This God-inspired servant of the word of Christ, Silouan, is the subject of today's lecture. The basic and main source that informs us about his life and teaching is the book *Saint Silouan the Athonite* by Fr. Sophrony. From the very first page, this book deals with deep issues and poses the question about the meaning of life in all its tragic gravity. It reveals the inscrutable abyss of the judgments of our God on the one hand, and on the other, the impossibility for man, in his present state, to fathom the divine will, and be incorporated in the pre-eternal design of the Holy Trinity concerning him. According to the testimony of his closest disciple, St. Silouan's exterior life does not present any special interest. A few events prior to his becoming a monk bear witness to his strong constitution, his dynamic character, and his religious profundity. Otherwise, his life passed by almost unnoticed. Even during his monastic years, comparatively few people recognized him for what he was. But blessed Silouan was an event so magnificent that he attracted God's attentiveness, and the love of all the saints in heaven. His whole being – soul, mind and body – became a scented vessel, full of the grace of the Holy Spirit. His heart was like a beautiful garden, full of flowers, in the depth of which the Lord was well-pleased to have a luminous and beloved dwelling.

St. Silouan was born in 1866 in the village of Shovsk, which was in the district of Lebedinsk in the province of Tambov. He came from a rather wealthy peasant family, which had been freed from serfdom but a few decades earlier. He arrived on Athos in 1892, and received the monastic tonsure in the Great Monastery of the Holy Great Martyr Panteleimon in 1896. He became a *great schema* monk in 1911. He fulfilled various obediences in the monastery of his repentance, where he also served as a steward for many years. There he led the ascetic life for forty-six years. The greatest spiritual event of his life was the vision of the living Christ, whom he was counted worthy of beholding six months after his entry into the monastery. During those months he had given himself over with great ardour to unceasing and agonizing prayer. This vision filled both his heart and his whole body with the strength of the Holy Spirit, and illumined his mind with the knowledge of the great mystery of Christ. In the ensuing long years of his life, he tirelessly and ceaselessly witnessed to the fact that "God is love" (1 John 4:8, 16) – indescribable and infinite love. Full of days, and replete with peace and grace, he departed to the Lord in 1938.

By God's providence, Fr. Sophrony also dwelt in the same monastery for about fourteen years. During the final years of St. Silouan's life, especially from 1931 until the day of his repose, it happened that Fr. Sophrony was his closest disciple and certainly the one most able to relate the saint's life. He assumed this undertaking after much thought and hesitation. Fr. Sophrony's exclusive aim in portraying the spiritual life of the saint was to benefit the faithful, for in the person of the saint the most precious aspects of the mystery of our faith were recapitulated. As the Elder mentions, it was in fear that he presented this testament. As all the works of the Lord are awesome and wonderful, so too is a spiritual testament awesome and wonderful, and in order for this testimony to divine love to be received, a readiness for struggle and self-denial is required. Our God is a difficult God, because He offers a cross; but that cross is the expression of His love "to the end" (John 13:1). That is why love is so terrible.

St. Silouan came from a pious family that was permeated with the spirit of evangelical love. This spirit also marked his own life, but he nevertheless did not escape the temptations of the world, nor the errors of youth. Two events precipitated his turning to repentance. The first was when he heard an account of the life and miracles of a Russian saint, John Sezenov (1791–1839). As he was listening to the story of the saint's holy life, he reflected, "If he was a holy man, it means that God is here with us, so there is no point in me going off to search for Him";[1] and his faith was rekindled. God had given him this thought in order to dispel the doubts concerning the existence of God that had been instilled into him by a travelling book-peddler, when he was but four years old. Thus, with this thought, he had regained his faith, and ardently clung to the memory of God, praying much and with tears. It was during this time that the desire for the monastic life was born in his heart. His father, though, firmly advised him to wait for a while, and to go to a monastery after finishing his military service. Meanwhile, he remained in this unusual state of grace for three months.

Thereafter, this first grace of God's calling departed, and Simeon, which was Silouan's name in the world, returned to the usual worldly ways of the youth of his village. It was then that God allowed him to fall into two grave sins for which he later repented all his life. Thus did the clamour of youth begin to drown the first summons to a monastic life of spiritual striving, and he lost the grace that initially visited him.

But God, who had chosen him, foreseeing his grateful fidelity, called him again, this time by means of a vision. As his biographer, the Elder Sophrony relates, after one of those days of wild living, having fallen asleep, he dreamt that he saw a snake crawl down his throat. Feeling revolted, he jumped up, whereupon he heard a voice saying to him, "Just as you found it loathsome to swallow a snake in your dream, so I find your ways ugly to look upon."[2] This voice was extraordinarily sweet and beautiful. St. Silouan was convinced beyond doubt that it was the voice of the Blessed Virgin. This voice, with its beauty, meekness and unutterable sweetness, transmitted to the youth the energy of divine grace, which overwhelmed him and shook him to the core of his being. To the end of his life he gave thanks to the Mother of God for not despising him in his sinful state, but deigned to come to him herself and to lift him from his fall. The fact that he had not been deemed worthy of seeing the Mother of God he attributed to the state of his impurity that possessed him at that time.

This new calling, which occurred a short while before his military service, radically changed his life and decisively determined the course of his future. He felt terribly ashamed about his past, and this shame was transformed into the most fiery and ardent repentance before God. *Aside:* It is the same in the sacrament of confession: the more shame we feel when we make ourselves naked before God, the more strength is given to us to overcome sin and the passions. *End of aside.*

With this repentance came a new outlook on life and the world. He became deeply aware of the fleetingness of the visible world, and the importance of eternity as the final destiny of our temporary existence. This outlook could be clearly seen in his conversations and in his behaviour as a whole with the people around him. During one of these village fêtes, as Fr. Sophrony relates, Simeon noticed a middle-aged fellow villager who was playing the accordion and dancing. This surprised him and drawing him aside he asked him, "How can you play and dance like that, Stepan – didn't you once kill someone?" He had indeed killed a man in a drunken brawl. Stepan answered Simeon and said to him, "When I was serving my sentence I prayed and prayed, begging God to forgive me. And He did. That is why I can now play and be happy."[3] Simeon, who was himself burdened by the guilt of his own sins, understood how it is that one can ask God for forgiveness and obtain it, as in the example of Stepan. This event confirmed him further in his own personal repentance.

He joined the army while in this ardent state of repentance, and his term went smoothly. He proved himself to be conscientious, kind and willing. He became a pleasant, amiable and precious counsellor to his companions. His mind, though, was preoccupied by the Last Judgment, and his care was how to please the Lord, who was increasingly revealing to him the vanity of the world. Towards the end of his military service, he went to visit St. John of Kronstadt in order to ask for his prayers and blessing for the future. The saint was absent and Silouan, or rather Simeon as he was then, left him a note with but a few words: "*Batioushka*, I want to become a monk. Pray that the world does not hold me back."[4] He returned to his barracks and, as he himself professed, from the very next day he felt the flames of hell roaring around him.

While in this state, he arrived on Mount Athos and entered the Russian Monastery of St. Panteleimon. There Simeon began his new life and his struggle for eternal salvation. He spent his first few days in complete quiet, remembering and writing down all his sins in order to make a general confession, as was the Athonite custom and practice. The tormenting awareness of hell which accompanied him, together with the grace from the sacrament of confession, engendered in the soul of the young novice an unrestrainable and ardent repentance. After his confession, the confessor encouraged him to rejoice for the forgiveness that he had received, and for the new life which the Lord had given him on Athos, that "haven of salvation."[5] Inexperienced as he was, Simeon accepted the advice of the confessor with simplicity and faith, and delivered himself to the joy of his new life. He did not realize that the spiritual warrior must be temperate even in his joy, and so it was not long before he lost the spiritual intensity of prayer that he had since his visit to Kronstadt. He was assaulted by carnal thoughts, and his mind was assailed by seductive images. Passionate thoughts suggested to him: "Return to the world and get married." When he went to confession, his confessor said to him, "Never let your mind linger on such suggestive thoughts as those, and if they come – drive them away at once."[6] *Aside:* Fr. Sophrony often repeated to us like a slogan: "Do not surrender your mind to the thought!" *End of aside.* The first fall in thought made Brother Simeon soberly watchful for the rest of his life. He was so shaken by this event that from that day not once during the forty-six years of monastic life did he ever accept a single carnal thought. The realization of human frailty and the possibility of perdition, even in the monastery, were a precious lesson for him. *Aside:* I think what shook him more than anything here was the contrast between the state of grace in which he was and the fall, even though only in the mind, by the carnal thoughts. The contrast was so enormous – that was the thing that shook him. *End of aside.* Yet again the enemy took advantage of Simeon's bitter remorse for his "slip" by suggesting to him that he should depart into the desert in order more easily

to find salvation. However, he understood the deception of
this thought, and in the depths of his soul he decisively said to
himself: "I will die here for my sins."[7] *Aside:* Man is strong when
he makes this decision. The greatest gift we have is to be able to
die the way we like; and if we die properly, the way which is right,
that is the greatest gift. *End of aside.*

Steadily, with time, Brother Simeon was taught the spiritual
science of the monastic tradition of Athos, which is permeated
by the unceasing remembrance of God. This tradition is cultivated daily in the life of the monks through the rich programme
of work, services, vigils, confession, Communion, and by the
verbal instructions of the Abbot, confessors, and generally all the
advanced ascetics in the monastery. The most prominent place in
the rule of life of the monks is given to the Jesus Prayer. Simeon
was also struggling to acquire this interior prayer, which can be
said everywhere and at all times. His biographer mentions that
after three weeks, while praying before the icon of the Mother
of God, the prayer entered his heart and continued there day and
night, of its own accord. This unceasing invocation of the name
of Jesus delighted his soul and gave him the strength to fulfil
with exactitude all the obediences and labours that constitute
the monastic polity. Nevertheless, he was not yet able to remain
steadfast in grace, and sometimes vacillated between thoughts of
vainglory and despair.

One night, after the vision of a strange light that had appeared
in his cell, and even penetrated into his chest, devils began to
appear to him. Naïve and inexperienced as he was, he would
converse with them as with ordinary people. These demonic
assaults increased. Sometimes they would say to him that he was
holy and other times that he would not be saved. Once, the novice
Simeon asked one of these demons: "Why do you contradict
yourselves, sometimes saying to me that I am holy, and at other
times that I shall not be saved?" The devil mockingly answered
him: "We never tell the truth."[8]

The novice, Brother Simeon, gave himself over to extreme
asceticism, and prayed with great zeal and ardour in order to

counteract the demonic assaults which tormented his soul. He
slept a total of two hours in the twenty-four hour cycle, and
that in snatches of fifteen to twenty minutes, while sitting on
a backless stool. He observed great abstinence in food. He was
immersed in a deep and prolonged mourning that reached the
boundaries of despair. He was further burdened by a heavy and
tiresome obedience at the mill, which he carried out beautifully
and with exactitude.

Simeon persevered in this trial for six months. The terror of
eternal perdition and the horror of despair crushed him all the
more until he foundered. Sitting in his cell before vespers, in
extreme despair he thought: "God is inexorable. He will not be
moved by entreaty." Following this thought, a very dangerous
thought, he felt utterly forsaken, and his soul plunged into the
darkness of an indescribable agony. He remained in this state for
around an hour. After a while, he made his way to vespers, in the
church of the Holy Prophet Elijah, which was close to the mill.
Despite the agony of his soul he managed to utter, "Lord Jesus
Christ, have mercy upon me a sinner." He then saw to the right of
the Royal Doors, in the place of the icon of the Saviour, the living
Christ. *Aside:* Utter, extreme self-emptying changed to a state of
divine vision, as we see in the life of our Lord; in one moment
he was saying, "My God, My God why hast thou forsaken me?"
(Matt. 27:46, Mark 15:34), and in the next He is saying to the thief,
"Verily I say unto thee, to day shalt thou be with me in paradise"
(Luke 23:43). *End of aside.* The Lord appeared to the young novice
in a manner surpassing all understanding, and his whole being,
even his body, "was filled with the fire of the grace of the Holy
Spirit – that fire which the Lord brought down to earth with His
coming". The vision exhausted Simeon and the Lord vanished.[9]
Aside: Here St. Silouan describes the vision like the Gospel
describes the Transfiguration of our Lord – in a few words. In
the descriptions of the Gospel there is no room for imagination, because the events that are described surpass anything that
man can imagine. So the Gospels are just very sober and simple
accounts. *End of aside.*

But however brief and simple the description of St. Silouan's vision (while still a novice) seems to be, nevertheless as a spiritual event it surpasses anything the created mind could imagine. The state he had experienced then is beyond description. According to the perceptive witness of his biographer, this event essentially constituted the true spiritual rebirth of the saint. This was accomplished through his illumination by the divine light and by his spirit being caught up "to heaven, where he heard ineffable words".[10] Henceforth, Silouan would never forget the serene, meek and humble gaze of Christ, all-forgiving and boundlessly loving, who is replete with inexpressible joy, and attracts man's entire being to Himself.

Elder Sophrony marvels how Simeon, simple and untutored as he was, during the vision immediately recognized both Christ, who had appeared to him, and the Holy Spirit, who acted within him. In his writings, he never ceases to repeat that he recognized Christ by the Holy Spirit, that he saw God in the Holy Spirit. He certified that when the Lord manifests Himself to the soul, she cannot but recognize in his Person both her Creator and her God.[11]

Aside: And Fr. Sophrony used to tell us that the proof of the authenticity of St. Silouan's vision was that immediately after the vision this illiterate peasant, who maybe never saw a world map, began to pray for the whole world; and not just in a sporadic manner as the peasants in the East do all the time: As they sit to eat they thank God for what He has provided for them, and beg Him that no one in the whole world be deprived of His bounties. This is very common in the East, where you hear the old people say, "Save my children and all the children of the world". Their prayer embraces the whole world. I used to hear that kind of prayer all the time when I was a boy. But Fr. Sophrony says that with St. Silouan, after he saw Christ, it was a more systematic and ardent prayer, as an urgency of his spirit. That was the proof of the authentic vision, because at the moment of the vision, when one beholds something divine, there is a communion of states; the state of Christ was imparted to St. Silouan at that moment. And as Christ is the New Adam, bearing in himself the whole

Adam, and intercedes before the Father for the whole Adam, he who receives His state (at the moment of the vision) cannot but have the same spirit and the same prayer. *End of aside.*

The appearance of Christ to Brother Simeon undoubtedly was the greatest and most important event of his life. It could not but have had a radical influence on the rest of his life. Christ is the way and the truth and the life (*cf.* John 14:6). Now Simeon knew *what* and *whom* to seek for, and *in what manner. Aside:* It is very important to meet the Lord even once. *End of aside.* From the saint's writings we learn that from the moment when God appeared to him, the Holy Spirit witnessed to him of his salvation. His whole being was apprised that his sins had been forgiven. The previous experience of the flames of hell was now turned into Paschal spiritual joy and delight. Simeon's *kenosis* before the vision was replaced with a wealth of divine love. He lived that great and blessed peace, the peace of reconciliation with God. Grace filled his soul and his body, and his heart could receive all men within it, with ease.[12] *Aside:* In Greek, forgiveness, *synchoresis,* means to be contained together in the heart. This comes from the word *synchorô,* which is made up of the verb *chorô,* meaning to occupy a space or place, and the prefix *syn,* which simply means together; and so *synchoresis* conveys the notion of being together in the same place, that is to say, in the heart. *End of aside.* His body became light and was no longer a burden; his mind was illumined and became familiar with the essential mysteries of the word of God.[13] His converse with God poured forth in sweetness and delight and his compassion urged him to ardent prayer for the whole world: "I pray Thee, O merciful Lord, for all the peoples of the earth, that they may come to know Thee by the Holy Spirit."[14] He prayed that every mortal soul be given the same and equal portion of the divine inheritance that had befallen him. Like the Lord during the Last Supper, he was full of sadness for the world. In the seventeenth chapter of St. John's Gospel there is one phrase that betrays, unravels His Spirit: "O righteous Father, and the world hath not known thee" (John 17:25), showing where the mind of the Lord was all the time. Sometime later, when Simeon was serving in the refectory, a similar grace to the first again visited him, but with a somewhat lesser force; thereafter the grace of God gradually began to diminish. The memory of Christ's visitation and the new awareness that it brought to his soul remained in his mind, but the sensation of peace and joy that his heart experienced now receded, giving way to fear, the fear of abandonment.[15]

After the lightning flash of divinity, the darkness of this present life becomes even more terrible and impenetrable. Simeon began to seek ways of restoring himself to the grace he had known. However, this is "not of yourselves: it is the gift of God", as St. Paul says (cf Eph. 2:8). Together with an enhanced spiritual struggle in all the sectors of his life, the young monk took recourse in the counsels of his Spiritual Father and in the ascetical writings of the Holy Fathers. It was then that he became aware that he had been made worthy of a rare gift, but he could not understand how his mind which had been enlightened by the boundless light of the knowledge of God could now be darkened again by demonic apparitions. These had ceased for a while after the visitation of the Lord. So why this change, especially now that he was struggling to the extreme to keep the Gospel commandments?

In order to solve this problem, Simeon visited the Elder Anatoly at the Old Russikon. *Aside:* Old Russikon is an hour's walk from behind the Monastery of St. Panteleimon, in the forest. *End of aside.* After listening to the novice's life story and to what he had suffered from the demons, the Elder counselled him and instructed him in the art of mental vigilance, which the novice did not yet possess. However, he failed to conceal his amazement at the novice's achievements, and at the end of his instructive and profitable discourse he exclaimed, "If you are like this *now,* what will you be by the time you are an old man!"[16] This remark of the Elder occasioned the temptation of vainglory and threw the young novice into the most subtle, the most complicated and the most difficult of spiritual combats. Vainglory and pride bring about every spiritual calamity and downfall. Now the eyes of the left hand of the young monk had been opened and beheld the gifts that the right hand of the Lord bestows.

Aside: The Desert Fathers used to say that if we praise our brother untimely, you know, out of season, it is like delivering him to the demons; it needs a lot of discernment to praise. We praise people when we want to encourage them, to support them, if they are in difficulty or crushed, but we need to be careful with monks. Do not praise monks. They lose their mind more easily than others. *End of aside.*

Simeon found himself delivered yet again into a highly unequal combat with the demons. Grace retreated, his heart grew cold, prayer lost its ardour, his mind was distracted and passionate thoughts began to assail him anew. The soul that has known the yonder life, the heart that has tasted of the sweetness of the Holy Spirit, the mind that has known purity, does not want to give in to impure thoughts that have laid siege to it. But how is this to be managed? The long and weary period of alternating grace and abandonment had now begun.

Simeon was tonsured a monk and was trained in the science of spiritual warfare, most especially in the domain of mental vigilance and in the guarding of the mind from the suggestions of the enemy. Neither the gift of unceasing prayer which he possessed, nor the great gift of the vision of Christ could lead him immediately to perfection. His nature had to be transformed, in order for him to be permanently established in a state of grace and dispassion. *Aside:* The Holy Apostles at the moment of the Transfiguration fell down to the ground, but after Pentecost they were standing upright and conversing with the Lord in the Holy Spirit. *End of aside.*

Therefore, Simeon valiantly immersed himself in a life of deliberate spiritual striving, realizing that the main purpose and conclusion of such striving is the acquisition of grace. However, because Silouan had come to know God in the Holy Spirit and had been lifted up to contemplation of the universe of the Eternal Light and then had lost that grace, he now found himself in a state unimaginable to anyone who has not had the same experience. The suffering and sorrow of his soul were indescribable. His pain was of a metaphysical nature. He was prepared to deliver himself up to every struggle and hardship in order to regain that lost treasure, and to maintain the height of the revelation entrusted to him. Words cannot convey the agony of even a single night of that wrestling for grace. Silouan himself confidentially said to his disciple, "If in the beginning the Lord had not given me to know how much He loves man, I could not have survived one of those nights, and yet they were legion."[17] *Aside:* In *The Ladder* of St. John we observe the same spiritual phenomenon in the case of the "prisoners".[18] How amazingly valiant they were in their repentance. For they had seen God's Light, and so this was not something they had planned themselves. Indeed, it was Providence that pushed them into that struggle. We cannot plan our life. The spiritual life is never planned. All we do is give ourselves to God, and His Providence makes a plan for us. *End of aside.*

Silouan's titanic battle against the evil spirits lasted fifteen years, and it led him to repentance like unto Adam's, and to extreme despair. Then the Lord intervened and saved him by His word. Fr. Sophrony relates Silouan's own story as follows:

"It was fifteen years after the Lord had appeared to him, and Silouan was engaged in one of these nocturnal struggles with devils which so tormented him. No matter how he tried, he could not pray with a pure mind. At last he rose from his stool, intending to bow down and worship, when he saw a gigantic devil standing in front of the ikon, waiting to be worshipped. Meanwhile, the cell filled with other evil spirits. Father Silouan sat down again, and with bowed head and aching heart, he prayed,

"'Lord, Thou seest that I desire to pray to Thee with a pure mind but the devils will not let me. Instruct me, what must I do to stop them hindering me?'

"And in his soul he heard,

"'The proud always suffer from devils.'

"'Lord,' said Silouan, 'teach me what I must do that my soul may become humble.'

"Once more, his heart heard God's answer,

"*Keep thy mind in hell, and despair not.*"[19]

This brief discourse with God during prayer was a new, extremely important event in Silouan's life. The Lord's word to Silouan: *"Keep thy mind in hell, and despair not"*, however paradoxical it may seem to be, brought to him the seal of spiritual victory. He himself attests to this: "I began to do as the Lord told me, and my mind was cleansed, and the Spirit witnessed to salvation."[20] *Aside:* Not only is the divine state transmitted to us when we see something divine, but also when we hear the word of God. That is why the Lord said to the Jews, "How can you claim to know anything about immortal life if you have not seen the shape of God and heard His voice?" (*cf.* John 5:37). So, seeing the shape and hearing the voice transmits to man the knowledge of eternal life. *End of aside.*

The Lord suggested the vision of hell to Silouan, and he immediately surfaced, possessing a great science which restored his life, enriching him with grace and further knowledge of God. The means by which the soul is humbled, the heart made contrite, evil thoughts vanquished, and the mind cleansed, was given to him. And so grace finds a place in the believing soul. The descent to hell is that humble way which, willingly and without sin, Christ Himself walked. Thus, by obeying this word of the Lord, Silouan put himself in the humble Way of the Lord. He became his companion on the way, and was taught Christlike humility. Thus, following the Lord, he successfully passed over from the oppressive domination of the passions to freedom in the Spirit of God, from death to life. Fifteen years previously God had shown His Son to Silouan and had concluded a covenant of love with him. Now, beholding the faith of His servant, he spoke to His heart in order to establish him in the Lord's humble Way, the way which leads to fullness of life.

These are the two most important events in Silouan's life. In the first, he saw the glorified shape of the Father, and in the second, he heard His meek voice. As the Lord assures us, this is knowledge of eternal life. All the subsequent writings of the saint are but an expression of the experience and the way of life that these two primary events inspired in him. The Lord said,

"By their fruits ye shall know them" (Matt. 7:20). In the case of
Silouan, the authenticity of the vision of Christ that was given to
him can be seen in the trend of his thoughts, and in the "fruits"
he bore in his spiritual life: He was almost illiterate, and yet after
the vision he began to pray with tears *for the whole world* as for
himself. Perhaps he had never even seen a map of the world. This
signifies that at the time of the vision, the state of Christ, the "new
Adam", was transmitted to him, for Christ bears within Him the
whole of humanity, and His Spirit wants all men to be saved. This
is the apostolic enlargement and prayer that Christ's genuine
disciples receive (*cf.* 2 Cor. 6:13). Throughout the rest of his life
the saint will now ask: "I pray Thee, O merciful Lord, for all the
peoples of the earth, that they may come to know Thee by the
Holy Spirit."[21] This state came to him as a surprise. *Aside:* There
is always a surprise, as we observe in the Second Judgment: the
righteous have a surprise, and the sinners have a surprise. There
is a good surprise, and a bad surprise (*cf.* Matt. 25:31–46). *End of
aside.* This state came to him as a surprise. "I began", he said, "to
beseech God for forgiveness and He granted *not only forgiveness
but also the Holy Spirit,* and in the Holy Spirit I knew God."[22]

For one small act of repentance he was given to know the great
love and boundless goodness of Christ; his soul was captivated in
the remembrance of the meek and humble Lord (*cf.* Matt. 11:29),
a thought which would no longer let him rest on this earth. This
unceasing remembrance, like a "worm" from God – again, there
is a bad "worm" of hell (*cf.* Mark 9:44) and there is also the good
"worm" of God – would eat away at his flesh, until it had totally
assimilated him to the Beloved. "O Lord, send down Thy Holy
Spirit on earth that all nations may know Thee, and learn Thy
Love."[23] During the vision he was given to know the indescribable humility of the Lord and in a manner true to the prophets
he was placed on the humble Way of the Lord. He says, "Thou,
O Lord, shewest me Thy glory because Thou lovest Thy creature,
but do Thou give me tears and the power to thank Thee. To Thee
belongeth glory in heaven and on earth, but as for me – I must
weep for my sins."[24] These words are reminiscent of the heartfelt

sighs of the prophets upon beholding the glory of the Lord. I mention but two examples: the word of the Prophet Daniel, "O Lord, righteousness belongeth unto Thee, but unto us shame of face" (Dan. 9:7 Lxx),[25] and the sigh of Isaiah, "Woe is me! For I am undone, because I am a man of unclean lips, and I dwell in the midst of a people of unclean lips: for mine eyes have seen the King, the Lord of Hosts" (Isa. 6:5).

With simplicity and rather naively, he said that before the vision he did not even know about the Holy Spirit;[26] afterwards though, he affirmed that the Holy Spirit discloses to the soul that she is saved.[27] This grace is felt in both soul and body.[28] The soul, having known the Lord in the Holy Spirit, yearns after Him, and this desire is so strong that it detaches the soul from everything earthly.[29] The words of Christ addressed to Silouan's soul, *"Keep thy mind in hell, and despair not"*, which occurred fifteen years following the vision, gave him the means by which to be delivered from the repulsive sight of the demons, to preserve grace, transcend the pride of this world, and finally place himself continually in the humble way of Christ, following Him wherever He goeth, even into hell. By condemning himself to hell without despairing, he could remain at the limits of ascetical humility and yearn continually for the indescribable humility of Christ which he had known at the time of the vision. By so doing, he could give an ever expanding space in his soul to the Holy Spirit, for Him to come and dwell within him.

Aside: St. Silouan distinguished between two kinds of humility: ascetical humility – the highest form of which is when man considers himself "the worst of all human beings"[30] – and divine humility – "the humility of Christ", which he knew at the moment of the vision of Christ.[31] The latter is a *charismatic* humility. *End of aside.*

After these two great events in the life of Silouan, he was steadily led by the Holy Spirit towards perfection. The thoughts preserved in his notes, written near the end of his life, are directly from the Holy Spirit. He himself witnessed to this during his encounter with the ascetic Stratonicos. Questioning Stratonicos, "How do the perfect speak?" he himself gave the answer: "The perfect never say anything of themselves . . . They only say what the Spirit inspires them to say."[32] This is a great word.

The word of Silouan is the fruit of a heart on fire with the grace of the Holy Spirit. His word is meek, sweet and acts therapeutically on the soul that receives it. For this reason, in her hymnography, the Church calls Silouan "most comforting of divines" and conformed in heart to the meek and humble Christ, his "Teacher in the way of humility".[33]

Elder Sophrony was of the same spirit, and had gained a similar experience in the spiritual life as his Father, St. Silouan. Divine providence revealed this kinship through the manner by which they met and became acquainted. Here is a summary of that meeting. Fr. Sophrony had already spent about five years in the Monastery of Saint Panteleimon before becoming personally acquainted with the saint. *Aside:* He had been ordained a deacon in 1930 by Bishop Nikolai Velimirovich, who was a great friend of St. Silouan and often visited him. Fr. Sophrony told me that St. Silouan worked in the bookshop as an obedience, and on one occasion felt terribly uncomfortable, because Bishop Nikolai came and bought many books, and asked Silouan to help him to put them into his bag. And in this way he made St. Silouan handle every book. St. Silouan realized what the Bishop was doing and felt uncomfortable. So, while he was doing as Bishop Nikolai had asked, he pointed to the *Homilies* of St. Makarios and remarked: "Here is a great Father, his homilies are full of grace." To which Bishop Nikolai replied, "Nowadays, there are also Fathers equal to Saint Makarios". And St. Silouan later confessed, "I felt terribly uncomfortable after his word", for he realized that the Bishop had been speaking about him.

At a later time when Nikolai Velimirovich was ill in London, Fr. Sophrony visited him and asked him, "What do you think about the book on Silouan?" Fr. Sophrony asked for his opinion, because Fr. Justin Popovich had written a letter to Fr. Sophrony, in which he likened the writings of St. Silouan to those of St. Symeon the New Theologian. Fr. Sophrony repeated the words of Fr. Justin Popovich to Bishop Nikolai Velimirovich, who remained thoughtful for a moment, then he lifted up his head and said, "*Nyet. Nyet.* No. No. He is greater. His word is healing." Yes, that was the witness of this holy Bishop, Nikolai Velimirovich.

The ordination of Fr. Sophrony took place in the Old Russikon, behind the Monastery of St. Panteleimon, one hour's walk away. St. Silouan was walking together with Bishop Nikolai Velimirovich; Fr. Sophrony followed from behind. But it was some time after his ordination that he first spoke with St. Silouan. *End of aside.*

A little while after the Elder's ordination, a hermit monk, Fr. Vladimir, visited Fr. Sophrony at the monastery, and they discussed several spiritual issues. Fr. Vladimir, moved by the conversation and the overall spiritual atmosphere it had engendered, suddenly asked: "Fr. Sophrony, give me a word for the salvation of my soul!" The Elder, who was preparing tea for Fr. Vladimir, without hesitation replied, "Stand at the brink of the abyss of despair, and when you see that you cannot bear it any more, draw back a little and have a cup of tea", whereupon he handed him a cup of tea. This word, and especially the energy of grace that it conveyed, struck the hermit who, filled with contrition, departed and went to St. Silouan, seeking counsel and confirmation as to the authenticity and safety of this saying. The day after this little meeting, Fr. Sophrony was descending the outside stairs of the Monastery building on his way to the central court. At the same time, St. Silouan was ascending in the opposite direction from the harbour of the Monastery. Normally, they would have met outside the entrance to the church of St. Panteleimon. The Elder however, out of respect for St. Silouan – I told you earlier how he felt when censing St. Silouan – changed course in order to avoid meeting him. But St. Silouan, too, changed course, thereby making their meeting in front of the refectory inevitable. There St. Silouan asked Fr. Sophrony, "Father Sophrony, did Fr. Vladimir visit you yesterday?" And Fr. Sophrony, passing over all the usual phrases of etiquette – the intermediate stages of speech that normally occur at an encounter – simply answered, "Was I wrong?" Similarly, St. Silouan said to him, "No. But what you said was beyond the measure and strength of the brother. Come tomorrow, and let us speak together." And so the Elder visited St. Silouan, who related his own life to him. He described to him his fifteen-year struggle against the spirits of wickedness. He confided the revelatory word of Christ to him: *"Keep thy mind in hell, and despair not."* This word, which was a milestone in the saint's spiritual struggle, was in essence the same as the word given by Fr. Sophrony to Fr. Vladimir. Through the power of this word he was saved from every demonic assault, and was purified from every suggestion of pride.

Fr. Sophrony acquired such faith and reverence for Silouan that, in spirit, he would even venerate his footprints. As he himself wrote, he believed that the acquaintance and the relationship that he had with St. Silouan was the greatest gift that God had given him. This monumental event was of determinative importance to his later spiritual development and theology. Through his contact with the saint he was assured that the spirit of repentance which had so engulfed him at that time was unerring and true. He was reassured about the verity of his teaching, and through unshakeable faith in the word of the saint he gained stability in his ascetical life, and was led to dispassion. He lived the rest of his days, both in the desert and in his service in the world (to which God led him), bearing witness to the fact that it is only via the voluntary descent into hell, in obedience to the commandment, that the believer can place himself on the humble Way of the Lord, learn the indescribable humility of Christ, and be joined to Him.

It is evident from the above description of the encounter between the Elder and the saint that Fr. Sophrony had the same spirit and experience as the saint. He too had known the living God, even from his childhood. He relates: "There were occasions when, coming out of church, I would see the city [Moscow], then the whole world for me, lit by two kinds of light. Sunlight could not eclipse the presence of another Light [the Uncreated Light].'[34] Later on, as an adult, the year before he entered the Monastery, the Uncreated Light visited him after Holy Communion, on Easter Saturday. He felt it like the touch of Divine Eternity on his spirit. This heavenly Light remained with him for three days.[35] When he had become a monk this same experience was so frequently repeated, even daily, that the cessation of the vision was perceived as a fall from true ontology, from eternal life. The vision of the Uncreated Light would inspire in Elder Sophrony that self-knowledge which existed in the prophets of old, and the acknowledgement of his own sinfulness to the degree that he would regard himself as being worthy of hell, while at the same time the Lord remained for him "blessed unto all ages". His spirit, as he himself confesses, would stretch between hell and the kingdom of heaven; between the awareness of the infernal darkness within him and the vision of the infinite sanctity of our humble God. *Aside:* I remember that he once said to me, "Nothing can surprise me in the spiritual life." That is to say, he knew all the stages, like Saint Paul, who says in the Epistle to the Corinthians that "he that is spiritual judgeth all things, yet he himself is judged of no man" (1 Cor. 2:15). *End of aside.* Moreover, he adds that between these two frontiers of hell and the kingdom, the whole spiritual life of reasonable beings oscillates. In other words, there was no spiritual phenomenon or experience that could surprise him. He knew the whole range of experiences from hell to the eternal kingdom. Possessing the experience of the Uncreated Light, he was driven to repentance through the grace of life-giving despair, "charismatic despair", as he calls it, which separated him from the sensory world and rendered him passionless.

For Elder Sophrony, theology was the state of being in God. Possessing the experience we have described above, theology was for him the description of the event of his meeting with Christ, at the time when he was caught up and saw the divine Light. (For him theology was the narration of an event.) According to his writings, authentic theology consists not in the conjectures of man's reason or the results of critical research, but in the state of the life into which man is brought by the action of the Holy Spirit. Theology is then a grace of the Holy Spirit which rekindles the heart of man. Whoever has acquired this gift becomes as a light in the world, holding forth the word of life. As St. Silouan's word was perfect, for it was given by the Holy Spirit, similarly, the word of his disciple was from God. He would always ask God in prayer for a word, and would conceive in his heart a word pleasing to God and salutary to his brethren. *Aside:* You know, whenever I went to accompany him for the few minutes' walk from his house to the monastery, in order to receive someone who had come to see him, I would look to profit by asking him something about myself, but he would not let me, saying, "Ask me no questions now. Now my mind is in that person." He was praying all the time for the meeting with that person to be blessed. He did not want to be distracted for a moment. *End of aside.*

Fr. Sophrony had only one desire, that through repentance all may be saved in Christ and by Christ. He was inspired by the aim and grandeur of the service of Spiritual Fatherhood, and desired in a spirit of repentance and humility to be a "fellow worker with God" in the creation of immortal gods (*cf.* 1 Cor. 3:9). *Aside:* He found the work of a spiritual father a most creative work, because man collaborates with God in the creation of gods.[36] When I became a spiritual father he would often say, "Do not put your trust in something you have read or in something you once said which was of help to someone. Before you say anything, always bring your mind to your heart, ask God's blessing, and then speak. Ask for God's word, and then utter. You must learn this way, otherwise it will be reduced to a blind human service." He would often say that if we prayed before meeting one another – a priest with a priest, or a person with his spiritual father, a believer with his priest, or a priest with his bishop – then the meeting can be a prophetic one, because God will give utterance. He said, "If there is prayer especially from both sides, from the one who comes and the one who receives, surely then God will speak." *End of aside.*

Elder Sophrony is fit to interpret St. Silouan because he has the same spirit. Through his own personal experience, he *re*-reads, that is to say, he *re*-cognizes the spiritual life of the saint. In other words, his experience was the repetition of that of the saint. In the life of the saints, "repetition" or "copying" is the most creative act: it is the mystery of the Tradition of the Holy Spirit. The way to the acquisition of this holy Tradition was first indicated by the great Apostle Paul, "Be ye imitators of me, even as I also am of Christ" (1 Cor. 11:1). Forgive me, Fathers. Forgive me, Bishop.

Bishop Basil's Afterword: You know, we are all sons of the twentieth century, we are all born in the twentieth century and if you noticed, a few moments ago, Fr. Zacharias very calmly spoke one sentence in which he mentioned *four* saints: Elder Sophrony, asking another saint, St. Nikolai Velimirovich, what he thought about his own book about another saint, Silouan, in which he quoted another saint, Justin Popovich, all sons of the twentieth century, commenting on St. Silouan. You bring great gifts to us, Father, and this is not to praise you; this is to say that you are a faithful son of Fr. Sophrony, and for that we are most grateful. You know how the Church's understanding of Tradition comes from that Greek word, *paradosis* – "a passing on" – one person passing on something unchanged, something very valuable and precious and important, utterly important, from one generation to the next. And we have just received something precious; we are participating in Tradition in a very "existential" way. And we ask God's blessing upon Fr. Zacharias, and we thank God who is "wondrous in His saints" (Ps. 67:36 Lxx).

NOTES

1. Archimandrite Sophrony (Sakharov), *Saint Silouan the Athonite*, trans. Rosemary Edmonds (Tolleshunt Knights, Essex: Patriarchal Stavropegic Monastery of St. John the Baptist, 1991; repr. ed. Saint Vladimir's Seminary Press, 1999), p. 11.

2. *Ibid.,* p. 15.

3. *Ibid.,* p. 16.

4. *Ibid.,* p. 19.

5. *Ibid.,* p. 21.

6. *Ibid.,* p. 22.

7. *Ibid.*

8. *Cf. ibid.*, p. 24.

9. *Cf. ibid.*, pp. 25–26.

10. *Cf. ibid.*, p. 26.

11. *Ibid.*

12. *Ibid.*, p. 34.

13. *Cf. ibid.*, p. 35.

14. *Ibid.*, p. 274.

15. *Cf. ibid.*, p. 35.

16. *Ibid.*, p. 36.

17. *Ibid.*, pp. 41–42.

18. Step 5, in St. John Climacus, *The Ladder of Divine Ascent* (Boston, MA: Holy Transfiguration Monastery Press, 1991), pp. 54–66.

19. *Op. cit.*, p. 42.

20. *Cf. ibid.*, pp. 431–432.

21. *Ibid.*, p. 274.

22. *Ibid.*, p. 270.

23. *Ibid.*, p. 276.

24. *Ibid.*, p. 299.

25. We prefer the Septuagint "shame of face" to the Authorized (King James) Version's phrase, "confusion of faces".

26. *Cf. op. cit.*, p. 320.

27. *Cf. ibid.*, p. 304.

28. *Cf. ibid.*, p. 394.

29. *Cf. ibid.*, p. 301.

30. *Ibid.*, pp. 299–300.

31. *Ibid.*, pp. 277, 273.

32 *Ibid.*, p. 57.

33. The first phrase comes from the Saint's *Apolytikion* or *Troparion*, found in the *Service for Our Holy Father Silouan the Athonite*, published by the Holy Monastery of Simonos Petras (Mount Athos, 1991), pp. 2 and 18: "As preacher of the Love of Christ, sweetest among divines, art thou given to the world, O thrice-blessed one". The second phrase comes from an alternative *Apolytikion*, found on the reverse side of the Saint's icon,

produced by the Patriarchal and Stavropegic Monastery of St. John the Baptist, Essex, England: "Through prayer thou didst receive Christ as thy Teacher in the way of humility".

34. *We Shall See Him As He Is,* trans. Rosemary Edmonds (Tolleshunt Knights, Essex: Patriarchal Stavropegic Monastery of St. John the Baptist, 1988), p. 37.

35. *Cf. ibid.,* p. 178.

36. *Cf. On Prayer,* trans. Rosemary Edmonds (Tolleshunt Knights, Essex: Patriarchal Stavropegic Monastery of St. John the Baptist, 1996), p. 88.

Man's Birth into Eternal Life

SCRIPTURE SAYS that the sin of one man, our forefather, and death which came as a result of it, passed on to the whole race of men: "for all have sinned, and come short of the glory of God" (Rom. 3:23). We find ourselves, therefore, in a state contrary to nature, and far from that which God preordained for us in the beginning. We are without God in the world, and, living according to the flesh, it is impossible for us to approach the Spirit of God. In order to be regenerated into the Kingdom of God, which is "incorruptible, undefiled, and fadeth not away" (*cf.* 1 Pet. 1:4), we have need of the grace and mercy of one man again, the New Adam – Christ. The Lord Jesus calls us to this spiritual regeneration with His words: "Ye must be born again" (John 3:7).

God's calling to man is in the mind of the Maker of the world, in the pre-eternal will of the Father, and of the Son, and of the Holy Spirit. He directs him with forethought at every moment of time and in every place. Remember Job, when he put the question: "What is man, that thou shouldest magnify him? And that thou shouldest set thine heart upon him?" (Job 7:17). He then gives the answer which, in the Greek version of the Septuagint, is extremely beautiful: man holds God's attention, because he can be *katenteuktés Theou*, an "accuser of God",[1] that is, someone who can stand before His Face and even quarrel with Him; not in a bad spirit, but in order to go deeper into the love of God, and fathom His judgments (Job 7:20 Lxx). This calling is incomprehensible, great and wondrous. Its acceptance brings the grace of the Holy Spirit, which preserves and adorns man, leading him to a never-ending likeness to Christ, the Son of God. Consequently, the calling of God in Trinity is a call of love. This love, though, is not of the earth, but of heaven. God is by nature completely free, and in His relationship with man remains free from every passion and necessity. But man, too, created according to the image of God, possesses an independence which cannot be constrained. The first visitation to man of divine love comes to fruition when God finds him well-disposed to receive the energy of His grace with a good will.

In a perfect Christian life two wills must conquer: the divine and uncreated along with the created and human. The cooperation of grace with the will of man accomplishes a mystery in the life of every man, foreknown however by God the Creator. God seeks man out, desiring to give him a share of all that is His, of all the wealth of His life: "All that I have is thine" (Luke 15:31). The measure of His gift depends on man's free agreement. Where He foresees that the energy of His grace will be received with humility and gratitude, He grants it richly. Having in mind the mystery of the cooperation of the divine with the human in the spiritual life of the Christian, Elder Sophrony classified people into three categories.

"The overwhelming majority of people fit into the first category. Drawn to faith by a small measure of grace, they live their lives in a moderate effort to keep the commandments. Only towards the end, because of the pain they suffer, do they know grace to a somewhat greater extent. A certain number of them do, however, strive harder and finally receive a larger measure of grace. This happens to many monks.

"To a second category belong those who, attracted by a relatively small degree of grace, yet zealously wrestle in prayer against the passions, and in this painful struggle know greater grace; and spending the rest of their lives in still more urgent striving arrive at a high level of perfection.

"In the third and rarer category belongs the man who at the outset of his ascetic path, for his fervour, or, rather, because he is foreknown by God, receives great grace, the grace of the perfect [cf. 1 Pet. 5:10]."[2]

The Elder places St. Silouan in the third category of ascetics, those who receive the perfect gift of God's love from the outset. This event, however, makes their life a martyrdom,[3] because fallen human nature is unable to retain the fullness of grace. And Christlike love, inevitably, always suffers and undergoes great trials in this world. *Aside:* Fr. Sophrony makes an allusion to what St. Paul says in Acts, that Christ in this world is suffering (cf. Acts 26:23). *End of aside.* St. Silouan accepted God's calling, which acted in his life repeatedly and in various ways. The first time was when he heard about the life and miracles of St. John Sezenov the Recluse. But he felt the energy of the call more strongly the second time when, during the vision of swallowing the snake, he heard the words of the Mother of God admonishing him. On the third occasion the call was more imperative, by which time he had help from the prayers of St. John of Kronstadt. With the acceptance of God's calling, the grace of faith and repentance were rekindled in him. The fire of his repentance is evinced by the experience of "the flames of hell roaring" round him,[4] and the deep consciousness he had of his sins. As his biographer says, the surprisingly deep awareness of sin that he possessed was a gift of grace. His belief in the future judgment of Christ, and the fear of future condemnation which arose in his soul drove him to seek reconciliation with God the Saviour, even before his departure from this life. *Aside:* He did not live this feeling on the psychological level, but on a spiritual one. *End of aside.* Because of his sins, he considered himself "worse than a noisome cur".[5] He perceived sin not as an infringement of moral codes, but as a turning away from divine love, for which he had been created and for which he was intended. In other words, as his disciple Archimandrite Sophrony would later express, he felt himself a criminal offender against the love of the Father.[6]

Thenceforward, he would stand before God in complete humility of prophetic self-knowledge and awareness of his sinfulness. He fulfilled in a manner pleasing to God the law of Christ's word in the Gospel which states: "He that shall humble himself shall be exalted" (Matt. 23:12). Following six months of such humble and intense repentance, he was made worthy of convincing God that he belonged to Him forever, and the Lord turned towards him. *Aside:* You know, each day during Matins we read Psalm 119, where we say to God: "I am thine, save me" (Ps. 119:94). But who is man to say to God, "I am thine"? It is first necessary to convince Him of this, and once he has convinced God that he is His, then God replies in the same way that He spoke of His only-begotten Son: "Thou art my son, this day have I begotten thee" (Ps. 2:7, Acts 13:33, Heb. 5:5). From that moment on, as we say in theology, man passes from the psychological mode of existence to the ontological. *End of aside.*

Studying the mystery of repentance, the Prophet David says in his psalm, "For I said in my haste [of repentance], I am cut off from before thine eyes: nevertheless thou heardest the voice of my supplications when I cried unto thee" (Ps. 31:22). In his repentance, St. Silouan came to complete despair. *Aside:* Fr. Sophrony calls this kind of repentance "charismatic repentance", because it detaches man from everything that is created, and attaches him to everything that is uncreated, that is, God's. *End of aside.* While sitting in his cell, shortly before Vespers, he was completely crushed and thought: "God cannot be moved by entreaty". Following this dangerous thought, he felt completely abandoned by God, and his soul was plunged into the darkness of an indescribable agony for about an hour.[7] *Aside:* Who is man to stand before God and say such a word? It is a very dangerous word. We cannot enter into judgment with Him. He is always victorious. But those who are humble are happy to be defeated by Him. *End of aside.* When he went into Vespers in the church of the Holy Prophet Elijah near the mill, he found the strength to utter, "Lord Jesus Christ, have mercy upon me a sinner." Then he saw to the right of the Royal Doors, in the place of the icon of the Saviour, the living Christ. The Lord's apparition was incomprehensible, yet the whole being and even the body of the young man, who was then still a novice, were filled with the fire of the grace of the Holy Spirit, that very fire which the Lord brought down to earth by His coming. The vision drained Silouan of all his strength and the Lord vanished.[8] The description of this spiritual event is very simple and presented without imagination. The imagination is annulled, abolished by the power of the Spirit of God, which is active, and is "able to do exceeding abundantly above all that we ask or think", says St. Paul (Eph. 3:20). *Aside:* The event of God surpasses all imagination, and whoever lives this event has no longer any need of it. *End of aside.*

The Transfiguration on Mount Tabor is one of the greatest appearances of God in holy history, and yet it is described with likewise simplicity. Moreover, all the Gospel narratives of the parables and Christ's teachings are expressed with this sobriety, with no imagination. Where the kingdom of God is revealed in power, there imagination ceases to operate, since nothing further remains which may excite it.

The moment of St. Silouan's vision was the Lord's time to act. By his deep and humble repentance, Silouan had convinced the Lord that he was "His servant" and the "son of His handmaid" (*cf.* Ps. 116:16), in the same spirit as the Psalmist who says, "I am thine, save me" (Ps. 119:94). The Lord accepted Silouan over every expectation and revealed His shape, His Face, as if saying to him, "Yes, Thou art My Son, this day have I begotten Thee by My grace" (*cf.* Acts 13:33, Heb. 5:5). Therefore, the moment of the vision was for Silouan the moment of his birth into the "grace of adoption" (*cf.* Gal. 4:5, Eph. 1:5) – it was his spiritual regeneration.[9] *Aside:* There are many degrees of spiritual regeneration. *End of aside.*

Reading the words of the saint himself, one clearly sees that this event was very great, the greatest in his life. He continually comes back to it, almost on every page, each time shedding new light on important aspects revealed by it. This was a great lesson given by the Lord to Silouan, and through him, to the whole Church. He was taught a "great science" in a single moment, the knowledge of the "great mystery of godliness" (1 Tim. 3:16). It would be extremely edifying and beneficial if we were to examine from the saint's writings what he says about his life before the vision, during the vision and after the vision. Then, in an astonishing way, the marvellous mystery would be made known: how in the person and life of one man, Silouan, who is, moreover, a man of our times, is reflected the whole history of the relationship between God and Adam's descendants.

Before his calling from God and his taking up of repentance, Silouan's life was sinful. He had not yet been regenerated by faith, and without wishing to judge the moral nature of a man's life, we can follow St. Paul and rely on his words: "whatsoever is not of faith is sin" (Rom. 14:23). Without faith, man does not receive grace; faith and the Holy Spirit go hand in hand. Man cannot be regenerated without faith and without the Spirit, and consequently remains a slave to sin, and lives according to the flesh. But the Spirit of the Lord neither delights in such a life, nor comes down to it.

By God's providence and thanks to the prayers of the saints, the gift of faith was rekindled and Silouan accepted the vocation of monasticism. He took up the labour of repentance; he returned to the Lord. All the natural gifts that he possessed – frankness, simplicity, intelligence, earnest endeavour, a big and affectionate heart, a strong body – he put to the service of the one decision he made in the first grace of his calling: not to subject himself to the vanity of this world, but to live in freedom, in God's presence. The grace of faith became the grace of repentance. *Aside:* It is similar to what we read in the Gospel, where the Lord says: "every scribe which is instructed unto the kingdom of heaven is like unto a man which bringeth forth out of his treasure things new and old" (*cf.* Matt. 13:52). That is to say, he puts at the service of the Lord everything he possesses, all his natural gifts, to be sealed by grace. *End of aside.*

Silouan's repentance was marked by his great desire for God and deep humility. The longing for reconciliation with God kindled in his heart the unceasing invocation of the Jesus Prayer, which the Mother of God had granted him three weeks after his entrance into the monastery, while he was praying before her icon. Through this longing, he kept fervent the sensation of God and the living presentation before His Face; with never diminishing zeal he "perfected holiness in the fear of God" (2 Cor. 7:1). As we have already mentioned, his repentance was humble, without boldness, and carried out with a deep consciousness of his sinfulness. It was for this reason, perhaps, that his mind remembered and cared for God's judgment even before he experienced the sensation of the "flames of hell". He unremittingly sought forgiveness from God, and nothing else. He would turn to God with the consciousness that he was worse than a "noisome cur".[10] He did not even dare to consider for himself the state of a "hired servant", which the prodigal son humbly longed for (cf. Luke 15:19). He was led to the depths of humility, but the Lord, true to His word, "giveth grace unto the humble" (Jas. 4:6). He regarded his servant, and Silouan suddenly saw the living Christ. For the humble, the appearance of the Lord is always unexpected, because they do not dare to think about it, even though it may correspond, in part, to their state.

The pre-eminent example of God's appearing to man, which also helps to explain what happened in Silouan's case, is the Annunciation of the Mother of God. According to tradition, the Holy Virgin was consecrated to the God of Israel at a very young age. While abiding in the Sanctuary of the Temple, she gave herself over to prayer, and was taught the Law of Moses and the Prophets by the priests. When, by God's providence, she read the passage from Isaiah which says, "Behold, a virgin shall conceive and bear a son, and shall call his name Immanuel" (Isa. 7:14), her heart was kindled with one desire, and her whole being became one prayer: "O Lord, God of my Fathers, make me worthy to become the handmaid of the woman who will bring forth Immanuel into the world." And in the fervency of this humble prayer, which was prophetically fulfilling the future law of her Son, that is to say, "he that shall humble himself shall be exalted" (Matt. 23:12), the Archangel appeared to her and said: "Hail, thou that art highly favoured, the Lord is with thee: blessed art thou among women"

(Luke 1:28). In other words, it is as though he was saying, "Not the handmaid, but the very Mother of Immanuel" – and there is logic to it. The Virgin was a treasure of purity, and "the king's daughter is all glorious within", says the Psalmist (Ps. 45:13). The inner glory and beauty of the Mother of God, for which God glorified her, was her deep humility, as she herself exclaims and confesses, "for he hath regarded the low estate of his handmaiden" (Luke 1:48). Why does humility bear such grace? Because, according to the teachings of St. Silouan, humility gives love all the space, and God is love. As we are told in the Gospel of the Last Judgment, the notable appearance of the Lord at the end of the ages will be ineffably terrible: blessed for the humility of the righteous, but unbearable to the obstinacy of sinners. *Aside:* So, before the vision, there was this state of humility and this "going down" before God. *End of aside.*

The event of the vision of Christ is wordless, since by it one is caught up out of this world. It is a meeting with the living Christ, and above all, a meeting of love. The saint himself repeatedly tells us that this love is indescribably humble and dear, and that we cannot retain its fullness in our present state. Regenerated by the Holy Spirit, he describes the event with humility. He desires to bequeath, as a precious treasure entrusted to his care, the knowledge given to him concerning the person of the Lord Jesus; yet, in such a way as to build up the Body of the faithful, not provoking the conscience of the weak, and falling into the condemnation of the devil. As a true prophet, he understands that "the spirits of the prophets are subject to the prophets" (1 Cor. 14:32). Those who bear in themselves the Spirit of the God of Love struggle to give all the space in their heart to their brethren, whom Christ purchased with His precious Blood (*cf.* Acts 20:28). They engage in a marvellous contest: Who will humble himself most for the commandment's sake, the commandment of love? That is why the saint testifies modestly:

"I know a man whom the Lord in His mercy visited with His grace. And had the Lord asked him, 'Wouldst thou have Me give thee more?', from weakness of the flesh his soul would have made answer:

"'Thou seest, Lord, that I cannot bear more and would die,' for man is compassed about and cannot carry the fullness of grace.

"Thus on Mount Tabor the disciples fell on their face before the glory of the Lord. And no man can conceive how the Lord gives grace to the soul."[11]

From his words, it is clear how the fullness of grace is beyond man, and that the way in which God reveals Himself remains inexplicable. *Aside:* What I am trying to say is that if we are really and truly charismatic, we should have a competition: who will humble himself the more before the other? This is the sign of those who are "born again" (John 3:3). We must not easily air our graces and our gifts, precisely so as not to provoke the conscience of our fellows; this is something that those who call themselves "charismatics" should bear in mind. *End of aside.* In another part of his writings, Silouan describes the same event more fully:

"One of the novices on Mt. Athos, in the Russian Monastery of St. Panteleimon, accustomed himself to pray God without cease that his sins be forgiven him. . . .

"And then one day during Vespers he lifted up his eyes to the ikon of the Saviour and said a little prayer – hardly more than half a dozen words, 'Lord Jesus Christ, have mercy on me, a sinner' – and he saw the ikon turn into the living Saviour, and his soul and body were filled with ineffable sweetness. Through the Holy Spirit his soul knew our Lord Jesus Christ, knew that the Lord is merciful, that the love of God causes a man to forget all else; and from that time forth his soul was afire with love for the Lord."[12]

From these two sober and short narratives, but also from the saint's repeated references to this great event, we can draw certain conclusions about man's state when regenerated from on High. First of all, from the context of God's operation, this is an inexplicable event; it is an extraordinary blessing towards man, and one which is rarely granted. It is out of this world, eternal, though it takes place in time, in a moment, like a flash of divinity. Although not sought for by man, nevertheless it was foreseen by God in His mind, before the world began, and according to His own purpose and grace, and foreknown by Him that this man, Silouan, would respond positively and with good will. From the point of view of the man who partakes in the energy of God, this event is inconceivable and indescribable. The renewal he undergoes in his life is witnessed to by radical changes in his soul and conscience, by works and fruits with which he is enriched. During the mystical vision of the Lord, Silouan knew God, and he knew Him in the Holy Spirit. Before the vision he did not even know that a Holy Spirit exists, as he himself confesses with convincing simplicity.[13] Of course, he did not mean what the disciples said to the Apostle Paul when he came to Ephesus: "We have not so much as heard whether there be any Holy Ghost" (Acts 19:2). Silouan had both received a canonical baptism and had been chrismated. Also, in the services of the Orthodox Church, one continually hears, "Glory be to the Father, and to the Son, and to the Holy Ghost." Of course, he knew about the Holy Spirit; simply, he did not know how the Holy Spirit operated. Now, despite being a poor sinner and a "sorry wretch",[14] as he describes himself, he has been given in the Holy Spirit to know that Jesus Christ is God and Creator of man.[15] The saint, therefore, verified the Lord's dogma by experience. "He [the Holy Spirit] shall testify of me", says the Lord (John 15:26). In other words, the Holy Spirit reveals the divinity of Christ, the gentle and compassionate countenance of the Lord and its beauty. Silouan came to this knowledge through a change in his whole being, for the Holy Spirit pervades the entire man: soul, mind and body, as he says.[16] The fullness which the Holy Spirit communicates to the soul is the fullness of Christ's love for man. Silouan writes: "Oh Lord, Thou dost love Thy creature; and who can fathom Thy love, or delight in it, if he be not taught of Thee Thyself by Thy Holy Spirit?"[17] And here again the Gospel word, "He shall teach you all things" (John 14:26), is verified. Through the Holy Spirit man becomes taught by God, and understands the boundless and indescribable love of Christ. But without the Holy Spirit man is but "sinful clay", Silouan says.[18] By the Holy Spirit he is guided into all truth concerning the love of Christ for every man. The Holy Spirit does not simply reveal the Lord's love for the world, but also inspires love for the Lord in the soul. The saint confesses: "The Lord loves us without stint, and I could not have known this love had not the Holy Spirit taught me Who teaches every good thing. My heart loved Thee, O Lord, and therefore I yearn for Thee, and seek Thee in tears."[19] In another place, he prays as follows: "O Holy Spirit . . . Thy gift is an ardent love of God."[20]

During the vision of the living Christ the Holy Spirit imparts to man the very state of Christ Himself,[21] and He transfers all His love to the beloved. This is clear from the abundance of sweet tears which the soul sheds. Tears are the best and most fitting expression of its love. The burning love for the desired Lord is so great that the spirit of man is caught up by the vision of God. Then the soul that is filled with the love of God is oblivious both of heaven and of earth. *Aside:* Man then does not care any more about heaven and earth, his only concern is to be with the Lord, who is the King of heaven and earth.[22] *End of aside.* With regard to this being "caught up", to which the saint often refers, we find a similar outline given by the Apostle Paul: "Whether in the body" – that is to say, *on earth* – "I cannot tell; or whether out of the body" – that is to say, *in heaven* – "I cannot tell: God knoweth" (2 Cor. 12:2). Of course, when man reaches these heights, he perfectly fulfils "the first and great commandment" (Matt. 22:38).[23]

The work of the Holy Spirit does not stop here; He strengthens man's nature to bear the fullness of love for Christ, and *enlarges his heart* to embrace all creation in his prayer,[24] even his enemies.[25] Therefore, with the help of the Holy Spirit, the believer fulfils the second commandment, which is similar to the first (Matt. 22:39).[26] In St. Silouan's case, the *enlargement* which the Holy Spirit wrought in him from the moment of the vision is amazing! For more than forty years he prayed: "I pray Thee, O merciful Lord, for all the peoples of the earth, that they may come to know Thee by the Holy Spirit."[27] *Aside:* There could be no more beautiful prayer for the world. If we honour the saints, really we do nothing else but pay a "little debt" to them, because they first loved us and interceded for us with such prayers. It is understandable why we honour the saints . . . and God is well pleased in this. *End of aside.*

At the moment of the vision, the state of Christ Himself was imparted to Silouan by the Holy Spirit.[28] Through the mutual love in the Spirit, the existential union of the saint with the Saviour of the world was realized, and as Christ "the New Adam" bears in Himself, and grants salvation to, the whole race of men, so likewise is the soul, which has joined itself to Him, infused with the same wisdom, longing and prayer: that all may be saved. In his writings, St. Silouan alternates between the terms humility and love; humility and love for one's enemies, as if they were the same. At the moment of the vision, the delight of divine love filled his soul and body, and he desired to suffer for Christ, as St. Paul says: "Unto us is given in the behalf of Christ, not only to believe on him, but also to suffer for his sake" (Phil. 1:29). When he saw how meek and humble the Lord is, his soul was humbled completely, and from then on he could have no other desire and no other yearning than for the humility of Christ, which, as he said, is incomprehensible: "No one can describe it, and it is made known only through the Holy Spirit."[29] He regarded humility along with love for one's enemies as the most excellent gift of the Holy Spirit.[30] This divine humility of Christ, as soon as it becomes active in man's spirit, wordlessly gives witness to the salvation of the soul.[31]

Despite his simplicity and lack of learning, at the time of the vision he came to know by experience the three Persons of the Holy Trinity. From contemplation of Christ, who is so meek and humble, the Holy Spirit pours forth plentifully, and man's spirit "melts with His grace",[32] as he experiences the greatness of the Father's love. The saint acknowledges that the Spirit proceeds from the Father, that without the Holy Spirit it is not possible to see Christ, and that the Holy Spirit is imparted to the whole man: soul, mind and body. He refers to the love of Christ as "fatherly", because he knows by experience that "every good gift and every perfect gift is from above and cometh down from the Father of lights" (Jas. 1:17). That is why the saint recounts in wonder: "What mercy is this – that the Lord desires us to be in Him and in the Father!", and "Our soul feels the Lord in us".[33] During the vision of Christ a great divine light shone about Silouan. The heavenly and Holy Spirit filled his whole being and bore witness to the divinity of the only-begotten Son of God, and to the salvation of his soul. The same Holy Spirit taught that the indescribably great love of Christ is the same as the Father's love. He came to know by experience the life of the Holy Trinity, in which he became a partaker with his whole being. As we sing at the end of the Holy Liturgy, he had found "the true faith", and for this reason he thankfully proclaims:

Glory be to the Lord God that He gave us His Only-begotten Son for the sake of our salvation. Glory be to the Only-begotten Son, that He deigned to be born of the Most Holy Virgin, and suffered for our salvation, and gave us His Most Pure Body and Blood to eternal life, and sent us His Holy Spirit on earth. Glory be to the Holy Spirit. The Holy Spirit reveals to us the mysteries of God. The Holy Spirit teaches the soul ineffable love toward mankind. The Holy Spirit so adorns soul and body that man becomes like unto the Lord in the flesh, and in heaven we will live for ever with the Lord, and behold His glory. In the life eternal all men will be like unto the Lord. And no man could know of this mystery, were it not revealed by the Holy Spirit.[34]

Aside: This is true theology. True theology, as we have said before, is a narrative, the story of an encounter, of a meeting with God. *End of aside.*

During the time following the appearance of the Lord, Silouan's soul became vivified by the grace of the Holy Spirit. His mind was enlightened and it was as though a "transformer" of divine love had been placed in his heart. Whatever he saw, whatever he heard, whatever he thought, everything that surrounded him, described the glory of God, and worked together towards a higher ascent of contemplation and greater fullness of love towards Christ and man: from love to love, from one fullness to a greater fullness. He felt that his body was no longer a burden and that it had the same pull and eager desire for ascent as the soul. The word of God became kin to his soul and his attentiveness to it renewed his nature. *Aside:* Our nature is renewed through the dwelling in us of the word of God. *End of aside.* He was living the feast of divine love. Paschal joy was in his soul. He entered spiritually into the everlasting place of Heaven, where the whole creation offers hymns with gratitude and thanks to "the Lamb slain from the foundation of the world" (Rev. 13:8). Overwhelmed by gratitude and amazement he exclaims: "Oh, what a Lord is ours!"[35] The Lord visited Silouan and he became "like them that dream", and was glad (Ps. 126:1). He concluded a personal covenant with the Lord; he became a "house of God". *Aside:* We know from the First Epistle of St. Peter that the judgment of God begins from the "house of God" (1 Pet. 4:17), and the key of David will be turned. We know from the Book of Isaiah that the Messiah will have the "key of the house of David" (Isa. 22:22), that is to say, messianic authority, and with this authority and grace all that He opens no one can close, and all that He closes no one can open, as is repeated in the Book of Revelation (*cf.* Rev. 3:7). Now, the "key of the house of David" is turned in the life of St. Silouan. *End of aside.* Encouraging Christians to be patient under the fiery trial of temptations, persecutions and sufferings of this present life, in view of the glory which will be revealed by Jesus Christ, St. Peter pronounces the following profound words: "For the time is come that the judgment must begin at the house of God" (1 Pet. 4:17). The judgment of God is the way of Christ, which reaches down even to the lowest parts of the earth. If, therefore, by the appearance of Christ, Silouan became a "house of God", that is to say, a dwelling-place of the grace of God, then the judgment of the Son of God should be first on him; and so there should also be a repetition in him of the way of Christ, which is narrow, but nevertheless leads to life (*cf.* Matt. 7:14). *Aside:* Fr. Sophrony used to say that suffering in this world is a sign of election, not of misery. *End of aside.* He must also submit to the fiery trials and endure the judgment of God's discipline. He must show his faithfulness and become an inheritor of Christ, as a lawful son and not as a baseborn child (*cf.* Heb. 12:5–8).

Elder Sophrony says that "to live a Christian life is impossible: all one can do is 'die daily' [1 Cor. 15:31] in Christ, like St. Paul".[36] It is impossible for one to see or meet Christ and not to undergo a certain "deadening", a kind of death. We see this spiritual phenomenon in Silouan: before the vision, through his desire for reconciliation with God and his burning repentance, he reached the depths of despair, and went through a horrible self-emptying. He completely emptied himself and became as "nothing", suitable material, from which God can create (*cf.* Ps. 51:10).[37] He gave all the space in himself to Christ who visited him. His complete self-emptying was followed by the fullness of perfect love, which he experienced in the Holy Spirit. His biographer says that after the vision Silouan "was drained of all his strength".[38] This is the mark of "being dead" in God, which takes place at the moment of the encounter with the living God. The great Paul described the mystery of this experience: "I am crucified with Christ: nevertheless I live; yet not I, but Christ liveth in me" (Gal. 2:20). After the vision, man is dead to passionate concerns and material goods. He does not pursue either high positions or power. He is not brought down by the contempt of others, and neither does he consider their praise. As Elder Sophrony says, in this state man forgets the past, does not become attached to the present, and neither does he worry about the earthly future. God has revealed to him a new life, one that is full of light; henceforth he will struggle to be faithful to the "heavenly vision". *Aside:* This is the same word that St. Paul spoke to King Agrippa, when asked to defend himself against the accusations of the Jews: "Whereupon, O king Agrippa, I was not disobedient unto the heavenly vision" – revealed on the way to Damascus (Acts 26:19). *End of aside.*

If man still has some strength in his soul, he does not cease to long for a greater fullness of love. If, however, this is beyond his strength, he remains peaceful in blessed silence, for in the depths of his heart there remains the peace from knowledge of the true God. *Aside:* This knowledge of the true God gives stability to our life. *End of aside.* What we described above is only the positive aspect of "being dead", which comes from a vision of the love and sweetness of the Holy Spirit, but there is also crucifixion with Christ, which is expressed negatively, through a multitude of sufferings.[39] This test is a mark of the believer's election by the Heavenly Father; and St. Silouan, who received such an excellent lesson from the ineffable favour of God's goodness, will undergo divine examination, "the chastening of the Lord" (cf. Heb. 12:5–8). *Aside:* That is to say, all those moments when God visits man are lessons to be kept for life. *End of aside.*

After the vision of Christ, the action of grace diminished slightly. The memory of what he had experienced remained in Silouan's consciousness, but no longer with the same force. Fear of abandonment and horror of losing the heavenly treasure began to come upon his soul. His soul was afflicted and longed for the Lord, now distant again. He intensified his personal struggle and used every means of asceticism so as not to yield to the increasing inner poverty. He had recourse to the advice of the spiritual fathers and the reading of ascetic works, so as to find the solution to, and the way out of, his predicament. The extremes of his experience were diametrically opposed. He went from contemplation of the light of the knowledge of God to even demonic darkness, which had disappeared after the vision. His reading of ascetic texts and the wonder which his spiritual father mistakenly expressed at him, threw him into a difficult, delicate and complex battle with thoughts. His eyes were opened to see on the left what the right hand of the Most High was doing with him on the right. Through the untimely praise of the spiritual father, there began a battle with thoughts of vainglory, and these thoughts rendered the heart arid. *Aside:* You see, even spiritual fathers are not infallible. *End of aside.* Despite the fact that he had delighted in the unutterable joy of salvation when he had seen Christ, and that he had received, very early on, the gift of unceasing prayer, nevertheless, his reason had not yet been proven in the ascetic struggle. This is why he was unable to preserve the state he had known. However, he could not resign himself to this new change – the withdrawal of the Light.

Then began a titanic struggle with states of alternating grace and aridity. Occasionally, he felt the consolation of grace, but this did not last for long. As time went by, these changes taught Silouan the workings of thoughts and grace. The main aim of his life became the acquisition of grace, and his chief concern was to find the reason why he was abandoned by it.[40] Many monks, but also Christians generally, receive great grace at the outset of their lives; few, however, wage an ascetic struggle to regain it. Silouan now embarked on a long stretch of spiritual aridity and trials. He was ready to give himself over to death for the sake of recovering the grace he had known. *Aside:* Fr. Sophrony used to say that we must not take the first visitation of grace psychologically, but it must be taken as the conclusion of a covenant, to which we must remain faithful and prove ourselves. *End of aside.* From the lives of the saints, especially evident in the description of the penitents in *The Ladder* of St. John of Sinai, and in the account of the life of St. Bessarion the Great, in *The Sayings of the Desert Fathers,* we can see that those who have contemplated divine light and then lost it are inconsolable in their mourning. Not even the lamentation of a widow who has lost her only son can be compared with the lamentation of these ascetics. The pain of their soul becomes metaphysical, and the cry of their distress resounds in all the deserts of this world. Since grace is incomparably higher than every earthly love and more precious than every treasure on earth, its loss gives birth to a torture which exceeds the torture of those who are bewailing their dead.[41] This asceticism for the reacquisition of grace is not planned by man in advance, but is inspired by the close knowledge of God which precedes it, and for this reason it is not something for everyone. However, for us it is useful to be aware of the order of the spiritual phenomena.

This torturous struggle in Silouan's soul lasted for fifteen years, following which the Lord intervened in his life, and after a brief prayer-dialogue with Him he heard the word in his heart, *"Keep thy mind in hell, and do not despair."* As we have already mentioned, the Lord gave Silouan the means by which he could become humble, hold fast to His way, and perfect grace could be restored.

By keeping his mind in hell, he could follow the Lord closely on His path, and be instructed in His Spirit. These two great events: the Lord's appearance at the outset, and then hearing His voice after the intervening trial, worked together so that Silouan finally became established in perfect and steadfast grace, which guided him to passionlessness and complete sanctification.

However, from a didactic point of view, it is important and of great value to have a correct understanding of the second phase which ranges between the two main events in Silouan's life. The same pattern and spiritual order is repeated to some degree in the lives of all the faithful. Without this understanding and knowledge, there is the danger of attributing the first grace of election to a state of psychological elation and euphoria, and the reacquisition of the first love to be an unattainable, imaginary hope, whereas through the lessons and the experience of this same stage, Christians can arrive at the perfect state of divine adoption. Why does God, therefore, withdraw His grace, and why does He abandon man? *Aside:* I dwell a little more on the second stage in the Christian life, because it is very important to have some idea of it, as it lends stability to our life; and then whether we are in euphoria or in affliction, in inspiration or in despondency, Christ is Lord and "sitteth on the right hand of the Father" (*cf.* Col. 3:1). This is what we see in the Person of our Lord: He was being delivered to death and at that moment He was saying to the thief, "To day shalt thou be with me in paradise" (Luke 23:43); because He knew the Father (*cf.* Matt. 11:27; Luke 10:22; John 10:15; 17:25), and He was united to the Father (*cf.* John 10:30). *End of aside.*

There are three ways in which man can experience abandonment: by God's providence, for the sake of punishment, or for instruction.

Abandonment by providence is something dispensed to all men. This first grace, which is the crowning of divine goodness, accompanies God's calling to man to set out on a new journey and a new life, and is a pure gift. Elder Sophrony, in an original spiritual interpretation of Luke 16:10–12, defines the first grace in the Lord's words as "unrighteous mammon", or "undeserved" and "another's riches" (*cf.* Luke 16:11–12),[42] a pure gift. Man, in order to acquire it, must freely show forth all his wisdom and fidelity as a good householder, and then His inheritance becomes his own for all eternity. He must submit to God's lawful training and be instructed by the Most High in the mystery of the law of adoption (*cf.* Gal. 4:5). He must struggle in order to conform his nature to the height of contemplation which has been revealed to him. When he is instructed in the will of God, abiding patiently in the heat and aridity[43] of this period of abandonment, then the riches given in the beginning, which are "another man's" and "foreign", become now truly his own: "all that I have is thine" (Luke 15:31).

In the case of the second kind of abandonment, it is because of man's independent will that God allows abandonment for the sake of punishment. When man is carried about by the proud inclination to "self- divinization", then the noble and meek Spirit of God is grieved and departs. The Spirit of God is so fine that it cannot bear even the return of man's mind to itself, in self-love.[44]

Abandonment for the sake of punishment also takes place when the Christian falls into sin or becomes slothful and no longer cares for his salvation. (Despondency means lack of care for salvation, in Greek *akedía*.) Nevertheless, the Lord permits this for the salvation of the believer, and as the Apostle says, "We are chastened of the Lord, that we should not be condemned with the world" (1 Cor. 11:32). Everything that God does with us is out of love.

The final kind of abandonment, for the sake of instruction, is a powerful gift of the Holy Spirit, as we see in the life of St. Silouan. It is usually reserved for those who received a great gift of grace at the outset of their lives.

The foundation of this spiritual phenomenon lies in the life of Christ. Christ patiently bore abandonment and death on the Cross to heal our abandonment and to make our death of no effect. Abandonment and death came into our life through disobedience to the commandment of God, which preceded them (*cf.* Gen. 2:17; Rom. 5:12). Christ's abandonment and death healed and saved man because they were voluntary and sinless (*cf.* Rom. 5:18). When we endure our abandonment lawfully, that is, with good will and following the example of the Lord, the death of our inner desert is conquered and we inherit the grace which issued forth from the Cross and the Resurrection of the Author of our faith. Since abandonment is a part of the life of the Lord, it is indispensable for us to pass through it, so that we may come to know every step of the Lord's Way, and attain to perfect knowledge of His Person. In other words, if we do not go through abandonment, we cannot know Christ fully.

The journey of man's spiritual life with the three stages: the first grace of the calling, the withdrawal of the grace or man's being abandoned by it, and finally its repossession, is foreshadowed in the history of Israel. In the beginning, God called the Hebrews and showed His power and protection with great and wondrous works. He freed the people from the Egyptians; He caused them to cross the Red Sea unharmed, and led them to the Holy Mountain of Sinai, where He gave them a revelation and grace, and the people celebrated their Passover, their Salvation. Then followed forty years of trial, temptations and hardship. Finally, those who proved themselves faithful to the commandments of God were led into the blessed entrance of the Promised Land.

During the second period, that of withdrawal of grace, the man who has discovered its light and seen the pattern of divine life cannot find rest in the present reality of the world. He suffers from inconsolable desertion and feels an ontological void, which brings metaphysical grief to his spirit, and which in his wounded heart is perceived as death.[45] Perplexity and the uncertainty as to whether He who has departed will ever return[46] strain the pain of his despair. The more intensely he experienced the delight of union with God, the more deeply he suffers the separation from Him.[47] His suffering corresponds to the measure of the enlargement of his heart wrought by grace.[48] Eternal life becomes an indispensable condition for the true fulfilment of his temporary existence.

The abandonment of this period places man face to face with all the consequences of our forefather's transgression, and reveals the real nature of this event. Knowledge of this apocalyptic truth spurs man on to give himself over to complete repentance, as far as possible, and voluntarily to bear self-emptying in order to be healed. When the prayer of repentance is prolonged, the believer is crushed and suffers on all levels of his being.[49] He is humbled and becomes a mere "nothing", "suitable material which our God can create from".[50] The dreadful pain which possesses man's whole being produces an abundance of tears. These purify, heal and unify his broken nature and draw him to deep humility.[51] In this state, he attracts the grace of the Holy Spirit which restores him to eternal communion with God. It would have been impossible for him to survive this period without the mystical and real protection of the good Heavenly Father.

During this time of repentance, man suffers from an inconsolable and metaphysical pain, yet God seems "merciless and deaf to entreaty".[52] Desire for God is active like a caustic flame. Because of the pain in his heart, man is crucified on an invisible cross. He examines himself severely under the light of the Lord's commandments,[53] and continually contrives ways of approaching God. But God makes Himself unapproachable so that the "hidden part" of man's deep heart (cf. Ps. 51:6) may become manifest. This reminds us of the prayer of the Holy Prophet David: "Cleanse thou me from secret faults" (Ps. 19:12).

Man's freedom is tested unto the end, and he arrives at a complete crucifixion. When he is on the Cross, he will either blame God and will be thrown down into the abyss of darkness, or he will surrender to the Heavenly Father who judges justly (cf. Rev. 16:7; 19:2 and Pss. 19:9; 119:75, 137), and so he will inherit the portion of His Son, like the Good Thief (cf. Luke 23:39–43). If he holds out on the death of the desertion he is living through, and is not frightened to follow Christ "whithersoever he goeth" (Rev. 14:4), then, thanks to the determination of his faith and the love which he bears, he conquers death and is regenerated into the eternal kingdom. When he finds grace before God, his experience of universal desertion is transformed into fervent intercession for the salvation of the whole world. When the believer submits to the instruction of the Lord, he not only grows spiritually, but also grants God the possibility of showing the greatness of His love for man; for God desires to make the ascetic in His image, that is to say, lord and king, and to transmit to him His holiness and the fullness of divine existence: He wills to be united to His image, man, and prove him victor over the devil.

Unless the believer emerges from the stage of abandonment by God triumphantly, as we see in the example of Job, he cannot "convince" the enemy of his likeness unto God. However, by fulfilling every righteousness of God's instruction through extreme sufferings and completely and freely placing himself on the level of eternity, he is received by the Heavenly Father, who honours him with all that He has (*cf.* Luke 15:31) "for our eternal use".[54] *Aside:* Put simply, when we are threatened by any kind of death and do not give way to fear, but cling to God and surrender to Him in faith, that means that the love and faithfulness we have towards God are stronger than the death that threatens us. Therefore, our faith and love overcome death.[55] *End of aside.*

The disciple of Christ is a disciple of the Cross, but also of blessedness. The blessedness springs from knowing the depth and height and length of the way of Christ (*cf.* Eph. 3:18). Through the crucifixion of this period, man's deep heart is cleansed from secret and unknown dishonourable passions and made ready to receive the spiritual and divine sensation, which, according to the wise Solomon, she seeks by nature: "The heart of an upright man seeks for a sensation," he says (*cf.* Prov. 15:14 Lxx). Then, according to the words of our saint, grace will love him and abandon him no more. In other words, the believer enters into the third stage of his spiritual life.

In his chapter *On Love*, St. Silouan outlines, in a poetic and inspired way, the return of grace *for good* to the heart of the saints. Here is what he says:

"The souls of the saints, O Lord, hast Thou drawn unto Thyself and they flow toward Thee like gentle streams.

"The minds of the saints attached themselves to Thee, O Lord, and are drawn toward Thee, our Light and joy.

"The hearts of Thy saints are confirmed in Thy love, O Lord, and cannot forget Thee for a moment, even when they sleep, for sweet is the grace of the Holy Spirit."[56]

This sensation of God in the heart and blessedness of knowing well the Way of Christ,[57] renders the shepherds and spiritual fathers of our Church perfect. They possess the treasure of the knowledge of the glory of God in the Face of Jesus Christ, and their heart gives birth to a good and perfect word, which bestows grace, regenerates the souls of the flock, and builds up the glorious Body of Christ, the Church. Forgive me.

QUESTIONS & ANSWERS

Question 1: Are the three reasons for abandonment that you have just described exclusive to one another or can they overlap, so that the same abandonment has more than one purpose or reason?

Answer 1: Yes, they can overlap, it is true. We sometimes try to systematize things which cannot be reduced to categories. But we do this for the sake of clarity and to transmit certain truths, but it is not possible to create a system in this case, for the Spirit of God "bloweth where it listeth", says the Lord (John 3:8).

Question 2: Last night you spoke about "charismatic humility", "charismatic despair", and today about "charismatic repentance". Could you help me to understand these terms and how they differ from one another, please?

Answer 2: Yes. There are several degrees of humility, as St. Silouan says. There is humility for which man strives, and the highest form of this is when one considers himself the worst of men, and puts himself beneath all creation. This is ascetical humility. "Charismatic humility", however, is when man beholds the Love of Christ and considers himself unworthy of such a Saviour, such a God. This kind of humility is given to those who are deemed worthy of the vision of Christ or of hearing His voice.

"Charismatic despair" is when man, in like manner as Abraham, with faith and "hope against hope" (*cf.* Rom. 4:18), hangs everything on the mercy of God; and without looking for any substitute, any support in this life, holds fast onto the word of God, and with this word follows Him to the end. He despairs of everything in this world, of everything that is created, and turns to God with all his being and attaches himself only to God, holding fast to His word. That is why this charismatic despair helps him to "divest" his being not only of the passions and sinfulness, but of everything that is created, even of his own body, because we have to "divest" ourselves before we can "invest" ourselves with the New Adam, the Heavenly Man. This "charismatic despair" is indispensable if we are to "change our skin" (cf. Gen. 3:21).

Now, "charismatic repentance" occurs when the grace of God co-works with us and in us, and we cannot forget God for a moment, but continually weep before Him over our spiritual poverty, thereby fulfilling the first of Christ's Beatitudes: "Blessed are the poor in spirit: for theirs is the kingdom of heaven" (Matt. 5:3). Unless we have this "charismatic repentance", which is inspired by our poverty, not only by a concrete sin of the past but by something which is existential, which we bear all the time, we cannot come to the second Beatitude: "Blessed are they that mourn: for they shall be comforted" (Matt. 5:4), by the comfort of the Comforter.

Question 3: You have mentioned despondency, *akedía*. Could you say a few more words about it?

Answer 3: Yes, *akedía* is the lack of concern, the lack of care for salvation. Sometimes monks, when they are in *akedía*, can move mountains, they become very active, they build, they demolish, they plant, they harvest, but all this activity is simply a form of *akedía*. All the sciences of our times are a product of the *akedía* of Medieval monks, who forsook the path of prayer, and gave themselves to experiments and observations of natural phenomena. Of course, they made discoveries and furthered the cause of science, but they themselves lost out in spiritual terms.

Actually, the highest activity for man is to remain still and stay the mind in God, as the Old Testament commands us: "Be still, and know that I am God" (Ps. 46:10). But that stillness is so intense that one has to learn to go into it very slowly. I remember when I first came to the monastery Fr. Sophrony advised me to try this no more than ten minutes each day, and gradually one learns more and more to stay in it, to stay the mind in the heart and in the presence of God, as St. Theophan the Recluse says very often in his writings.[58] In his chapter on monks, St. Silouan says that those who really have the gift of repentance should not occupy themselves with any other work; they should not be exhausted, "spent" with other activities, but rather should be protected to pursue this rare gift. This gift of repentance will surely lead them to the fulfilment of their vocation, that is to say, to become intercessors for the whole world. If someone truly repents, then he will find grace, and in that grace he will discover two things: first his deep heart, and then, in the deep heart, he will discover God and his neighbour. This is the discovery that the Mother of God made in the Temple, when she was in the Holy of Holies, as St. Gregory Palamas says. Through prayer, she discovered her deep heart, and there too she discovered her unity with the whole world, and thus began to intercede for the whole world, already at that young age.[59]

Therefore, the first movement is towards God, with repentance. Having found God, we return to the world in intercession, bringing the world before God, and interceding before God for every creature. This vocation is not only for monks; this is for every human being created in the image and likeness of God. I have mentioned this passage in Job, where he says, "What is man, that thou shouldest magnify him?" (Job 7:17); and he goes on to say, "Why hast thou set me as a *katenteuktés* before thee?" (Job. 7:20). In the Septuagint, a *katenteuktés* is someone who stands before God and intercedes, and even quarrels with God.[60] But he must be passionless to do that. And God is not angry or irritated by such a quarrel; He even bestows great grace, because that quarrel is selfless, it is not for our satisfaction, for our passion, but it is of the same spirit that God has given us, who desires the salvation of all. Such was Moses' quarrel with God, when he asked the Lord to save all the Hebrews or blot him out of the book of life (Exod. 32:32). St. Paul preferred to be accursed, but that the Israelites be saved (Rom. 9:3); and in like manner do all the saints of every age intercede before God. *If someone truly repents, he will not escape this path of intercession.* We priests have to do this by the nature of our ministry. I have discovered something: many times I feel that my prayer is of no avail, for myself at least, but when I pray for other people, I sometimes feel that it brings a benefit, and it is not because of me, but because God wants to help the other people, and He helps them through the grace of the ministry He has given us. A priest is there to intercede for his people. Just as the Lord, who, when ascending on Golgotha, bore in His heart the whole of mankind; and when He prayed in the garden of Gethsemane, He prayed for all mankind. When He died on the Cross, He died bearing all mankind in His heart. When He went down into the grave, without seeing corruption, as it is written in the Book of Acts (*cf.* Acts 2:27, 13:35; from Ps. 16:10), because He was sinless, and "God . . . raised him up from the dead" (1 Pet. 1:21) with the same content in His heart, the *whole Adam* found salvation, because the *whole Adam* was in the heart of Christ.

It is the same in the Liturgy: whatever we bring, whatever our prayer embraces when we stand before God, when we present ourselves before the altar of the Lord; whatever our conscience embraces, the moment of the Consecration will bring a grace upon the content of our prayer. That is to say, if in the Liturgy we embrace the whole world with our prayer, we will spread a blessing upon the whole world, because we must not forget that it is not we who celebrate the Liturgy, but Christ Himself. In the Liturgy we are but poor instruments of Him who "offers and is offered". So, when we say to God, "Thine own of thine own, we offer unto Thee, in all and for all", we do not offer Him just a small cup of wine and a tiny piece of bread, for in *that* bread and in *that* wine we put all our love, all our faith, all our intercession for our beloved, for the people who suffer, for the whole world. We put all our life in that bread and in that wine, and we say to God: "Thine own of thine own, we offer unto Thee, in all and for all." And He does the same, because He is a God of love, and He condescends, because He gave the commandment, "Do this in remembrance of me" (Luke 22:19). So He does the same: He receives those gifts and He puts all His life in them, the Holy Spirit, and He says to us: "The holy things unto the holy". In the Liturgy there is an exchange of lives. Man offers his life to God, and God offers His life to man, and who can compare, or rather measure this exchange of lives? For ours is temporal, corruptible, earthly, and His is incorruptible, heavenly, eternal. Therefore, in the Liturgy there is an unequal exchange of lives.

In fact, the Liturgy is the greatest event in our life. Fr. Sophrony had a passion for the Liturgy. On the day before celebrating he would fix his mind on it, and was in eager anticipation of it. He was nearly ninety-seven years old, and celebrated the Liturgy two months before he died. Every time was like his first. He had such an expectation that when he would come before the altar he would be rapt in God. For him everything else was a preparation for the Liturgy. Even unceasing prayer of the heart was but a preparation for a good presentation before the altar of the Lord. He had such a passion for the Liturgy!

Therefore if our presentation, be it in prayer, in repentance or in the Liturgy, is fruitful before the Lord, sooner or later we will meet this necessity: to spread the same grace upon the whole of creation, to intercede for others, and the greatest exercise for this is priesthood, which God has given us; and I do not think that there is another gift upon earth that God has given us greater than the priesthood. We cannot thank Him enough, "worthily", as St. Basil says in his Liturgy just before communion: "Instruct us how we may worthily gives thanks unto thee . . ."[61]

Question 4: Could you comment on the relation between the three stages of the spiritual life that you mentioned earlier: great imparting of grace, abandonment and then restoration, and the three stages of *theosis*: purgation, illumination and union with God?

Answer 4: I make use of the schema of purification, illumination and *theosis* less frequently, because I prefer the way Fr. Sophrony presents the three stages of the spiritual life, and the way they were prefigured in the history of Israel, since, from the first moment, the grace of God is at once purifying, illuminating and deifying. Every touch of the Spirit of God is light, but there are different degrees. Every time we have a little contrition and we can pray with ease and comfort, that is a touch of the light of God, a touch of grace. If that brings a greater strength so that we can feel that our life is all transferred into Christ and Christ is in us by the action of the Holy Spirit, then that is a greater light. But to experience this kind of vision or ravishing by the Spirit of God is a very rare gift. Truly spiritual people do not consider themselves worthy of any spiritual gift; they only try to learn one thing, namely, to go down before God, because then surely they will be exalted in due time. Because, when we have expectations of gifts, there is a danger lurking within us – a temptation – there is a hidden pride, that we consider ourselves worthy of receiving them, which means that we can fall into demonic delusion. The best thing to do is to pray humbly and commend our lives to God as we say in the Liturgy, "Let us commend ourselves and one another, and our whole life to Christ our God."[62] So at every stage I think you get all three (purification, illumination and *theosis*), and there is simply a varying degree of intensity of one kind over the other.

Question 5 (Bishop Basil): Father Zacharias, you used a very interesting phrase, that man "needed to convince God that he was His", which sounds like something very important. How do we do that? Or how did St. Silouan or Elder Sophrony do that? How do we convince God? What is it that we must do?

Answer 5: In the English translation of his book, St. Silouan speaks about a "noble love", which in the original is called, "the great science" – the science, that is, of learning to go down before God, because all the gifts of the Holy Spirit came by the Lord's coming down. As we read in the Epistle to the Ephesians, "When he ascended up on high, he [the Lord] led captivity captive, and gave gifts to men" (Eph. 4:8). And the Apostle says in wonder: "Now that he ascended, what is it but that he also descended first into the lower parts of the earth?" (Eph. 4:9). Therefore, if we want to follow Christ and know *totus Christus*, the whole Christ, we must learn this way of Christ of "going down". Only this gives us the possibility of convincing Him that we are His.

Question 6 (Bishop Basil): Is self-emptying a part of it?

Answer 6: Yes, and self-emptying, as we said before, comes through repentance.

Question 7 (Bishop Basil): Is that an act of my will or is that something that God does before He comes in?

Answer 7: I think it is always a combination of the two. But given the fact that God always wants to give us all that He has, it is up to us to respond to His wish, to His desire, and, by accepting His Cross, to convince Him that we are His. You see, our God is a "difficult" God, and that is why many fall away from Him. He is difficult because He has conceived something very great for us, and He wants to give us everything; but how can He entrust to us all heaven, all eternity, before we are tried? In order to receive something very great we need to be tried. In common life, for instance, we have to prove ourselves in order to receive something – say, a promotion of some kind – so how much more do we have to prove ourselves if we are to receive the divine life? And this is not because God is mean or unkind, but because He doesn't want to give us the divine life and then for us to give "that which is holy unto the dogs" (Matt. 7:6), thereby bringing on ourselves even greater desolation. God does all this for our sakes. He has conceived something exceedingly great for us: He created us in His image and likeness, giving us the capacity for receiving the revelation to come at the end of time through His Son.

Question 8: Father, what advice would you have for people living in the world, either priests or lay people, to get started on what you were talking about?

Answer 8: Yes, we spoke about these words of Christ to Silouan: *"Keep thy mind in hell, and despair not."* This is not for everybody – not even for all monks. I remember when I first became a spiritual father I began to grasp a little how this is carried out in life, and I wanted to share it with all my fellows, and

I was trying to teach this to one of the sisters; and Fr. Sophrony said to me (forgive me for speaking so openly): "You are stupid! This is not for everybody, not even for all monks. Tell this person to carry out her obediences and to do the work of the Hegoumen, that is to say, the work of the monastery, and she will be saved." But, people slowly, slowly, with time, become stronger; grace strengthens their nature, and they begin to practise this in some measure. But there is another way, for people living in the world: to keep thanking God continually, thus: "I thank Thee, O Lord, for all the things that Thou hast done for me", and so on, adding at the end, " . . . though I am unworthy." This brings the same result, the same state. Psychologically, it is more acceptable and has the same effect, because thanking God continually intercedes for our weakness before Him, makes up for our weakness. I believe that this is a more accessible way for people living in the world. And when we are strengthened by grace, the same grace will teach us. We must never forget that "one is our Teacher, even Christ" (Matt. 23:10).[63]

Question 9 (Bishop Basil): I just wanted to share with you some words from St. Silouan that speak to this great responsibility and gift, to which Father Zacharias referred, especially to you as priests, intercessors. St. Silouan says, "The Lord moves the soul by His grace to pray for the whole world – or sometimes to pray for one particular person". He emphasizes how effective and pleasing such prayers are before the Lord: "When the Lord would have mercy on a man, He inspires others with the desire to pray for him, and helps them in their prayer. Therefore we must know that when we feel a wish to pray for someone, it means that the Lord Himself wants to show mercy on that soul and will graciously hear our prayers."[64] It is like He wants to do good for a person, but He wants you to be a partner with Him in doing good for that person. I want to ask Fr. Zacharias to relate one short story, one short vignette; I think it will be a good example. Father, you mentioned that there was some nun who recently asked some spiritual father for a word, and it has to do with poverty and spirit. Do you remember what the word was?

Answer 9: Yes, I was telling the Bishop that some of our people often want a word to inspire their prayer, and sometimes I am very poor, I haven't got such a word. Sometimes, when God has given me to pray with a certain word, and I give it to others, I see that it has an effect. But sometimes I am poor and haven't repented properly, and the word doesn't come. Once, one of the sisters asked for a word. I felt very poor, but still I had to "play my role" as a priest, and I said to her: "Well, tell the Lord: 'Lord, You deserve better, I am sorry I am so poor and have nothing to offer Thee.'" And that inspired her so much to pray! The Bishop also reminded me to add that as priests we must always be very careful with what we say to the people, as one word from us can be of such great help and inspiration to them, because we are all sharers in the priesthood of Christ, and bearers of the priesthood of Christ. We may say a simple word, but the Lord infuses it with strength, and He helps the people. Once I was in Greece and a nun phoned me late in the night to tell me of some problems she was having with a person who was very precious to her, and who had become displeased with her, and punished her. I took the phone, even though I was absolutely dead after a very intense day of working. (At that time, I was proof-reading one of my translations of Fr. Sophrony's books, with the help of a former Professor of mine from Thessalonica, who used to help me check all my translations from Russian into Greek.) And this sister phoned me late one night and told me about her problem, and as I was holding the receiver I was thinking to myself, "Lord, you know that I am dead now, but give me a word for Thy servant." Suddenly, a word came to my mind, which Fr. Sophrony mentions, and which had been given to him by his Hegoumen, Archimandrite Missail, and I told her: "Never mind, be happy that you received a judgment by this person who is responsible for you – that you have been judged by this person. If you accept his judgment, then you are free from the judgment of God, because God does not judge twice."[65] And that sister knew the monastic way, and said to me: "Thank you very much. This is enough for me. I am freed from my problem." I was dead tired, but because I was a priest, God had given me a word and the sister managed to see through her difficulty without any problem afterwards. So, do not be afraid when you are asked for a word! We do not have to be saints: I am an abomination before God, I am the worst of all, but we must not be afraid; we must have the daring of faith to ask God for a word when people are in need of it, because they are His people, He purchased them with His Precious Blood (Acts 20:28, 1 Pet. 1:19). He will give something, and even if He does not give anything, you can say something trivial, because if you ask Him beforehand, He will give you the grace to inform the heart of that person and cause the regeneration of His people. Forgive me, can I be more stupid and say something more? Once I was in Greece, translating the book of Fr. Sophrony, *We Shall See Him as He Is*, and I was living in the mountains, near a convent, because the Gherondissa of the convent there is one of the best Greek philologists and a very good friend of ours. I was translating and giving my work to her to check. (I am not an expert in anything; I don't know anything.) We had the Liturgy two or three times a week, no books to read, I only had my dictionaries with me and the text of Fr. Sophrony; and the people started coming for the Liturgy, in the beginning fifteen or twenty. I started speaking to them in every Liturgy and, except for the Anaphora – I read the prayers of the Liturgy – but except for the Anaphora, all the time during Matins, or even during the Liturgy, whenever I was able, I was just praying in this manner: "God, Lord, give me a little word for these Thy people, whom Thou hast purchased with Thy Precious Blood." That was my prayer, all the time, and – may God forgive me that I say this; I am very scared but nevertheless I shall say it – the moment I took the Gospel from the Holy Table and turned to the people saying, "The reading is from the Holy Gospel according to . . . St. John", let's say, the word that I had to say to them after the reading of the Gospel would appear in front of me. More people started to come, and we reached – I shalln't say how many – but I was very afraid, and when I came back to the Monastery I told Fr. Sophrony what had happened, and he said to me, "This was not for you; it had nothing to do with you. God wanted to help those people, and He made you a sharer of that." So, we must not be afraid to ask God. Priesthood is such a great and dynamic gift from God, and if we ask Him to quicken it, it can accomplish things which are beyond us. Forgive me for being so stupid.

NOTES

1. The Greek *katenteuktés*, which is a translation of the Hebrew *miphga'*, can mean either *target* or (as in Job. 7:20) *accuser.* Thus, the uppermost meaning here is *one who can call God to account.*

2. Cf. *Saint Silouan, op. cit.*, pp. 27–28.

3. *Ibid.*, p. 197.

4. *Ibid.*, p. 19.

5. *Ibid.*, p. 270.

6. Cf. *We Shall See Him, op. cit.*, p. 33.

7. Cf. *Saint Silouan, op. cit.*, pp. 25–26.

8. *Ibid.*

9. *Ibid.*, p. 344.

10. *Ibid.*, p. 270.

11. *Ibid.*, p. 362.

12. *Ibid.*, pp. 458–459.

13. *Ibid.*, p. 320.

14. *Ibid.*, p. 362.

15. *Ibid.*

16. Cf. *ibid.*, p. 394.

17. *Ibid.*, p. 345.

18. *Ibid.*, p. 328.

19. *Ibid.*, pp. 283–284.

20. *Ibid.*, p. 348.

21. Cf. *On Prayer, op. cit.*, p. 56.

22. Cf. *Saint Silouan, op. cit.*, p. 56.

23. That is to say, Matt. 22:37: "Thou shalt love the Lord thy God with all thy heart, and with all thy soul, and with all thy mind."

24. *Cf. Saint Silouan, op. cit.*, p. 104.

25. *Cf. ibid.*, p. 105.

26. *Thou shalt love thy neighbour as thyself.*

27. *Op. cit.*, p. 274.

28. The saint himself acknowledges that "the grace of the Holy Spirit makes every man like unto the Lord Jesus Christ while still here on earth." *Ibid.*, p. 281.

29. *Ibid.*, p. 310.

30. *Cf. ibid.*, p. 105.

31. *Cf. ibid.*, p. 304.

32. *Cf. ibid.*, p. 282.

33. *Ibid.*, p. 332.

34. *Ibid.*, p. 383.

35. *Ibid.*, p. 363.

36. *We Shall See Him, op. cit.*, p. 73.

37. *Ibid.*, p. 124.

38. *Saint Silouan, op. cit.*, p. 26.

39. *Ibid.*, pp. 200–201.

40. *Cf. ibid.*, p. 40.

41. *Cf.* Step 5, in St. John Climacus, *The Ladder, op. cit.*, p. 59.

42. *We Shall See Him, op. cit.*, pp. 206, 218.

43. *Cf. ibid.*, p. 55.

44. *Cf. On Prayer, op. cit.*, pp. 30–31.

45. *Cf. ibid.*, p. 13: "He has withdrawn and I am left empty; and I feel my emptiness like a death."

46. *Cf. ibid.*

47. *Cf. We Shall See Him, op. cit.*, p. 128.

48. *Cf. ibid.*, p. 61.

49. *Cf. Saint Silouan, op. cit.*, p. 201.

50. *Cf. We Shall See Him, op. cit.*, p. 124.

51. *Cf. ibid.*, p. 50.

52. *Saint Silouan, op. cit.*, p. 457.

53. *Cf. We Shall See Him, op. cit.*, pp. 122, 127.

54. *Cf. ibid.*, p. 85.

55. *Cf. ibid.*, p. 72.

56. *Cf. Saint Silouan, op. cit.*, p. 383.

57. *Cf. We Shall See Him, op. cit.*, p. 64ff.

58. "The mind in the heart stands consciously before the face of God, filled with due reverence and begins to pour itself before Him. This is spiritual prayer, and all prayer should be of this nature." *What is Prayer* in *The Art of Prayer*, compiled by Igumen Chariton of Valamo, trans. E. Kadloubovsky and E. M. Palmer, edited with an introduction by Timothy Ware (London: Faber and Faber Limited, 1966), p. 53.

59. See esp. St. Gregory Palamas, Homily LIII, 49 and 53, *On the Entry into the Holy of Holies of Our Exceedingly Pure Lady, Mother of God and Ever-Virgin Mary, and Her Divine Manner of Life There.* English trans. in *Mary the Mother of God: Sermons by Saint Gregory Palamas*, edited by C. Veniamin (South Canaan, PA: Mount Thabor Publishing, 2005), pp. 41–42 and 43–44.

60. See n. 1 above.

61. *Cf.* prayer of the *Anaphora* beginning, "Our God, God of salvation . . .", *Divine Liturgy of St. Basil the Great.*

62. *The Divine Liturgy*, petition of the *Offertory.*

63. Gk. *kathegetes*, lit. *guide, teacher, professor.*

64. *Saint Silouan, op. cit.*, pp. 492 and 493.

65. *Cf. On Prayer, op. cit.*, pp. 52–53.

"Keep Thy Mind in Hell and Despair Not"*

CHRIST IS THE "SIGN" OF GOD to men in every age, and His Way is the only true way leading to the eternal kingdom of the Father, and of the Son, and of the Holy Spirit. When the Jews erroneously asked Jesus for a "sign from heaven" (Luke 11:16), He repeatedly spoke of "the sign of Jonas the Prophet", which was given to the generation of the Ninevites, as being the *only* sign of God for the world (*cf.* Luke 11:30).[1] The sign of Jonas prophetically foreshadowed Christ's descent into the lower parts of the earth, followed by His ascent above the Heavens. In Christ's Person, in His life and in His example, was given the answer to all man's questions. He became the eternal sign of God for every age and generation. This event of His descent and ascent constitutes also the fount of every grace flowing from the Holy Spirit (*cf.* Eph. 4:8–9).

A "friend" of God is one who receives this sign with faith, taking it as a model and pattern for his life. "I have called you friends; for all things that I have heard of my Father I have made known unto you", says the Lord (John 15:15). As Jonas was a sign to the Ninevites, so also are the friends of Christ in every age a sign for their generation, according to His unfeigned promise that "I am with you alway, even unto the end of the world" (Matt. 28:20). They are the sign of God for their generation, because God speaks through them, and by their words they provide an answer to all the problems of their own age. They become the sign of God when, by the grace of the Holy Spirit, the Way of Christ is revealed to them: descent, even unto hell, and ascent, according to the example and way which Christ showed. One cannot be holy, a friend and a disciple of the Teacher, of the Master, that is to say, of Christ, if one has not traversed this road to the end and "known the mysteries of the kingdom of God" (cf. Luke 8:10). It is only on this condition that one may become a "light in the world", proclaiming "the word of life" for one's generation (cf. Phil. 2:15-16). If according to the word of the Apostle Paul, "the saints shall judge the world" (1 Cor. 6:2), this is right simply because they first became the mouth of God the Word, and by their word they gave light to the world. Christ spoke through them, and He himself states: "The word that I have spoken, the same shall judge him in the last day" (John 12:48).

According to the spiritual law which we have set forth above, if the Church, guided by the Holy Spirit "into all truth" (John 16:13), glorified Silouan as an "apostolic and prophetic teacher" – as he is called in the *Act of Canonization*[2] – what should we seek in his person, life and word as being the characteristics of one who is a sign of God for his generation? What is "the word of life" which God revealed to our generation through him? If one has ears to hear and a mind to understand the words of the "unlettered" Silouan, he will recognize their divine origin, despite their simplicity. He will remember the answer St. Silouan gave to Fr. Stratonicos' question: "How do the perfect speak?" – that "the perfect never say anything of themselves ... They only say what the Spirit inspires them to say."[3] He will see that his words are given by the Holy Spirit, and that *not even one of his words* is a product of human reasoning, but all of them are born of a pure heart, a heart which is "enlarged" (2 Cor. 6:11), according to the gift of Christ. In a short talk such as this it is not possible to examine all the words of St. Silouan, which are offered as words of God for our generation. It is enough for us to hold on to one word only, and try to go to its very depths. This word then, may become, by God's grace, a lens through which we can gaze fixedly at the endless horizons of the "great mystery of godliness" (1 Tim. 3:16), which has been revealed to us. So, today the word under consideration is the word of Christ to Silouan: *"Keep thy mind in hell, and despair not"*, which came as God's answer to his prayer, "Lord, teach me what I must do that my soul may become humble."[4] We shall speak about this word, *"Keep thy mind in hell, and despair not"*, because it is central to the teaching of St. Silouan, and also to the understanding of the Way of Christ, that way which first descends and afterwards ascends, and which gives birth to all the gifts of the Holy Spirit.

Chronologically, our generation is nearer to the Second Coming of Christ than ever before. That is logical. Moreover, the words of Christ, "Nevertheless when the Son of man cometh, shall he find faith on the earth?" (Luke 18:8), imply that our generation finds itself in greater want and tribulation, and has need of salvation, more than ever before. What are the tribulations which emphatically constitute the common and distinctive mark of our generation? We can name a few, which according to our poor opinion are the chief ones: pride, the darkening of the mind and its captivity by the spirit of wickedness, despair and the multitude of involuntary afflictions which accompany it, and finally, despondency – the manifest lack of concern for the salvation which God offers every day to the world. This revealing word from Christ Himself: *"Keep thy mind in hell, and despair not"*, offered by St. Silouan to his contemporaries who are of like passions, provides the answer to these and many other symptoms.

After this short introduction to the subject and before proceeding to analyse it, I should like to briefly refer to some points in the saint's life which preceded these revelatory words. St. Silouan was born in a village in Russia in 1866. While still a young man, a series of intense and alternating states of the grace of God and an acute sense of hell, gave birth in him the desire for monasticism. He set out for Mount Athos at the age of twenty-six, and after six months of even more intense struggle he was deemed worthy to behold the "living Christ" before the icon of the Saviour. Although this event only lasted an instant, it had such an effect on him that from that moment his prayer embraced all the peoples

of the earth. He suddenly acquired a universal conscience. But
how could this happen to a simple villager, barely educated, who
perhaps had never even seen a map of the world? This happened
because at the time of his vision of Christ, the very state of Christ
Himself was transmitted to him, and we know that Christ, as the
"second Adam" and the true "High Priest" of the New Testament
(*cf.* Heb. 4:14, 7:26, 8:1), carries in Himself the whole of mankind
of every age. The grace that St. Silouan received during his vision
was great, and filled not only his soul but even his body, which, as
he said, "longed to suffer for Christ".[5]

This grace, however, gradually diminished and Silouan was
attacked by thoughts from the enemy. He lost that indescribable
peace which he had felt with the grace of the vision, but it was
not possible for him to accept this change in himself passively.
From the lives of the saints we see that when man has known such
a measure of grace, he remains inconsolable following its diminution or loss. At that moment, Silouan was ready to endure every
sacrifice for the sake of reacquiring the lost treasure. Just like the
Apostle, who says: "Not as though I had already attained, either
were already perfect: but I follow after, if that I may apprehend
that for which also I am apprehended of Christ Jesus" (Phil. 3:12).

So, Silouan could not have resumed a normal way of life after
the vision. He went to seek help from an experienced spiritual
father of the monastery, Fr. Anatoly, to whom he told all that
had happened to him. This spiritual father helped him by his
advice, but did not hide his amazement for the young novice,
and said to him: "If you are like this *now*, what will you be by
the time you are an old man!"[6] These words gave Silouan over
to a delicate and difficult war with vainglory, something complicated and dangerous for the young novice. The Desert Fathers
would say that praise to our brother, without discernment, can
deliver him into the hands of the enemy, that is to say, can make
him a victim of conceited self-love. In this way, by God's permission, Silouan was engaged in a titanic war against vainglory and
pride. The episode is described by his biographer vividly and
with understanding, as follows: "At all events, the young and

still inexperienced monk Simeon set out on the most difficult, complex, subtle battle against conceit. Pride and vainglory entail every disaster and downfall – grace departs, the heart grows cold, prayer feeble. The mind is distracted, and wrong thoughts set to work. The soul contemplating another life, the heart that has savoured the grace of the Holy Spirit, the mind that has known purity are unwilling to accept the base thoughts that attack. But how is this to be managed?"[7] This is our question now.

This difficult period of alternating states and vacillations lasted fifteen years, during which time Fr. Silouan tried every form of asceticism and way of life he could think of, which might restore him to the grace which he had known. During the night, he would sleep on a stool for only one and a half to two hours and this only in snatches of about fifteen to twenty minutes.[8] As far as his prayer of repentance is concerned, we can catch a glimpse of it from these words of *Adam's Lament*, in which he speaks of himself. In this chapter, he actually gives us a portrait of himself.

"Adam, father of all mankind, in paradise knew the sweetness of the love of God; and so when for his sin he was driven forth from the garden of Eden, and was widowed of the love of God, he suffered grievously and lamented with a mighty moan. And the whole desert rang with his lamentations. His soul was racked as he thought: 'I have grieved my beloved Lord.' He sorrowed less after paradise and the beauty thereof – he sorrowed that he was bereft of the love of God, which insatiably, at every instant, draws the soul to Him.

"In the same way the soul which has known God through the Holy Spirit but has afterwards lost grace experiences the torment that Adam suffered. There is an aching and a deep regret in the soul that has grieved the beloved Lord." *Aside:* That is real hell! *End of aside.*

"Adam pined on earth, and wept bitterly, and the earth was not pleasing to him. He was heartsick for God, and this was his cry:

"'My soul wearies for the Lord, and I seek Him in tears.
"'How should I not seek Him?

"'When I was with Him my soul was glad and at rest,
and the enemy could not come nigh me.'"[9]

In St. John of the Ladder's wonderful description of those living in repentance in the "Prison" outside the monastery in Alexandria, it is clear that all who have known the light of the grace of Christ, and then lost it, are ready to give themselves over to death at any moment, in order to regain with knowledge the first grace of their calling, and not be shut out of the "bridal chamber" of Christ. As St. John of the Ladder says, their repentance takes on the form of those lamenting over their dead.[10] In *Adam's Lament*, St. Silouan says the following:

"Adam wept:
"'The desert cannot pleasure me;
nor the high mountains, nor meadow nor forest,
nor the singing of birds.
"'I have no pleasure in any thing.
"'My soul sorrows with a great sorrow:
"'I have grieved God.
"'And were the Lord to set me down in paradise again,
there, too, would I sorrow and weep –
'O why did I grieve my beloved God?'"[11]

Living like this, and passing the nights with the tormenting thought, "O why did I grieve my beloved God?", and not departing from the love he felt for God at the time of the vision, he would come to the point of asking, "Where art Thou, O my Light? Where art Thou, O my joy? Why hast Thou forsaken me?"[12] Silouan's biographer gives the following explanation in the saint's own words: "If in the beginning the Lord had not given me to know how much He loves man, I could not have survived one of those nights, and yet they were legion."[13]

I cite now Fr. Sophrony's description of the last night of his fifteen years of martyrdom, which is also the most dramatic, when God intervened and gave the solution:

"It was fifteen years that the Lord had appeared to him, and Silouan was engaged in one of these nocturnal struggles with devils which so tormented him. No matter how he tried, he could not pray with a pure mind. At last he rose from his stool, intending to bow down and worship, when he saw a gigantic devil standing in front of the ikon, waiting to be worshipped. Meanwhile, the cell filled with evil spirits. Father Silouan sat down again, and with bowed head and aching heart he prayed,

"'Lord, Thou seest that I desire to pray to Thee with a pure mind but the devils will not let me. Instruct me, what must I do to stop them hindering me?'

"And in his soul he heard,

"'The proud always suffer from devils.'

"'Lord,' said Silouan, 'teach me what I must do that my soul may become humble.'

"Once more, his heart heard God's answer,

"*Keep thy mind in hell, and despair not.*"[14]

Strange and incomprehensible is God's word to Silouan. Strange and incomprehensible, moreover, is Silouan's reaction to the word which he heard in his heart. He says: "I began to do as the Lord taught me, and my soul was rejoiced by rest in God."[15] This grace realized his passing over "from death to life", and rejoicing, Silouan sings a song of victory, echoing the just men of all ages:

"O the compassion of God! I am an abomination to God and men, yet the Lord so loveth me, giveth me understanding and healeth me, and Himself doth teach my soul humility and love, patience and obedience, and hath poured out the fullness of His mercy upon me. . . . O wonder!"[16]

As soon as the Lord lays His hands upon the soul, she becomes *a new being*: "Who shall describe the joy of knowing the Lord and reaching out toward Him day and night, insatiably? O how blessed and happy are we Christians!"[17] The Lord spoke the words in Silouan's heart, offering him the vision of hell, and amazingly, he immediately emerges possessing great knowledge, and his life is restored with a wealth of grace and of the love of God.

But what is the mystery of God which is enclosed in these words: "*Keep thy mind in hell, and despair not*"? It is evident that knowledge of this mystery brought Silouan victory over the power of the enemy, and a perfect likeness to his master, our Lord Jesus Christ. This is what Silouan witnesses to in another part of his writings:

He who has humbled himself, has conquered the enemy. *No enemy can come near* the man who in his heart esteems himself deserving of eternal fire. No earthly thoughts find place in his soul – heart and mind he lives entirely in God. And the man who has come to know the Holy Spirit, and learned humility of Him, has become like to his Teacher, Jesus Christ, Son of God, and resembles Him.[18]

Why did this word of the Lord free Silouan from the struggle with the enemy, and add to his stature such strength of Spirit and stability of life? This happened because God's word placed Silouan on the very Way of the Lord Himself. By following the Way of the Lord, one's heart is "enlarged", and man becomes unapproachable to his enemies.

As we said at the beginning of our talk, the sign of Jonas represents the way the Lord walked, and the Apostle says that victory came into the world by Christ's descent into hell and His ascent which followed (*cf.* Eph. 4:10). Hence, when the Lord proposes hell to Silouan, and through Silouan, to our despairing generation, He is offering him the possibility for descent, for going down; and reveals to him the means and path to humility, so that having become like the Lord, he may obtain spiritual victory. This is a spiritual journey, and the saint's biographer, Archimandrite Sophrony, says that "those who are led by the Holy Spirit never cease condemning themselves"[19] in their journey *downwards*, towards Christ, who is the head of the "inverted pyramid", and holds all the weight of the pyramid on His shoulders, and takes away the sin of the world.[20] *Aside:* Fr. Sophrony, in his book on St. Silouan, presents this theory of the "inverted pyramid". He says that the empirical cosmic being is like a pyramid: at the top sit the powerful of the earth, who exercise dominion over the nations (*cf.* Matt. 20:25), and at the bottom stand the masses. But the spirit of man, by nature, demands equality, justice and freedom of spirit, and therefore is not satisfied with this "pyramid of being". So, what did the Lord do? He took this pyramid and inverted it, and put Himself at the bottom, becoming its Head. He took upon Himself the weight of sin, the weight of the infirmity of the whole world, and so from that moment on, who can enter into judgment with Him? His justice is above the human mind. So, He revealed His Way to us, and in so doing showed us that no one can be justified but by this way, and so all those who are His must go downwards to be united with Him, the Head of the inverted pyramid, because it is there that the "fragrance" of the Holy Spirit is found; *there* is the power of divine life. Christ alone holds the pyramid, but His fellows, His Apostles and His saints, come and share this weight with Him. However, even if there were no one else, He could hold the pyramid by Himself, because He is infinitely strong; but He likes to share everything with His fellows. Mindful of this, then, it is essential for man to find the way of going down, the way of humility, which is the Way of the Lord, and to become a fellow of Christ, who is the Author of this path. *End of aside.*

Such was the importance to the Lord of this "going down" that when the sons of Zebedee asked for thrones, He said that this was madness (*cf.* Mark 10:35–45). That is to say, to ask to "go up" is madness. This is the way of Lucifer, who wanted to set his throne above the throne of God. The true way of a master is to become a servant, to go down, to become the last. [21] To all those who think themselves worthy of ascent without drinking the cup of descent, Christ said once and for all time, "Ye know not what ye ask" (Mark 10:38). As for Capernaum, which arrogantly "sought after a sign" (*cf.* Matt. 12:39), the Lord said, "And thou, Capernaum, which art exalted to heaven, shalt be thrust down to hell" (Luke 10:15). However, He raised and justified the publican, who "would not lift up so much as his eyes unto heaven" (Luke 18:13), but fulfilled Christ's law, which says, "Whosoever shall exalt himself shall be abased; and he that shall humble himself shall be exalted" (Matt. 23:12, *cf.* Luke 18:13). The publican lowered his head and his mind and went *downwards*, and in "going down", he found his heart, and in his heart he found God (*cf.* Luke 18:10-14). *Aside:* When the Lord was praised by men for His miracles, He did not fear pride, but always sought to give us an example of His Way. Hence, every time He was glorified, He would reveal to us the way of humility by saying, for example, "The Son of man must be delivered into the hands of sinful men, and be crucified, and on the third day rise again" (Luke 24:7). That is to say, He would give us an example not to exercise ourselves in lofty matters. *End of aside.*

Therefore, the Way of the Lord stretches out through death on the Cross to the infernal regions of hell. It is like descending into the waters of baptism. Baptism is an imitation of the Lord's Way. We meet Christ and put Him on (Gal. 3:27), and ascend reborn "in newness of life" (Rom. 6:4), since He first descended into the waters and blessed them. By first going down into the waters, in obedience to His commandment, we come up renewed. "Going down" signifies His death, and this is a real death, because we die to sin, and "coming up" signifies our rebirth "in newness of life". In baptism, we have this tracing of the Way of the Lord, and so it is also when we are commanded to descend into hell: not that we may perish, but so that we may explore even there the wondrous mystery of the divine and humble love which reaches down even into those dreadful regions. This is so that, before the greatness of this love, we may humble ourselves unto the end and, in our turn, respond with gratitude to Christ, so perfectly and so powerfully that nothing, no place, not even hell, can separate us from God the Saviour (*cf.* Rom. 8:35–39). Man will never have full knowledge of the mystery of Christ if he, too, has not been through hell.

This humble journey downwards is the way that the Holy Church points out to us. If we carefully examine her thought as it is expressed in her prayers, we shall see again this twofold movement of descent and ascent. For example, before the service of baptism or of the Divine Liturgy we see the celebrant humbling himself and descending in spirit so that he may be clothed with strength to perform the service of God, and thereby be raised on High, together with the faithful whom the Spirit of the Lord has entrusted to him. *Aside:* I have in mind the prayer before the Cherubic Hymn. *End of aside.* Almost every significant prayer of the Church is divided into two parts: the first part is the descent of the spirit, and the second is the ascent with the cry of faith, trusting in the boundless mercy

of our bountiful Lord. To confirm this truth it is sufficient for one
to read the prayers before Holy Communion.

The life of the faithful is a life of repentance. Through
repentance we have the humble descent "under the mighty
hand of God, that he may exalt us in due time" (1 Pet. 5:6). That
wonderful teacher of *The Ladder*, St. John, says at the end of his
chapter "On Repentance", that by voluntarily accepting retribution and punishment we escape the punishment which is
everlasting.[22] *Aside:* "God does not judge twice."[23] If we judge
ourselves voluntarily, we are free from the second judgment
(*cf.* 1 Cor. 11:31). The judgment in this present time is always
to examine ourselves in the light of His commandments. *End
of aside.* Hence, by descending into hell we do nothing other
than follow the Lord. This is the way of the Lord Himself.
However, the Way of the Lord leads to life, and for this reason
we should not despair. The three holy Hebrew children, whom
Nebuchadnezzar threw into the fiery furnace, wonderfully
foreshadowed the mystery of the Lord's descent and ascent.
The devout youths took upon themselves the sins and iniquities
of their people, and in spirit condemned themselves as being
worthy of the furnace for their injustice. They humbly prayed
to the God of their Fathers: "We have sinned, and have transgressed in departing from Thee, and in all things have we greatly
sinned; and thy commandments have we not heard ... And all that
Thou hast brought upon us, and every thing that Thou hast done
to us, Thou hast done in true judgment" (S. of III Children 5–7).[24]
Since they were prophetically on the Lord Jesus' humble path of
descent they were for that reason made worthy of having the Son
of God, who was as yet without flesh, as their fellow-traveller
and companion. *Aside:* They put themselves in the Way of the
Lord, and they begat Christ as their companion. *End of aside.*
He descended into the furnace and walked with them "in the
midst of the fire" preserving them unharmed (Dan. 3:25).[25] Of
course, the power of this mystery was then active *prophetically*.
However, after the Lord's incarnation, His descent into hell and
ensuing ascent, the power of this same mystery is incomparably

greater, because there is no longer a place in the created world which has not been filled by the energy of His countenance.

Having now spoken about the theological basis of the Lord's word to Silouan, *"Keep thy mind in hell, and despair not"*, it remains for us to explain how to carry this out in practice.

Before continuing, we should clearly stress that all the power of the mystery hidden within this word is due to the fact that the descent of the Lord into hell was voluntary and sinless. It was due only to His obedience and love for His Father and for the desire of salvation for fallen man. For this reason, in order that our descent be blessed and bear fruit, it must be voluntary and by the commandment of the Lord. St. Silouan's experience of hell was a charismatic one, full of grace, and that is why the Lord's revealing word corresponded perfectly to his state. *Aside:* St. Silouan's case is exceptional, that sensation of hell enveloped even his body, not only his spirit. He was experiencing hell piercing even his body. *End of aside.* It is difficult for us to conceive its depth without having had a similar experience. However, since it expresses the tradition of the Church's ascetic life, we shall try, by referring to the Holy Fathers, to go to its root and comprehend its power, even if only in part.

This word, *"Keep thy mind in hell, and do not despair"*, is a commandment of the Lord with the intention that we might imitate Him in His descent, whilst at the same time, trusting in His mercy and the eternal salvation which He obtained for us by His ascent. The mere disposition in us to receive this word and fulfil it in our life attracts the grace of God. *Aside:* The disposition to receive the word of the Lord always attracts grace in us. *End of aside.* Being a divine Light, this grace discloses and confirms this truth: hell is where man finds himself separated from the God of love. It also discloses sin, injustice, and spiritual poverty. This knowledge brings contrition to the soul. Contrition is a precious gift from God to man; it is the beginning of humility and prepares a "dwelling-place" for God in us. As a property of grace, this contrition gives birth to spiritual courage. *Aside:* You see, we can go to a psychologist for psychoanalysis, and he will analyse us, and bring to the surface all our infirmities and defects. And so what? Afterwards we fall into despair! But when the grace of God strips man naked and reveals to him all his infirmity, all his poverty, this same grace gives him the courage to overcome it. There lies the difference! We can go to a psychologist to learn about ourselves, and this may be good, but it is of very limited value. But if God reveals to us our true state, He will also give us the strength to overcome it, and this is very precious. That is why the Prophet would say "Lord, know me that I may come to know Thee" (cf. Jer. 11:18 Lxx). True self-knowledge comes with the knowledge of God. *End of aside.*

As a property of grace, this contrition gives birth to spiritual courage. St. Symeon the New Theologian says the following: "What is more courageous than 'a humble and contrite heart' (Ps. 51:19)? Without difficulty it routs the massed troops of the devils and pursues them to their end."[26] This contrition is spiritual courage, since it is the only state in which man, inspired by the grace of God, dares to stare at His spiritual poverty without despairing, whilst hoping that He who revealed to him the depths of his desolation is also able to carry him across, unharmed, to the other bank where God is. He achieves this through self-condemnation, and the following prophetic attitude: he attributes every justice to God, whereas his own face is covered with shame (cf. Dan. 9:7 Lxx). It is for this reason that St. John of the Ladder says that spiritual courage is victory.[27] It is victory because without the courage born of contrition it is impossible for us to behold clearly our spiritual poverty. Then spiritual poverty becomes a gift which lays the foundation for our spiritual ascent: "Blessed are the poor in spirit: for theirs is the kingdom of heaven" (Matt. 5:3). St. Symeon the New Theologian wonders, "What is more glorious than spiritual poverty, which is the means of obtaining the kingdom of heaven?"[28] St. Silouan knew the power of this spiritual phenomenon – contrition – through Christ's word to him: "*Keep thy mind in hell, and do not despair.*" He would find it by taking refuge, as he says, in his "beloved song":[29]

Soon I shall die, and my accursed soul will descend into the blackness of hell. I shall languish alone in the sombre flames, weeping for my Lord. 'Where art Thou, O Light of my soul? Why hast Thou forsaken me? I cannot live without Thee.'[30]

In the first half of his beloved "psalm", he would place his soul in the fire of hell, which extinguishes every passionate thought, whilst in the second part he would turn his spirit to the love and mercy of Christ, which he knew and bore in his heart. In the first half, he would humbly make his way down, a way of descent, which the proud enemy was unable to follow. *Aside:* The enemy always wants to go up; when we try to go down, he leaves us alone – he can't go down. That is why when we are tormented by thoughts, it is more effective than prayer to stand, bring our mind to our heart and say, "Lord, you know I am the worst of all men." This thought "bites" the heart, and then the enemy departs. It is more efficacious than prayer: it is prayer, but of a different kind. *End of aside.*

Having made his way down, the saint, free of worry from the enemy and inspired by the memory of the Lord's mercy, would turn with all his heart to God, who by His grace would vouchsafe him to ascend. In the same perspective, St. Silouan advises that in order for man to retain the salutary power of contrition he must always remember his sins, humble himself and mourn over them, even if God has forgiven them. Thus is the enemy vanquished! With His word, the Lord revealed to Silouan the way to acquire contrition and humility, and in this way to defeat the enemy. Contrition is spiritual courage and light for the soul, through which man discerns each thought that approaches him. *Aside:* St. Barsanuphius the Great says that if we have contrition, then we can discern the thoughts. At the moment of contrition we can see immediately the alien thoughts that approach; but without contrition we do not always see them. *End of aside.* Contrition leads to humility, which is victory over the enemy, and prepares the soul to become God's dwelling-place. It is a precious gift of grace and is maintained by self-condemnation, the extreme form of which is self-condemnation to hell. St. John of the Ladder verifies this when he describes the "prisoners", who repented in a small monastery outside the larger monastery of Alexandria, praying like this: "We know, we know that in all justice we deserve every punishment and torment." This prayer was able to move to contrition even the very hardness of stones,

says St. John of the Ladder.[31] In another place, he says again
that condemning oneself to hell preserves the mind unruffled
by demonic suggestions.[32] We see, therefore, that putting into
practice the words of the Lord, "*Keep thy mind in hell, and despair
not*", bears the fruit of humility and purity of mind, which are
vital conditions for freedom from passions and union with our
Holy God.

St. Silouan was taught this science by this word of the Lord,
as he himself writes: "I began to do as the Lord taught me, and my
soul was rejoiced by rest in God."[33] As mentioned earlier, he also
says: "He who has humbled himself has conquered the enemy.
No enemy can come near the man who in his heart esteems himself
deserving of eternal fire. No earthly thoughts find place in his
soul – heart and mind he lives entirely in God."[34] And elsewhere,
he adds, "But when my mind emerges from the fire, the suggestions of passion gather strength again."[35]

We have noticed with sadness that nowadays men suffer
dreadfully because their mind is fragmented. Imagination, which
is only one of the mind's activities, is overindulged and dominates
men's lives, leading some to hardness of heart due to pride,
and others to mental illness. According to the teaching of the
Gospel and the Scriptures, the mind works naturally only when
it is united with the heart. Mind and heart are naturally joined
together when the fire of contrition is in the heart. *Aside:* In the
hesychast tradition, it is very important to find the place of the
heart. And this is a way of finding the place of the heart. We have
a "circular" movement, as St. Gregory Palamas says: in the first
instance, the mind, through the fall into sin and the passions,
moves towards creation, is scattered or dispersed over it and, as
it were, becomes "stuck" to the world. We must bring the mind
back to the heart, and when the mind is established in the heart
and dominates the whole of our nature, it then turns our being
towards God. Therefore, there is a triple movement: firstly, an
outward movement, that of the fall; secondly, the return back to
the heart, and thirdly, the movement from the heart to God.[36]
When they speak about the Jesus Payer, Fr. Sophrony and all the

hesychasts greatly emphasize repentance of *this* kind, because it is an infallible way of finding the heart, of bringing the mind back to its natural base. *End of aside.*

That is why St. Silouan recommends the following therapy for the soul. He gives a principle, a method for the therapy of the fragmented mind and soul, and he says, "Keep your mind in your heart and in hell. The more you humble yourself, the greater the gifts you will receive from God."[37] From the words of St. Silouan it is clear that self-condemnation to hell is not only harmless, but becomes a fount of great gifts. Which are the "greater gifts from God", acquired by keeping the mind in hell? As he says, it gives birth to repentance unto the remission of sins in the soul, and brings the joy of salvation to the heart. Moreover, the saint witnesses that the Lord gives the Holy Spirit to those who work at condemning themselves. This should not be at all surprising, since self-condemnation to hell can only take place in a spirit of humility. The saint writes:

I was thinking to myself, I am an abomination and deserving of every punishment; but instead of punishment the Lord gave me the Holy Spirit. O sweet is the Holy Spirit above all earthly things![38]

These words of St. Silouan are in accordance with the spirit of the New Testament. The Lord gives the following commandment to His disciples, for the moment when they will be persecuted and brought before judges: "Settle it therefore in your hearts, not to meditate before what ye shall answer: For I will give you a mouth and wisdom, which all your adversaries shall not be able to gainsay nor resist" (Luke 21:14–15). The Lord gives the wisdom of the Holy Spirit to all who *willingly* place themselves before the judgment-seat of God, and anticipate His judgment by their voluntary self-condemnation to hell. *Aside:* You know that now we are not brought before any judgment-seat for our faith – though there may come a day when that will happen – but the word of the Lord, which I have just mentioned (Luke 21:14–15), is true for all ages and for all circumstances. Therefore, though we are not persecuted or brought to courts, we voluntarily put ourselves before the judgment-seat of God, and then "we shall be given a mouth and wisdom", that is to say, a prayer of repentance that justifies us and confounds our enemy. *End of aside.*

God does not judge twice,[39] as the Apostle Paul says: "If we would judge ourselves, we should not be judged" (1 Cor. 11:31); and in another place, he says that "we shall all stand before the judgment seat of Christ" (Rom. 14:10), but we shall not all be condemned. It is possible, by willingly condemning oneself even unto hell, to anticipate God's judgment, and by this to be justified even in this life, and become a partaker of God's word and wisdom; and this is the grace of, and betrothal with, the Holy Spirit. Archimandrite Sophrony writes, "God does not judge twice",[40] and St. John of the Ladder says that by voluntarily accepting retribution and punishment we escape the punishment which is everlasting,[41] and elsewhere he says that by present shame we are delivered from future shame.[42]

Aside: I said elsewhere that the more shame we feel in confession, the greater the grace and comfort of the Holy Spirit we receive after our confession. Why? Because the way of shame is the way of the Lord, and when we put ourselves in the way of the Lord, we immediately beget Him as our companion. It was through the Cross of shame that He saved us; so, when we bear a little shame for His sake, in order to repent and come to confession, He considers it as a thanksgiving to Him, and in return He gives us the comfort of the "Comforter". This is one reason why the sacrament of confession is so powerful for our regeneration. We see a demonstration of this in the case of Zacchaeus, a noble man of Jericho, a notable personage who made himself a laughing-stock by climbing up a sycamore tree to fulfil his desire to see Christ. He did not consider the taunts of the people; and because he suffered shame to see Christ, the Lord immediately noticed him and harkened to him. The Lord was on His way from Jericho to Jerusalem to suffer the Cross of shame, and He saw something akin to that in Zacchaeus who, by bearing shame in order to see Him, put himself in the way of the Lord, and attracted the Lord's visitation by this kinship of the spirit. And what happened when the Lord visited Zacchaeus? Zacchaeus was restored to a fourfold dimension, that is to say, the mystery of the forthcoming Cross and Resurrection of Christ became active in Zacchaeus' life. He put himself in the way of shame, and because of the little shame he bore, he received the fourfold grace of the Cross, as St. Paul says (*cf.* Eph. 3:18).[43] Zacchaeus went down by shame; he was brought up by the visitation of the Lord; he was enlarged by His grace to restore every injustice, and by this enlargement embraced all mankind in his heart (*cf.* Luke 19:2-8). The mystery of the cross was active in the life of Zacchaeus at that moment. *End of aside.*

And so, by present shame we are delivered from future shame, because shame is the Way of the Lord. That is why we must always examine: "Is this the Way of the Lord?" Then surely, if it is the Way of the Lord, we will have Him as our companion: He will visit us; He will raise us up; He will enlarge our hearts. We see the same golden thread of tradition unceasingly unfolding in the teaching of the ascetic fathers. It is clear that self-condemnation to hell is the most powerful means for one to be delivered from hell. *Aside:* I am sorry to speak about this "infernal" asceticism. We cannot speak about these things to those "outside", to the people in the world. This is not for the general public. But you are teachers of the New Israel, and so it is good for us to know these things, and for each one to apply them in his own measure. *End of aside.*

Self-condemnation is inspired by the grace of the Holy Spirit: it brings contrition, cleanses the mind, leads to humility, defeats the enemies, gives freedom from sins, and makes man a participant of the Holy Spirit. I shall pass over the words of the Desert Fathers, which are well known to many, and just quote a shorter extract from St. Gregory Palamas, where he expresses the same science that we have seen in St. Silouan. St. Gregory Palamas says in his homily on the Sunday of the Publican:

If someone really accounts himself guilty of eternal punishment, he will courageously endure not just dishonour but also harm, disease and, in fact, every kind of misfortune and ill-treatment. He who shows such patience, as though in debt and guilty, is delivered by a very light condemnation, temporary and ephemeral, from truly grievous, unbearable and unending punishment. Sometimes he may even be delivered from dangers threatening him now, because God's kindness begins from that point, due to his patience. Someone chastened by God said, 'I will bear the chastening of the Lord, because I have sinned against Him' [cf. Micah 7:9 Lxx].[44]

Aside: Here, we find the same science as we see in St. Silouan, but from the psychological point of view, and it is important that we see this phenomenon from every angle. What St. Gregory Palamas means by this is that when man condemns himself to hell, which is the greatest voluntary self-condemnation, he will not notice insults or some other hardship in life, because he has already "descended to the bottom".

This attitude is very helpful especially in common life. Once someone confessed to me that she was suspecting that some other person did not like her, and she became upset about it. I said to her, "Our Fathers used to sell themselves into slavery in order to free their fellows; and you, by the suspicion that maybe this person does not like you, have grown cold. How can this be?" And she was healed, simply by recalling that some of the saints sold themselves into slavery in order to free others. I think one such example was St. Serapion, who would do this again and again. *End of aside.*

We see, therefore, in one unbroken tradition the same experience formulated in a variety of ways. The excellence of the principle given to St. Silouan consists in the fact that it proceeds as a direct revelation of the Lord, and in its brevity. It is in two parts: the first, *"Keep thy mind in hell"*, suggests the Lord's descent. The second part, *"and despair not"*, balances the first part with hope, for the Way of the Lord is full of Truth and Life (cf. John 14:6). *Aside:* According to our state and strength, we can place our emphasis, either on the first part, or on the second part. There are monks who feel that their heart is hard, and dwell longer on the first part, saying, "I am not going to be saved and I do not deserve God's salvation." And by doing so, they try to crush the arrogance of their heart, and soften it. Others, who are already softened by other tribulations and afflictions, put the emphasis on the second part. But the healthy sign is always the following: if prayer goes well, this means that it is inspired by God. If prayer does not go well, we must stop and reconsider things. The sign of God's pleasure in this exercise should be the fact that prayer goes with comfort and ease. *End of aside.*

The word of the Lord to Silouan is proffered in the form of a commandment. This reveals the necessity of its fulfilment in our time. Nowadays, the seduction of carnal pleasures has spread and augmented to a high degree, offering subtle and intense enjoyment in order "to seduce, if it were possible, even the elect" (Mark 13:22). Through this commandment, man is given the possibility to follow the Lord in humble descent, and thereby make his own the spiritual gifts which gushed forth from the Lord's ascent. In other words, he is given the ability to weigh up the temptation of his time decisively and victoriously, since he bears the fullness of the true and incorrupt comfort of the Holy Spirit, which crowns the descent and ascent of the Lord.

Aside: We find an emphasis on the theme of the sacrifice of the Lord in the apostolic preaching, and I think this is a central theme in the Gospel, because our Lord became for us "the Lamb slain from the foundation of the world" (Rev. 13:8), and also because in those times people appreciated the notion of sacrifice, sacrifice for one's country, family, friends, and so on. Nowadays, all these values are levelled out. Nothing remains in our times. Today people want pleasure, but this too can be a way of evangelising them, to say to them, "Do you want pleasure? All right! There is no greater delight than in the gift of the Holy Spirit." Of course, this can be a bit dangerous, because we need to add a corrective when saying this. Nowadays there is an emphasis on the charismatic movement and such things. People want pleasure. People want delight. People want comfort. And we say to them: "Yes, come! Here is the comfort of the Comforter. This is the gift of Pentecost." But we must always warn the people and add the corrective that this is achieved only by putting ourselves in the Way of the Lord. *End of aside.*

Our times are marked by a strong "lust of the flesh" and "pride of life" (1 John 2:16; *cf.* 2 Tim. 3:2), as well as by the pervasive feeling of fear and general despair. The first half of the Lord's word to

St. Silouan leads to humility and prevents the first temptation of fear. The second, touches on the final redemption, thereby strengthening hope and overcoming the second temptation, that of despair.

Archimandrite Sophrony believed that the word given to Silouan was a gift of God's divine providence. The Lord deigned to provide mankind with a spiritual counterbalance to the danger of complete annihilation contained in Einstein's scientific discovery. These two events approximately coincided in time.[45] *Aside:* That is to say, the providence of God gave Einstein the formula by which all matter can be transformed into energy ($E = mc^2$). But implicit in that is the danger of complete destruction of the universe. At the same time, God gave Silouan this word that counterbalances this danger and this fear. That is to say, a man who is ready to place himself in the Way of the Lord, which goes down, cannot be affected even by that. *End of aside.*

In the conditions of today's world the experience of hell is a reality for many people. They often come face to face with titanic impulses and confusion of intellect. The human mind falters, and remains in this pitiful state. It is held captive by the pain of the reality which surrounds it, and easily seeks to break away from it, so as to find comfort in the substitutes which the passions of a world alienated from God offer. This tendency, often encountered in our day, leads to a continually increasing estrangement and diffusion. *Aside:* That is to say, man does not want to face the hell in which he finds himself, and seeks to escape from it through substitutes, only to find himself more entangled in it than before. *End of aside.*

The stress on the verb "keep", *stay* your mind in hell, in the first part of the commandment, shows that if one voluntarily and persistently keeps in one's mind a vision of the general hell of this present life, one is on the way to salvation and healing. This vision should inspire repentance and prayer for the salvation of all those who are in a similar state of suffering. The negative energy which comes from this experience of hell is transformed by this prophetic attitude of self-condemnation into energy for converse with God, which conquers the passions, bringing our life to the ontological level. *Aside:* Therefore, we should find this to be a formula given to us by the way of our Lord, a formula that converts all energy that assails us to spiritual energy, giving us the strength to converse with our beloved God. *End of aside.*

St. Silouan's word truly expresses a great spiritual science, the only one which can effectively oppose the all-destroying corruption and devastation, apocalyptically being perpetrated in these last times by the spirit of wickedness. Through the greater pain of voluntary self-condemnation to hell, and by virtue of the Lord's commandment, the believer can triumph over every other pain and temptation, and prove the love of Christ to be stronger than death, as is He who "conquered death by death".[46] Whatever is done willingly and in fulfilment of a commandment of God is inspired by divine wisdom, and leads to eternal victory. This victory renders man above this world, like unto Christ, who, by His extreme humility, overcame the world (*cf.* John 16:33).

And I would like to finish by remembering the words of St. Basil the Great, who exhorts, "Make voluntary that which is involuntary. Do not be sparing of the life which of necessity we shall be deprived of."[47] That is to say, we must chose either to live in order to die or to die in order to live (*cf.* Matt. 10:39). Forgive me.

Questions & Answers

Question 1 (Bishop Basil): What are we to understand by the word "mind"? I know the Lord did not speak English, or maybe He did. My question is: Are we to understand "mind" as *Nous*?

Answer 1: In Greek mind is *Nous*, in Russian *Um* (as in the Lord's word to Silouan: *"Dyerzhi 'um' tvoy vo adye, i nye otchaivaysya"*, that is, *"Keep thy* mind *in hell, and do not despair"*). This is the faculty by which man beholds God. It is the faculty that God gave man from the beginning, which, ineffably, enables us to enjoy God's presence. It is the *nous* of man that is called Israel in Jacob. "Israel" is the *nous that beholds God.* Because Jacob wrestled the whole night, and in the morning saw God, he was given the name Israel, that is to say, *the mind that beholds God* (*cf.* Gen. 32:24–30). Therefore, it is that inner faculty which God gave to man at the moment of creation, by which he can ineffably enjoy the vision of God, the presence of God – a presence that was lost with his falling into sin.

Question 2: How would you define shame? And could voluntary condemnation be understood in a way that is detrimental to us, and which might even lead to despair?

Answer 2: Yes, self-condemnation can become a morbid thing if it is not accompanied by faith, by trust in God. But if we know to whom we present ourselves, we shall have the courage to take some shame upon ourselves. I remember that when I became a spiritual father at the monastery, Fr. Sophrony said to me, "Encourage the young people that come to you to confess just those things about which they are ashamed, because that shame will be converted into spiritual energy that can overcome the passions and sin." In confession, the energy of shame becomes energy against the passions. As for a definition of shame, I would say it is *the lack of courage to see ourselves as God sees us.*

I remember a remarkable lady who came to confession. She used to take people to her house for six months in order to help them when they had a crisis. One day she came and told me, "I am not at peace, and I do not know where I have stumbled. I examine myself and I see nothing wrong." Fearful and ignorant as I am, I did not know what to say to her. Somehow I managed to bring my mind to my heart and ask for a little word, and I said to her, "But it is not enough to see ourselves as *we* can see ourselves, we must see ourselves as God sees us. So, pray to Him: 'Lord, deliver me from my secret sin.'" She was a very pious woman. She started praying like that, and after two days she came back and said, "Now I know where I stumbled", and she told me. It was good, because she discovered it herself, and so she was courageous to confess it and, by the strength of the Lord, she had already overcome it.

I do not like to ask questions in confession. I hear whatever the people wish to tell me, I read the prayer, and if I have a little word, I give it. We must try to say a word to inspire people, and this inspiration will reveal their state. It takes longer but it is surer.

Question 3: Father, could you tell us something about Fr. Sophrony in his last days?

Answer 3: I do not know what to say. We had such ease of access to him! Myself, I had the key to his house; I could enter any time, day or night. If I wanted to ask him something, and he was asleep, I only had to shake his armchair and he would open his eyes and say, "*Shto?* What?" and in the twinkling of an eye I would have a word that really informed the heart. We had such access to him, but we never lost sight of the fact that he was different, that he was "a man of God", all his being was rapt in God.

Very noble and kind as he was, when he was speaking with me in Russian or in Greek, he would never address me in the singular, but always in the plural. Usually we do this for people who are older than we are. (In English, though, there is no distinction between formal and familiar speech.) He was strict with us when he perceived pride in us, because he knew that if he did not "service us", we would have a crash. Otherwise, he was very loving and very kind. We used to go and "tire" him, especially myself, because I was very talkative and I had a lot of questions. Sister X and I were the ones who tired him most. Fr. Sophrony named her "a barrel of questions", and another sister said to me, "That's why she's become 'a barrel of answers' now!" When he got tired, in order to tell us that it is enough, he would say a very nice rhyme in Russian, like a poem: "Allow me to express my gratitude and, with heartfelt satisfaction, take my leave."

So, I went to see him two weeks before he died. At that time we were building the Crypt, where we are going to be buried and, of course, Fr. Sophrony was going to be the first. The walls and the roof were ready, but it was still muddy underneath, as there was yet no floor. As he was accompanying me to the door, he looked at the Crypt and asked, "How long will it take for it to be finished?" I answered, "Father, two more weeks, I suppose." He replied, "Hum. For me it is difficult to wait even one hour: I have said everything to the Lord; now I must go." It must be wonderful to feel in your heart that you have spoken to the Lord to the end, and that remains in eternity, and you are ready to go. Myself, I have the feeling that I have never spoken to the Lord.

I went to see him again, about a week before he died. He was already lying in bed, whereas before he was always sitting in an armchair. He said to me, "Have you written the book I have asked you to write?" He had asked me to write a book, which I managed to bring out only last summer. I told him I had written two chapters, and I explained to him what their content was. He said, "You must put them at the beginning," and then he added, "I will tell you the four central points of my theory about personhood." In brief, he gave me all his theory about the "hypostatic principle", as he says. It was about a page long, but *very* fundamental – four points. And he was telling me how to proceed in writing the book.

Four days before he died, he closed his eyes, and would not speak to us any more. His face was luminous and not pathetic, but full of tension; he had the same expression as when he would celebrate the Liturgy. Not all of us went in to see him, only Fr. Kyrill, myself, Fr. Nicholas and Fr. Seraphim. Two or three weeks before he died, he invited all the brethren, one by one, to go and sit with him for about an hour in his kitchen, for their last conversation with him. But the four of us had the key to his door, and would go to see him every few hours. We would go in and say, "*Blagoslovitye, Otche*", "Your blessing, Father." He would not open his eyes or utter a word, but he would lift up his hand, blessing us. He blessed us without words, and I understood that he was going. So, myself, I did not want to detain him. Before I used to pray that God extend his old age, as we say in the *Liturgy of St. Basil the Great*: "*to geras perikrateson*", "succour the agéd."[48] But during those days I saw that he was going, and so I began to say, "Lord, grant unto Thy servant a rich entrance into Thy kingdom." I prayed using the words of St. Peter, as we read in his second epistle (*cf.* 2 Pet. 1:11). So, I was constantly saying, "O God, grant a rich entrance to Thy servant, and place his soul together with his Fathers," and I named all his fellow ascetics that I knew he had on the Holy Mountain, starting with St. Silouan, and then all the others.

The last day, I went to see him at six o'clock in the morning. It was a Sunday, and I was celebrating the early Liturgy, while Fr. Kyrill together with the other priests were to celebrate the second. (For practical purposes, on Sundays we have two liturgies at our monastery.) I realized that he was going to leave us that day. I went and started the *Prothesis*; the Hours began at seven o'clock, then the Liturgy followed. During the Liturgy, I said only the prayers of the *Anaphora*, because in our monastery we have the habit of reading them aloud; for the rest, my prayer was continually, "Lord, grant a rich entrance into Thy kingdom to Thy servant." That Liturgy was really different from all the others. The moment I said: "the Holy things unto the Holy", Fr. Kyrill entered the Altar. We looked at each other, he began to sob, and I realized that Fr. Sophrony had gone. Asking what time he departed, I knew that it was the time I was reading the Gospel. I went aside, because Fr. Kyrill wanted to speak with me, and he told me, "Take Communion, give Communion to the faithful, and then announce the departure of Fr. Sophrony and serve the first *Trisagion*; and I will do the same in the second Liturgy." So I parcelled the Lamb, I partook; I gave to the faithful, and I finished the Liturgy. (I don't know how I managed.) Then I came out and I said to the people, "My dear brethren, Christ our God is the sign of God for all the generations of this age, because in His word we find salvation and the solution of every human problem. But the saints of God are also a sign for their generation. Such a Father God gave us in the person of Fr. Sophrony. In his word we found the solution to our problems. And now we must do as the Liturgy teaches us, that is, "to give thanks" and "to make entreaty", "to supplicate". Therefore, let us give thanks to God who has given us such a Father, and let us pray for the repose of his soul. Blessed is our God . . .", and I began the *Trisagion*.

We put him in the Church for four days, because the Crypt was not yet finished and the tomb was not yet built. We left him uncovered in the Church for four days, and we were continually reading the Holy Gospels, from beginning to end, again and again, as is the custom for a priest. We read the Holy Gospels, and we read the *Trisagia* and other prayers; we had the services, the Liturgy, and he was there, in the middle of the Church for four days. (It was really like Easter, such a beautiful and blessed atmosphere!) No one showed any hysteria. Everybody prayed with inspiration. I had a friend, an Archimandrite, who used to come to the monastery every year and spend a few weeks during summer time: Fr. Hierotheos Vlachos, who wrote, *A Night in the Desert of the Holy Mountain*. He is a Metropolitan now. He came as soon as he heard that Fr. Sophrony had died. He felt the atmosphere, and said to me, "If Fr. Sophrony is not a saint, then there are no saints!" We happened to have some monks from the Holy Mountain who came to see Fr. Sophrony, but they did not find him alive. Fr. Tychon from Simonos Petras was one of them.

Every time the Greeks came to England for medical purposes, they had the habit of coming to the monastery to be read a prayer by Fr. Sophrony, because many were healed. They all relate such things. Two of them, out of gratitude, even built a Church in Greece, dedicated to St. Silouan. The second or the third day after Fr. Sophrony's death, a family came with a thirteen year old child. He had a brain tumour, and his operation was due the next day. Fr. Tychon, from Simonopetra, came to me, and said, "These people are very sad, they came and did not find Fr. Sophrony. Why don't you read some prayers for the child?" I said to him, "Let us go together. Come and be my reader. We will read some prayers in the other Chapel." We went and read the prayers for the child, and at the end Fr. Tychon said, "You know, why don't you make the child go under the coffin of Fr. Sophrony? He will be healed. We are wasting our time reading prayers." I told him that I could not do that, because the people would say that he has only just died and we are already trying to promote his canonization, "So, you do it!" I said to him, "You are an Athonite monk; nobody can say anything." He took the child by the hand, and made him pass under the coffin. The next day they operated on the child and found nothing. They closed his skull and said, "Wrong diagnosis. It was probably an inflammation." It happened that the child was accompanied by a doctor from Greece, who had the X-ray plate, showing the tumour, and who told them, "We know very well what this 'wrong diagnosis' means." The next week, the whole family of that child, who were from Thessalonica, came to the monastery to give thanks at the tomb of Fr. Sophrony. The child has grown, he is twenty-one years old now, and he is very well. When they came to give thanks the week after, they found in the middle of the Church the coffin of Mother Elisabeth, the oldest nun of the monastery, a hundred and one years old. She died exactly thirteen days after Fr. Sophrony. The family said, "Hum! Every time we come here we find somebody dead in the middle of the Church."

This was something from the last days of Fr. Sophrony. I have never been so open in my life as I have been with you during these days. Forgive me for being like that. Although our dear Bishop warned me that his clergymen are so good that they will make me open up, I did not take any precautions.

Bishop Basil's Afterword: A sign of a monastic's love for his fellows is that he puts himself "in danger". We thank Fr. Zacharias for putting himself in danger by sharing with you, because you are his fellow priests, things that he would not share with others. And really, treat these things like they are – pearls – and pray that God will preserve him as he is, and not let any condemnation come upon him because of his love for us.

NOTES

* Paper read at the *Twenty-Seventh Annual Adult Education Series* under the general theme *A Modern-Day Saint and His Disciple: Saint Silouan the Athonite and Father Sophrony* (Saint Tikhon's Seminary, September 2, 1997). First published in *Alive in Christ,* Vol. XIII, no. 3 (Winter 1997), pp. 15–21, and 34; also in *The Tikhonaire* (South Canaan, PA: St. Tikhon's Orthodox Theological Seminary, 1998), pp. 46–52.

1. The verse in question runs as follows: "For as Jonas was a sign unto the Ninevites, so shall also the Son of man be to this generation."

2. *Patriarchal Act of Canonization*, Protocol Number 823/26.11.1987.

3. *Saint Silouan, op. cit.*, p. 57.

4. *Ibid.*, pp. 42, 460.

5. *Ibid.*, p. 320.

6. *Ibid.*, p. 36.

7. *Ibid.*, pp. 36–37.

8. *Ibid.*, p. 39.

9. *Ibid.*, p. 448.

10. Step 5:9, in St. John Climacus, *The Ladder, op. cit.*, p. 56; and see also *Saint Silouan, op. cit.*, p. 41: "The husband who has lost his beloved wife, or the mother her precious son, can but partially understand the grief of one who has lost grace."

11. *Saint Silouan, op. cit.*, p. 450.

12. *Ibid.*, p. 374.

13. *Ibid.*, pp. 41–42.

14. *Ibid.*, p. 42.

15. *Ibid.*, p. 431.

16. *Ibid.*, pp. 430–431.

17. *Ibid.*, p. 431.

18. *Ibid.*, p. 411.

19. *On Prayer, op. cit.*, p. 174.

20. *Saint Silouan, op. cit.*, pp. 237–239.

21. Christ, who "came not to be ministered unto, but to minister, and to give his life a ransom for many" (Matt. 20:28), bade His disciples to follow His example: "Ye know that the princes of the Gentiles exercise dominion over them, and they that are great exercise authority upon them. But it shall not be so among you: but whosoever will be great among you, let him be your minister; And whosoever will be chief among you, let him be your servant" (Matt. 20:25–27).

22. *Cf.* Step 5:42, in St. John Climacus, *The Ladder, op. cit.*, p. 66.

23. *On Prayer, op. cit.*, p. 52.

24. *The Song of the Three Holy Children* is included among the Old Testament Apocrypha in most English editions of the Bible. See also Dan. 3:26–30.

25. "Lo, I see four men loose . . . and the form of the fourth is like the Son of God."

26. *Discourses (Catecheses)* II, 2, in *Symeon the New Theologian: The Discourses,* Eng. trans. C. J. deCatanzaro, in the series *Classics of Western Spirituality* (New York: Paulist Press, 1980), p. 48.

27. *Cf.* Step 14:36, in *The Ladder, op. cit.,* p. 103.

28. *Discourses, loc. cit.*

29. *Saint Silouan, op. cit.,* p. 46.

30. *Ibid.*

31. Step 5:12, in *The Ladder, op. cit.,* p. 56.

32. *Cf.* Step 7:10, *ibid.,* p. 71.

33. *Saint Silouan, op. cit.,* p. 431.

34. *Ibid.,* p. 411.

35. *Ibid.,* p. 212.

36. See I, ii, 5, in *The Triads: Gregory Palamas,* ed. J. Meyendorff, trans. N. Gendle, in the series *Classics of Western Spirituality* (New York: Paulist Press, 1983), p. 44.

37. *Saint Silouan, op. cit.,* p. 497.

38. *Ibid.,* p. 435.

39. *On Prayer, op. cit.,* p. 52; and *Saint Silouan, op. cit.,* p. 81.

40. *Ibid.*

41. *Cf.* Step 5:42, in St. John Climacus, *The Ladder, op. cit.,* p. 66.

42. *Cf.* Step 4:12, *ibid.,* p. 24.

43. That is to say, "the breadth, and length, and depth, and height" of Christ's love for mankind, of which His Cross is the sign.

44. Homily II, 20, *The Homilies of Saint Gregory Palamas,* Vol. 1, ed. C. Veniamin (South Canaan PA: St. Tikhon's Seminary Press, 2002), pp. 20–21.

45. *Cf. We Shall See Him, op. cit.,* pp. 236–237.

46. *Ibid.,* p. 94.

47. Homily XVIII, 8, *On the Martyr Gordius,* in *Patrologia Graeca* (PG) 31:505C.

48. *Anaphora, Liturgy of St. Basil the Great.*

God's Work of Salvation and Man*

L AST YEAR WE CELEBRATED the two thousandth anniversary of the manifestation of Christianity in the world, through the Incarnation of our Lord Jesus Christ "of the Holy Ghost and the Virgin Mary". If, according to the word of the wise Solomon, "To every thing there is a season, and a time to every purpose under the heaven" (Eccles. 3:1), is it not now, perhaps, the time and the season for us to call to mind and reflect upon the greatest event under the sun, the appearance in the flesh (cf. John 1:14) of our great God? This event is "the great mystery of godliness" (1 Tim. 3:16), and has its roots in the mind of God, where it "kept secret since the world began" (Rom. 16:25). It was prepared by means of prophetic events, utterances and holy scriptures, to an incredibly great degree of detail. "But when the fulness of the time was come" (Gal. 4:4), this mystery was made manifest with glory and made known unto all nations through Jesus Christ. In other words, the prophecy was fulfilled "after the eternal purpose" (Eph. 3:11), in accordance with which, "unto us a child is born, unto us a son is given" (Isa. 9:6). This is an opportunity, therefore, for the spirit of each and every Christian to "call to remembrance" (*anamnesis*) all of God's works from the beginning of sacred history down to the last times. This will challenge our minds to go deeper into God's providential decrees with regard to

Creation, His providence and His justice, so that we may rekindle within ourselves the life-giving breath of the Creator, and become partakers of His divine benefices. Holy remembrance of the wondrous works of God softens man's heart and fills it with sentiments of gratitude.

Aside: We said that the Liturgy is the fulfilment of the commandment of the Lord: "This do in remembrance of me" (Luke 22:19, 1 Cor. 11:24). When we come to celebrate the Liturgy, because we are fulfilling the commandment, the mystery of the Cross is at work, and we receive grace. When we remember in this way, when we have *anamnesis* of all the benefits of God, whether manifest or hid, whereof we know or we know not,[1] when we remember all His benefits, this sense of gratitude again softens the heart and brings grace. Through this grace we enter into eternity, this grace *is* eternity, and through this grace we become contemporaries of those events, and able to say "today" at every feast.

So this sacred *anamnesis*, the thanksgiving, the fulfilment of the commandment and the performance of the Liturgy, bring grace to our life. However, we need a certain inspiration in order to maintain this grace, and we derive this inspiration by placing ourselves in an eschatological perspective, in the Way of Him who has come and is coming again (*cf.* Rev. 1:4, 8; 4:8; 11:17). We human beings very easily get used to everything, even to the Liturgy and to Holy Communion. But there is one event which we cannot get used to, which is the Second Coming of our Lord, because it has not yet happened; and when we have that in mind we can maintain the necessary inspiration. We receive Holy Communion in the Liturgy, and we say: "Lord, thou hast accounted me worthy today, but cast me not away from Thy sight in that great and notable day when You will come again."[2] And so, "Yes, maybe I have deceived you today in receiving Communion, but how shall I then? Please accept me also in the day of Thy Second Coming." Having this conscience, we can maintain our inspiration, and the Liturgy can always be fresh. *End of aside.*

Holy remembrance of the wondrous works of God softens man's heart and fills it with sentiments of gratitude. Gratitude brings an increase of God's charisms in man and leads him to the perfection of "an honourable disposition" (*philotimia*), an honest endeavour according to God. It inspires him to prayer and glorification of God, and gives birth within the soul to dispositions and streams of divine love, which are stronger than sin and death.

The remembrance of God's works is not a psychological exercise, and it is not made in order to serve psychological needs, not even the most noble of these. The "wonderful works of God" (Acts 2:11) that we bring to mind are eternal events, wrought by the operation and grace of God; and when they are brought to mind in a spirit of thanksgiving and grateful confession we become partakers of the creative grace and work of God. They prepare us and lead us into a greater fullness of the divine love.

Scripture teaches us that God, from the moment He created man, has concerned Himself with him. He fashioned us and bestowed upon us the talents of His goodness; He brought us into being and gave us life (*cf.* Gen. 2:7), endowing us with a body and soul, a spirit, heart and senses. He established the earth as our footstool (*cf.* Isa. 66:1), the wondrous canopy of the heavens as a cover over our heads (*cf.* Ps. 104:2). He gave us the sun "to rule by day" (*cf.* Gen. 1:16), and for the welfare of our life, and also air to breathe. He placed the beasts of the field, the fowls of the air, fish and plants under our rule (*cf.* Gen. 1:26–28), and provided us with "diverse fruits" of the earth (*cf.* Gen. 1:29), to satisfy our needs and for our enjoyment, and also with clothing and the materials for our homes. In an amazing way, He has fostered the development of industry in order to meet the needs of the earth's growing population, and has made our survival possible and also pleasant. God has placed an immeasurable quantity of material wealth and energy at our disposal. As the Holy Fathers say, we have our whole existence "on loan" from God,[3] a loan without end. Every molecule of the air we breathe is a new loan; everything we have is a loan and a gift. What do we have that we have not received (*cf.* 1 Cor. 4:7)?

Not only are the bounties of the created universe a loan, in addition to this we have the generosity of the Provider of every good thing (*cf.* Jas. 1:17) in the richness of His providence. For at every moment He watches over us for the preservation of our health and strength, He cooperates in every good deed, and by His surpassing wisdom, orders our lives. He gives us parents, friends and above all wise instructors. He is the protector of our outward lives, and the success of those of our undertakings that are for our benefit. It is He who shields us from invisible evils and the fever of death, and does so with "mathematical precision",[4] even when, on man's side, there is no hope of salvation. It is He who said, "My Father worketh hitherto and I work" (John 5:17).[5]

What more can we say about the priceless loans that He credits us with by means of the riches of His spiritual gifts? God honoured man by creating him "in His image and likeness" (cf. Gen. 1:26). The very first breath that he breathed into man's nostrils (cf. Gen. 2:7) crowned him with glory and honour and, in a prophetic way, prepared him to receive the revelation of the Good Tidings that His Son was to bring into the world (cf. Luke 2:10).

In his original state, man was, as the Apostle says, "the image and glory of God" (1 Cor. 11:7). But when he chose to usurp this glory and "to become as God" (cf. Gen. 3:5), he found himself estranged from his Origin, since this glory proceeds "from God only" (John 5:44), and rightly must return to God. This estrangement gave the transgressor over to corruption and death (cf. Rom. 5:12); nevertheless, God, faithful and steadfast to His original design – to make man a partaker of His divine glory and beatitude – does not cease to devise ways, humbly, to visit His creature. But in order for the wealth of His spiritual graces to reach man, it was necessary that this be preceded by a long period, during which God would make ready the Coming of His Son into the world.

Looking at the history of God's relationship with man, we see nothing other than the tender, loving care of the former for the latter. Job, in his titanic struggle to understand the depth of God's judgments, and to stand firm in His truth, says that this is precisely why man is such a great wonder: because God has fixed His Spirit upon him, visits him every morning, and tries him every moment (cf. Job 7:17-18). God's continual visitations are indeed blessed and indescribably beneficial. Man himself becomes a "deep heart" (*cf.* Ps. 64:6) with divine and spiritual awareness. He becomes the object of God's tireless operation, which perfects him and makes him a reasonable creature fashioned after His image. The righteous were aware of the privilege and beatitude of these visitations, and yearned to receive God's salvation. The Lord bears witness to this, saying, "Many prophets and kings have desired to see those things which *ye see*, and have not seen them; and to hear those things which *ye hear*, and have not heard them" (Luke 10:24). And He also said, "Your father Abraham rejoiced to see my day: and he saw it, and was glad" (John 8:56). Of course, all the righteous received God's visitation in a prophetic manner, and rejoiced in the hope of the coming salvation. Each time they demonstrated virtue and righteousness in their lives, they received a foretaste of the blessing of the things to come. All of God's visitations on man proved to be fruitless in the long run, and in reality were only preparations (somewhat at a distance and "in part") for the effectual and permanent advent of God's grace, which was so desirous to those who had been deprived of it, since "all had sinned" (*cf.* Rom. 3:23).

However, many of God's visitations on the Old Israel were so strong and rich in divine presence and power that they proved to be of great value for the formation and moulding of God's people. Moses himself instituted annual feasts for their commemoration. Most distinguished among these was the Feast of the Passover, the commemoration of the deliverance of the children of Israel "out of the hand of the Egyptians", and their passage upon dry land in the midst of the Red Sea (*cf.* Exod. 14:15–31). By this great and wondrous event, God revealed His power and glory, and also His special favour for His people, saving them from certain disaster and annihilation. By celebrating the Passover each year with all solemnity and over seven days, the Israelites bore witness to their gratitude to God their Saviour (*cf.* Exod. 12:1–14), and thereby received the blessing and grace to continue in the knowledge of the true God, even in the midst of great and powerful idol-worshipping nations. And each and every Jew had as his highest bounden duty to tell "to the generation following" (Ps. 48:13) of the mercy and care of God for His people, and that the Lord of Hosts is He Who watches over and saves Israel. In short, man is the object of God's visitations, and he, guided by the spirit of prophecy, instituted feasts so that, by recalling the wondrous deeds performed by God in the past, he might rekindle in them the grace for the present, and also draw power from them for new feats of faith and piety.

The twofold striving of God's mercy, on the one side, and man's faithfulness on the other, continued over the wearisome flow of the ages. The Lord, "who alone fashioneth the hearts of men" (*cf* Ps. 33:15), looked down "upon all the inhabitants of the earth" (Ps. 33:14) and surveyed their works. From the very first moment of Adam's fall God sought after the transgressor: "Adam, Where art thou?" (Gen. 3:9). And He continued to seek among the sons of men for at least one with understanding, who would seek God and do good (Ps. 14:2). The Psalmist, in desperation, tells us that such a one could not be found, because "They are all gone aside, they are all together become filthy: there is none that doeth good, no, not one" (Pss. 14:3; 53:3).

But when "the fulness of the time was come" (Gal. 4:4, *cf* Eph. 1:10), such a person was found on earth, the Holy Virgin, who possessed every sovereign beauty and glory "within" (Ps. 45:14). Her presence before God was so bright and sublime, that the King of heaven "desired her beauty" (*cf* Ps. 45:11), overshadowed her with His Holy Spirit, made her the Throne of the Cherubim, and "bowed the heavens also, and came down" (Ps. 18:9; 2 Sam. 22:10). According to the teachings of the Holy Fathers, the Holy Virgin was a perfect vessel, which contained all the spiritual charisms and divine virtues. Three virtues, however, stand out in particular.

First, her "hesychastic" withdrawal into the Holy of Holies and her hesychastic prayer. That is to say, her perfect dying to this present world, and her Cherubic appearance before the Living God, the God of her Fathers. She forgot her people and the house of her father (*cf* Ps. 45:10), and instead, offered to God unceasing supplications for the salvation of the whole world. She became receptive to perfect revelation, drew the Most High towards her, and showed herself to be a Bethlehem – a house of the "bread of life" (John 6:48)[6] – the Mother of Christ, of God. Just as Abraham, by obeying the voice of God and forsaking his kinsmen, received the promises, just as Jacob, while being persecuted, came to that fearful place, "the gate of heaven" (Gen. 28:17), and just as Israel, exposed to the dangers of the desert, received revelations, so too did the Holy Virgin, who was dead to the world, become the dwelling-place of the Godhead.

The second virtue is her humility. As she says herself, the Lord "hath regarded the low estate of his handmaiden" (Luke 1:48), that is, her humility. The "nothingness" of her profound and extreme humility became the "stuff" by which the Highest wrought the recreation of the human race. By means of this humility the Most Holy Virgin, prophetically, set herself on the Way which her Son was to reveal, and was fulfilling the law of His Spirit: "he that humbleth himself shall be exalted" (Luke 14:11; 18:14), and thus He that is mighty "hath done" for her great things (Luke 1:49), and raised her up higher even than the angelic powers.[7]

Thirdly, her purity, which was never violated, neither by a glance, nor by thought, nor even by the slightest movement of the heart. Her heart was completely given over to God, and it was this "handing over" (*paradosis*) that made her worthy to converse with God, and made God await her consent, "Behold the handmaid of the Lord; be it unto me according to thy word" (Luke 1:38), as indispensable for the work of the salvation of the world.

The Son and Word of God "was made flesh, and dwelt among us, and we beheld his glory, the glory as of the only begotten of the Father, full of grace and truth" (John 1:14). The Word of God "tabernacled" in the Virgin's womb, the Son of God was born of the Holy Ghost and the Virgin Mary. The event of the incarnation of God is also the greatest and most sublime visitation of all, by which God has honoured the race of men. He united Himself with them, He became like them, and "through the eternal Spirit" (Heb. 9:14) gave Himself as a sacrifice on behalf of those held captive and them that were condemned, and found "eternal redemption" for all (Heb. 9:12). A great and glorious mystery is revealed, therefore, in infinite and glorious love. God gives his Only-begotten Son to the world, so "that we might live through him" (1 John 4:9). But the Son too gives Himself "for our sins, that he might deliver us from this present evil world, according to the will of God and our Father" (Gal. 1:4). And the Holy Spirit also offers Himself, in order to "guide you into all the truth" (John 16:13) of the fullness of the Trinity's love. *Aside:* That is to say, the Holy Spirit will strengthen our nature to bear the fullness of divine love, which is the fullness of Truth. *End of aside.*

It is in this blessed tradition of God's "giving" to man that the happiness of reasonable creatures is to be found, and in which God's plan "before the world began" (Titus 1:2) for His image, man, is fulfilled. At the very moment in which the Divinity was united with humanity in the Person of Our Lord Jesus Christ, all the charisms of the divine power – "the things that pertain unto life and godliness" – were transmitted to us, and in this way the most precious and greatest of God's promises were fulfilled, so that we might become partakers of the divine nature and escape the corruption that is brought about by fleshly desires (*cf.* 2 Pet. 1:3-4).

Our weakness became intertwined with divine power, our falsehood blotted out by the divine truth, our darkness illumined by the divine light, and our death abolished by divine life. And truly, as the great Apostle exclaims with wonder at the incomprehensible righteousness of divine love, "He that spared not his own Son, but delivered him up for us all, how shall he not with him also freely give us all things?" (Rom. 8:32).

Thus, the tradition of God's giving (*paradosis*) to man, by which all the good things of life and salvation have been bestowed upon us, signifies the weakness of the flesh assumed by Christ. *Aside:* We must remember that God did not save us by His omnipotence, but by His weakness, for "the weakness of God is stronger than men", says St. Paul (1 Cor. 1:25). *End of aside.* This is His profound poverty, by which He hid His boundless eternity on the day of His Nativity. It signifies the self-emptying, the *kenosis*, of His divine power and wisdom. And what is more, it signifies His unspeakable love, which is "unto the end" (John 13:1). And who can measure the distance from the height of His divine nature to the depth of

His humiliation, that infinite distance which He travelled in order to find and save the "lost sheep", fallen man? The limited human mind can follow Christ neither in His ascent beyond the heavens, nor in His descent into the abyss of fallen nature. Christ's descent into the infernal regions and His ascent beyond the heavens constitute a single work, thanks to which the world was reconciled with God (cf. Rom. 5:10, 2 Cor. 5:19), and the gifts of the Holy Spirit were given so that they might bear witness to the participation of men in the "greater abundance" (cf. John 10:10) of the life of God. Christ's prayer of agony in Gethsemane, His Passion, Cross and Resurrection are the focal point and "summing up" (recapitulation) of this work. By the "precious blood of Christ, as of a lamb without blemish and without spot" (1 Pet. 1:19) our race was redeemed from all the lamentable and tragic offspring of sin. As the Apostle says, man's grandeur consists in the honour which Christ bestowed upon him when he was bought with the price of His precious blood (cf. 1 Cor. 6:20 and 7:23).

"Having been set free by a ransom", man ought to measure up to Christ's salvation and not debase his worth to the passions of dishonour; neither should he become a slave to the desire to please people. Christ, through His passion and death, which "by the grace of God" He tasted for every man, brought "many sons unto glory" and perfection (Heb. 2:9–10). But just a few hours before He sealed the work of the salvation of mankind with His blood, He willed to give a practical way and means by which the faithful could always remain in the grace of eternal salvation. As He was handing down the mystery of His sacrifice to His disciples, and through them to Christians of all ages, He said: "This is my body which is given for you . . . This cup is the new testament in my blood, which is shed for you . . . this do in remembrance of me" (Luke 22:19–20). In other words, the Lord, as the new and spiritual Lawgiver, gives us the commandment to "call to remembrance" the work of His sacrifice, from which spring eternal redemption and salvation. The work of His sacrifice was accomplished by the power of the eternal Spirit (cf. Heb. 9:14), and as an event remains for ever in eternity, and His grace saves those who believe "unto perpetuity"

(Heb. 10:14). The remembrance of these awesome events in the life of Christ is made on a daily basis by the Church in the Mystery of the Divine Eucharist. Why did the Lord command us to perform the daily enactment of His sacrifice "in remembrance" of Him? He knew that we are inclined towards ingratitude. Christ healed ten lepers and only one of them returned to give thanks, and with sorrow He said: "Were there not ten cleansed? but where are the nine?" (Luke 17:17).

The Lord's sacrifice is sufficient, indeed more than sufficient, to save the whole world. Thus, the Lord did not want us to appear ungrateful and fall short of the grace of salvation. Through the remembrance of His sacrifice He wished to inspire gratitude in us, and for that gratitude to prepare our hearts to receive the grace of His salvation with humility. His Cross wiped out sin and His death became the fountain of life. By calling to remembrance Christ's victory, we raise up the trophy (the *tropaeon*) of His victory in our hearts, and by His grace we too are shown to be victors over sin and also, consequently, over death; and this rejoices not only the Author of our salvation, but also all the saints of heaven (*cf.* Luke 15:7).

It behoves us, therefore, if we do not wish to be deceived but to remain true in this transient world, to confess, in accordance with the Apostolic preaching, that "Jesus Christ is come in the flesh" (1 John 4:2–3; 2 John 7). If we desire to make Christ's victory over sin and death our own, we should be resolved not to know any thing other than "Jesus Christ, and him crucified" (1 Cor. 2:2). Fixing the mind's attention on the crucified God brings the grace of salvation, which accompanies this remembrance with power, and transforms it into the living memory "of Jesus Christ raised from the dead" (2 Tim. 2:8). The Apostle Paul, when speaking of the same mystery, adds certain new elements, and sets forth the remembrance of Christ's Sacrifice as a pattern for our life. The great Paul says: "For I have received of the Lord that which also I delivered unto you, That the Lord Jesus the same night in which he was betrayed took bread: and when he had given thanks, he brake it, and said, Take, eat: this is my body, which is broken for you: this do in remembrance of me. After the same manner also he took the cup, when he had supped, saying, This cup is the new testament in my blood: this do ye, as oft as ye drink it, in remembrance of me. For as often as ye eat this bread, and drink this cup, ye do show the Lord's death till he come" (1 Cor. 11:23–26). And the Church, by the mouth of Saint Basil the Great, that "revealer of heaven" (*ouranophántôr*),[8] adds that by this remembrance not only do we show His death, but we also confess His resurrection. And this is our work *par excellence* "till he come", so that we might remain steadfast in the grace of redemption and show ourselves to be "a new creation" in Christ, with a pure conscience, free from the dead works of sin, worshipping the living God "in spirit and in truth" (John 4:23; *cf.* Heb. 9:14). The grace which is given in return for the gratitude of this remembrance opens up the heart to embrace yet another eternal event, that of Christ's Second Coming. Christ came, and remains with us "unto the end of the world" (Matt. 28:20), but He shall come again with glory to judge the living and the dead (*cf.* 2 Tim. 4:1). And the event of Christ's Second Coming is in part present and at work even now, but will be revealed then in all its majesty and glory.

If now, therefore, two thousand years after having received the perfect revelation of the Spirit, written "in fleshy tables of the heart" (2 Cor. 3:3), we wish worthily to give thanks to God our Benefactor and Saviour, we should go deeper into the mystery of His Eucharistic remembrance. This remembrance which takes place in the Eucharist is the fulfilment of the commandment of Christ the Lord. It also introduces the eschatological dimension into our lives, since we are enjoined to keep this remembrance "till he come". And it places us on the Way of the Lord, and the Way is none other than Christ Himself, He Who comes and is to come, for as He said: "I am the way" (John 14:6). The Way of the Lord revealed the nature of His being, that is, that "God is love" (1 John 4:8, 16), and indeed love "unto the end" (John 13:1). And man, by calling to remembrance the Way of the Lord, expresses his own love and gratitude for God's saving work. And this he does "till he come". Man, in placing himself on the Way of the Lord by fulfilling His commandment, has the Lord as a fellow-traveller and becomes united with Him. The Lord's commandment is "exceeding great" and "life eternal". Its culture remains unattainable to the man who loves himself. Truly, "Who then can be saved?" (Luke 18:26). But the Lord said, "The things which are impossible with men are possible with God" (Luke 18:27). In other words, Christ has fulfilled the impossible – all of God's commandments to the point of perfection: "I have kept my Father's commandments, and abide in his love" (John 15:10). For us, it is enough to follow Him, as He bade us to do, when He said: "Come, follow me" (Luke 18:22). And all the things that He has achieved by His obedience to the unoriginate Father, freely become ours. That is how the impossible is fulfilled.

By following the Lord, we inherit the eternal salvation that He obtained for us by giving Himself over as a ransom unto death, by which we were held captive (cf. Matt. 20:28, Mark 10:45). Remembrance of His death, which the Lord endured for our sake, and His Resurrection, is synonymous with the struggle to follow Him "whithersoever he goeth" (Rev. 14:4).[9] In order that their zeal and fervour not be diminished, His disciples must always call to remembrance His impending Coming, not grow slothful before His bridechamber, nor should they content themselves with any talents that they might have. Expectation of the things to come lends a certain tension to their lives, and makes His disciples well-pleasing to the Holy Spirit, to whom they have commended their lives. The "place" (topos) where we are instructed in the remembrance of the Lord and become practised in the expectation of the Lord's Coming is the Divine Liturgy, which is celebrated by the people of God in church.

Each day is a gift of God's goodness, which is given to us that "we might perfect holiness in the fear of God" (cf. 2 Cor. 7:1). In the Liturgy we embrace the past and the future and refer all things back to God in full and all-embracing thanksgiving for all those things which God has done for us in order to set us before His Face. Along with a thorough confession of all our sins and a petition for forgiveness, we entreat that we might be received into a worthy and continuous attendance before Him. That is, we offer all our life to God, and God is pleased with our offering and returns the gifts back to us, accompanied by His life, the Holy Spirit. Having placed in these gifts all the expectation of our life, we say to God, "Thine own, of thine own, we offer unto thee in all and for all".[10] And God replies to us, saying, "The holy things unto the holy",[11] having rendered unto us "the true Light", "the heavenly Spirit", "the true faith", and the whole salvation of God the Holy Trinity.[12]

An exchange of lives takes place in the Divine Liturgy. Man offers his limited and transient life to God, and God, in return, grants him His limitless and eternal life. In this way, each day is filled with the fullness of life, and our whole lifetime becomes an "acceptable year of the Lord" (Luke 4:19).

Aside: All our life can be brought into this pattern of the Liturgy, or in more general terms, into the pattern of the sacraments of the Church. In every sacrament of the Church an alliance is concluded with God. In Baptism we make an alliance that we shall be "dead unto sin", and "alive only unto God". In the Liturgy we conclude an alliance with Him, as we read in the sixth chapter of St. John's Gospel, "As the living Father hath sent me, and I live by the Father: so he that eateth me, even he shall live by me" (John 6:57). We make an alliance so that we shall no longer live unto ourselves, but unto Him who has redeemed us (*cf.* 2 Cor. 5:15), who has "bought us with a price" (*cf.* 1 Cor. 6:20). The understanding of the Liturgy is based on a text of St. Paul, in the *Letter to Timothy*, where he says that "every creature of God is good . . . if it be received with thanksgiving: For it is sanctified by the word of God and prayer" (1 Tim. 4:4–5), and the Liturgy is God's word and entreaty. We base ourselves on God's word, "Take, eat; This is my body . . .", and the entreaty of the Church, "Send down Thy Holy Spirit upon us and upon these gifts here set forth;"[13] and the miracle happens: everything is sanctified by the word of God and by entreaty. All the prayers of the Church are according to this pattern. If we want to pray for a blind man, we say: "Lord, as Thou didst heal the man who was blind from his birth then, now also send Thy grace and strength and give light to our darkened hearts." We always base our first thought on the word of God, and then we can make entreaty. So everything is sanctified through the word of God and prayer. *End of aside.*

In accordance with the figure or pattern of the Liturgy, where the exchange of our life with the life of God takes place, our every deed and operation must preserve the tension and the intensity of the Apostle's "till he come" (1 Cor. 11:26). With these things in mind, it behoves the faithful to love the Lord's manifestation: firstly, by meditating on the coming of Jesus Christ; secondly, by tirelessly awaiting Him; thirdly, by desiring Him with all their hearts; and fourthly, by preparing themselves for Him with diligence. Without expectation there is no hope. Without hope there is no salvation, "For we are saved by hope," says St. Paul (Rom. 8:24). And without salvation there is no Christianity. Christians know that Christ worked the redemption of the world by means of His blood and death. They know, moreover, better than do unbelievers, that the law of sin lives among its members. It has a clearer view of sin, because its inner sense has not been extinguished by the desires of the passions, nor by the dullness of the conscience. Consequently, it is perfectly natural for the Christian to await the Coming of Christ, who "shall change our vile body, that it may be fashioned like unto his glorious body" (Phil. 3:21) and rid him of every trace of impurity, all rebelliousness of sin, every temptation.

The Christian suffers in this world, and suffers perhaps even more than other men do, because, apart from sufferings, which are the common lot of our nature, he also inherits and bears a special cross, the cross of faith, by which he becomes like his Teacher, Christ. How unfortunate would be the believer in his suffering, if he had not all his faith in Christ, who entered into His glory through sufferings, and who will come again to clothe in glory those who suffer for His sake. This hope causes man to rejoice in the sufferings of this present time, and to regard them but as small and unworthy "to be compared with the glory which shall be revealed in us" (Rom. 8:18). All the saints of the last twenty centuries, from the time of Peter, the Leader of the Apostles, down to our own times, through their hope in Christ's Coming, regarded sufferings as a sign of divine election and as an indispensable prerequisite "for the spirit of glory and of God" to rest in our hearts (1 Pet. 4:14).

As the day of Christ's Coming draws near, so will the negative signs which announce His Coming (His *parousia*) increase: the grief of nations, sicknesses, scandals, betrayals, multitudinous injustices, love's growing cold, the destruction of the environment, and above all widespread indifference and inattentiveness to the fact that, in accordance with the prophecies, the Lord will come "as a thief" (Rev. 3:3). But despite the turmoil of evils Christians hear the Lord's voice clearly, which tells them: "And when these things begin to come to pass, then look up, and lift up your heads; for your redemption draweth nigh" (Luke 21:28). *Aside:* The end is coming in such a tragic manner, yet the Lord says that this is the moment "to lift up our heads". There is always a contradiction of this nature, because our faith is beyond the rational mind. *End of aside.*

As the day of Christ's Coming draws near, so the privilege of "believing on Christ" and "suffering for his sake" becomes greater (*cf.* Phil. 1:29). *Aside:* The Ascetic Fathers of the fourth century spoke about the end of the world. Once, a novice asked his elder, "What have we done, Abba?" and the elder replied, "We have done half of what our Fathers did." "But what will the monks who come after us do?" he asked again. "They will do half of what we are doing." "And what will the last Christians do?" asked the novice. "They will just be able to keep the faith, but they will be more glorified in heaven than our fathers who could raise the dead."[14] *End of aside.* That is why the faithful must also "Look for and hasten unto the coming of the day of God" (*cf.* 2 Pet. 3:12), giving thanks to the Lord, who for our sake became the Passover and "righteousness, and sanctification, and redemption" (1 Cor. 1:30). At the same time we must not cease to supplicate for a more perfect and unshakeable participation in His eternal kingdom, together with the "clouds" and choirs of all the saints, which, by His grace, have been given to us as tokens of the incorruptible consolation that awaits "them that love his appearing" (2 Tim. 4:8).

QUESTIONS & ANSWERS

Question 1: Could you expand on what you said about how the last generation will live the faith?

Answer 1: There are many prophecies about the end of times in our Fathers, and the saying I mentioned earlier is just one of them. It said that the tribulations will be so many that the Christians of the last times will be barely able to keep the faith, and that they will receive more glory in heaven than the fathers who could raise even the dead. In another saying of the *Desert Fathers* there is the following story: A novice goes to an elder and asks him, "What do you think of a certain great elder, a great ascetic?" And the elder answers, "In comparison with his generation, he is great." After some moments the disciple asks him again, "What do you think of this father?" and the elder replies, "I told you, compared to his generation, he is great." Then he asks him a third time, "What do you think of this father?" And the elder says: "Compared to his generation, he is great," and he continues, "but I knew some fathers in the Upper Thebaid who could make the sun stand still in the middle of the sky."[15] That is to say, God always judges us compared to the great tree of humanity, of which we are but a few leaves. We cannot but be influenced by this great tree of humanity, so we are like a drop of water trying to flow against the current of a great river. It is impossible with men, but with God it is possible (*cf.* Matt. 19:26). He has done it; we only have to follow Him, and we shall inherit the fulfilment. But nevertheless, God reckons to us the general situation of the world. This is a consolation for us, not so that we relax, but to help us not to lose our bearings. God always judges us compared to our generation, our surroundings. He Himself states: "The Father judgeth no man, but hath committed all judgment unto the Son" (John 5:22), and the Father hath "given him authority to execute judgment also, because he is the Son of man" (John 5:27). The Son of Man, Christ, because He became man and lived the conditions of life we live, is a great judge. But even He does not judge anybody: He gives all judgment to His saints. "The saints," says St. Paul, "shall judge the world" (1 Cor. 6:2). But I think the saints of every generation will judge their own generation. I do not think that the Apostles will judge us, we will be judged by the saints of our generation and of our surroundings, who lived the same life with us, and yet found the way. Then God remains truthful in all His judgments. And we can even go further and say: I will not be judged by an American saint; I will be judged by a saint of my monastery, because who can enter into judgment with God? (cf. Ps. 143:2). He judges compared to our generation.

Question 2: St. John Chrysostom says in one of the prayers of the Holy Liturgy: "Remembering therefore this saving commandment of salvation, and all those things which came to pass for our sakes: the cross, the tomb, the resurrection on the third day, the ascension into heaven, the sitting on the right hand, *the coming again a second time in glory* . . ."[16] How can we have that in remembrance?

Answer 2: We do have that in remembrance, and this is not a psychological remembrance. St. John Cabasilas says that the Liturgy is a portrait of the life of Christ, and it is an expression also of the gratitude of man for everything He has done. By performing this act, we are given grace, and that grace helps us to enter an eternal event, which is always present: in eternity there is no past and no future, there is the eternal "today", the eternal present. So, by remembering all the benefits of God and, more especially, by basing ourselves on His word and performing His commandment – because we must not forget that the Liturgy is a commandment – the mystery of the Cross is at work. We receive the grace of the Cross and Resurrection of Christ, and that grace introduces us into eternal events; we become contemporaries of eternal events. That is why we can say, "Today Christ is born." Having entered eternity through the grace we are given, we are contemporaries to these eternal events, and we can say, "*Today* Christ is born", "*Today* Christ is crucified", "*Today* Christ is risen", and of course, "*Today* Christ is come." We do not passively wait for the Lord's Day, says Saint Peter, but we "hasten" towards it (*cf.* 2 Pet. 3:12). What is the second coming? It is the day when the Lord will shine in glory, but unto us "the ends of the world are come", says St. Paul (1 Cor. 10:11). Beholding the glory of the Lord means that He is here, He has come. And so His saints behold even the second coming.

Question 3: My question is linked to the previous lecture you gave: "*Keep thy mind in hell, and despair not.*" I went to the chapel this evening, like everybody else and, you know, I have to take medicine for my health. While I stood there, it was very hot and I almost fainted, but I kept my mind on just what you had said. A couple of times I wanted to leave, but I remembered the words "*Keep thy mind in hell, and despair not,*" and I felt I had to stay to the end, even if I fell down. I wanted to ask: Is there a limitation to this, or what?

Answer 3: I think what you did is correct: it is a matter of faith and there are many degrees of faith. In every word of God there is a bottomless depth. The word of God is like a sphere, which has many points of contact, and wherever you touch it, you touch the whole sphere. There are many aspects to this. When you read the interpretation of the Scriptures by the saints you find many interpretations for the same passage, because the word of God is eternal and has infinite aspects, an infinite number of points of contact, and it is a matter of faith to go into it, to penetrate it. The thought that you had is, of course, an honourable one.

Question 4: You have mentioned about today's people desiring pleasures and comfort, so what is the place of the emotions for us?

Answer 4: We all have emotions, but the emotions really are an expression of the "old man", and God asks us to divest ourselves of this "old man" (Eph. 4:22) and the emotions. We must convert these emotions, which are of a psychological nature, into spiritual feelings and sensations.

Question 5: Could you define emotions?

Answer 5: For example, something happens to me and because of that I feel a great joy. I can live it psychologically and enjoy myself and be really happy, or I can transform this emotion of happiness that I have because of what happened to me and make it a spiritual sensation. Immediately, I open a conversation with God, and I begin to give thanks to the Lord, there and then, so that instead of it being a psychological emotion it becomes a spiritual joy, it becomes an energy of conversing with God. If I have an emotion of sadness and I am terribly afflicted because, let us say, my mother has died or my best friend, or some other catastrophe has befallen me, I will pour out my heart to God like the Prophetess Hanna (cf. 1 Sam. 1:4–28), and use this energy of sadness and make it an energy of prayer before God.

Fr. Sophrony used to say to us that we cannot live a monastic life properly unless we learn to change our psychological states into spiritual states. And how do we do that? We allow any energy to come to us, but we change the thought and turn towards God, to converse with Him. For example, I remember my grandmother, how pious she was; how she would be the first in Church, and the last to leave. During the night she would make prostrations continually, and my mother used to watch her, through the door, as she was making her prostrations; and she would say to me, "You know, your grandmother is making prostrations all the time." I recall all that and I feel emotional. Never mind, let the emotion come, but then I lift up my mind to God, and use that energy of emotion for what I want. "The spirits of the prophets are subject to the prophets", says St. Paul (1 Cor. 14:32). So, I turn that energy towards my sinfulness, and I begin to entreat for the forgiveness of my sins, or for something else. I change the focus of my mind, and give it something else to fix on.

Fr. Sophrony sees this kind of "transformer of energy" in the life of our Lord. He used to say to us that the Lord did not think about the people who were going to crucify Him, who were coming to arrest Him in the Garden of Gethsemane – whether they were Greeks or Romans or Jews – but He was conversing with God, saying, "The cup which my Father hath given me, shall I not drink it?" (John 18:11). He knew that He was going to be crucified; yet He did not think psychologically: "But why, if they are Jews, are they ungrateful? I have done so much for them, so many wonders to save them from their enemies. Why are they now unjustly going to crucify me?" He did not descend to that level, but was conversing with His Father – "The cup of my Father, shall I not drink it?". So it is the same with us: we have many energies, positive and negative, of sadness, tragic energies, energies of pleasure, noble energies that befall us. But we do not remain on that level of emotion: we exploit the energy they bring. We take the energy and direct the thought to God according to our needs, and we pray.

I will give you an example. I was in Cyprus and my friends were coming to take me from my mother's house to a village for the Liturgy. We arranged that they would come at six o'clock to collect me; the Liturgy was going to start at seven, and it was an hour from Nicosia to the village. I was very busy in Cyprus, because many priests were inviting me to speak at their parishes, on the television, on the radio. I got so completely tired and drained that I went to bed late and got up early to prepare for the Liturgy. I got up at four o'clock, because, as I said, at six o'clock they were coming to pick me up. But I could not pray. My heart was torn into pieces; it just would not follow me. I thought to myself: "I have no energy, I have no strength, I will go and wash my clothes." I had some T-shirts to wash because I sweat a lot during the night, and maybe that will waken me up a bit more and then I will try again to pray and see if I can manage. I went into the bathroom for half an hour and finished the laundry, and at half past four I came out and heard some whispering. The door was a little open, and I could see my mother, who cannot walk, on the bed. She was making small bows on the bed and praying, and with each prayer she would say, "The whole world and my children". She was doing this with fervour, and I felt so ashamed that my heart was healed, and for an hour and a half I prayed also. I prepared for the Liturgy, and it was one of my best Liturgies. My own elderly mother put me to shame that day.

Sometimes we think that we have no energy, but we have an incredible amount of energy in us. The secret is to find a humble thought which will put us to shame, which will bring contrition to us and release that spiritual energy in us. That is why we have to put ourselves in the humble way of "going down", in order to be able always to "fish out" those humble thoughts that release the internal spiritual energy that will enable us to do the work of God. I have a fellow priest and one day he was very tired from his ministry with the people. It was a Sunday and he was completely exhausted. He told me, "In the night when I am so exhausted, I usually just go to my room, look at the icons and say, 'Good night to all of you', and go to bed." But that night he felt ashamed of doing that, instead he walked up and down the corridor saying, "Sorry Lord, I cannot pray tonight. Forgive me." "Sorry Lord, I am tired, I cannot pray tonight. Forgive me." For half an hour he went up and down the corridor saying these words, and in that way God enabled him to perform the rule of his prayer. So we can always discover in ourselves an incredible amount of spiritual energy, if we find the right key, "the key of David" (*cf.* Isa. 22:22, Rev. 3:7), and make the right movement to release it, that is to say, a humble thought, given to us by the Lord, when we put ourselves in His judgment, by "going down". He gives us "a mouth and wisdom" (Luke 21:15), the humble thought that releases spiritual energy.

NOTES

* Originally published in Greek in *The Orthodox Herald: Official Publication of the Greek Orthodox Archdiocese of Thyateira and Great Britain,* no. 138–139 (March-April, 2000), 14–18. English trans. C. Veniamin.

1. *Cf. The Liturgy of St. John Chrysostom,* prayer of the *Anaphora*: "For all these things we give thanks unto thee, and unto thine only-begotten Son, and unto thy Holy Spirit; for all whereof we know and whereof we know not; for benefits both manifest and hid which thou hast wrought upon us."

2. See the *Prayers of Thanksgiving After Holy Communion*, the beginning of the first prayer: "I thank thee, O Lord my God, for that thou hast not rejected me, a sinner, but hast suffered me to be a partaker of thy holy things . . ."; and the end of the fourth prayer: "And at thy dread second

coming, account me, a sinner, worthy to stand on the right hand of thy glory: By the prayers of thy most holy Mother, and of all the Saints."

3. *Cf.* St. Maximus the Confessor, *On the Lord's Prayer*, in *The Philokalia*, vol. 2, ed. G. E. H. Palmer, Philip Sherrard and Kallistos Ware (London: Faber & Faber, 1981), p. 297.

4. *We Shall See Him, op. cit.*, p. 196.

5. *Cf.* St. Filaret of Moscow, Homily VI, in *Choix de Sermons et Discours de S. Ém. Mgr Philarète*, Vol. 1, trans. A. Serpinet (Paris: E. Dentu, 1866), p. 110.

6. *Cf.* Heb. *bethlechem*, lit. "house of bread".

7. In one of the most important Orthodox hymns dedicated to the Most Holy Mother of God the Church calls her "more honourable than the Cherubim and past compare more glorious than the Seraphim."

8. *Cf.* Amphilochius of Iconium, *The Life of Basil of Caesarea* 2, in F. Combefis, *SS. Patrum Amphilochii Iconiensis, Methodii Tyri et Andreae Cretensis opera omnia* (Paris, 1644), col. 168D; found in *A Patristic Greek Lexicon*, W. G. H. Lampe et alii (Oxford University Press, 1961), *s.v. ouranophántôr.*

9. In the Book of Revelation, the Apostle John sees those who were redeemed from the earth, dressed in white robes, and the Lord tells him that they are those who have whitened their garments in the blood of the Lamb, and they follow Him "whithersoever he goeth"; and Fr. Sophrony adds, "Even to hell."

10. *The Divine Liturgy of St. John Chrysostom*, prayer of the *Anaphora*.

11. *Ibid.*, prayer of *The Communion*.

12. *Ibid.*, prayer before *The Dismissal:* "We have seen the true Light . . ."

13. *Ibid.*, prayer of the *Epiclesis*.

14. *Cf.* Abba Ischyrion, in *The Sayings of the Desert Fathers: The Alphabetical Collection*, trans. B. Ward (Kalamazoo, MI: Cistercian Publications, 1984), p. 111.

15. *Cf.* Abba Elias, 2nd Saying, *ibid.*, p. 71.

16. *The Divine Liturgy of St. John Chrysostom*, prayer of the *Anaphora*.

PRAYER
THE WAY OF CREATION*

PRAYER IS THE SPIRITUAL MAN'S WORK *par excellence*, by which the fact of his creation "in the image and after the likeness" of God is brought to light. *Aside:* We pray because we are created "in the image and after the likeness of God" (Gen. 1:26). *End of aside.* So intimately is man's union with God realized in prayer, that he mirrors the divine perfection in his corporeal existence, and reflects it in his imitation of God's life.

Prayer as Personal Communion

Prayer signifies man's turning towards God, the creature's reaching forth to receive the light of the Uncreated. As bearing within himself God's creative breath, and by the invocation of His name, man attracts God's "visitation" (*cf.* Job 7:18). The man of prayer becomes a "temple of God" (1 Cor. 3:16). God turns His eyes and heart towards him perpetually, and seals him with His name (*cf.* 1 Kgs. 9:3). This reciprocal action of man's turning towards God, and of God's turning towards man, effects a personal relationship or communion between them. For man's part, this relationship is deep and life-giving. Prior to the Fall, this relationship was bright and direct. God, as St. Gregory Palamas writes, "appeared visibly before man . . . that [he] might imitate Him."[1] When, however, man lost the vision of God, He Himself came into the world as man. As a result, prayer is the most precious and indispensable means for man's communion with God. Fr. Sophrony defines prayer as "infinite creation",[2] since by means of it man is granted the privilege of becoming a collaborator with God in realizing his personhood. He receives the grace to reveal himself as effecting the perfection of the hypostatic principle in him.[3] *Aside:* What does Fr. Sophrony mean by "hypostatic principle" and "person"? Though he says that the person cannot be defined, we could say that personhood is the gift of God to man, by which he possesses his nature. In more simple words, when we have even the least contrition from the Holy Spirit, we exercise control over all our senses, and on every movement of our heart and mind; thus is man quickened by the grace of God. When this gift of God is perfected in man, through this gift he possesses his whole nature. This is personhood. I have not defined it, but rather described it. *End of aside.* Man receives the grace to reveal himself as effecting the perfection of the hypostatic principle in him. *Aside:* The hypostatic principle is this gift that God gave us to be able to embrace all the divine Being (of course, in its energetic form) and all the human being. *End of aside.* By means of prayer, the energy of the true God penetrates man's being and endows him with the strength to strive for the fulfilment of his calling. The longer he remains in prayer, the greater is his resistance to whatever corrupts or hinders the flow of its action. *Aside:* Prayer generates prayer. *End of aside.* The work of this striving is sublime and creative,[4] full of wisdom and inspiration, beauty and majesty.

In the heart, which is the place where God's communion with man is cultivated, the Spirit of God is revealed, operates and prays. The heart's opening up to prayer heals man's personhood. Man's mind is concentrated in, and becomes united with, the heart. Thus the heart is enlarged to contain all the fullness of Christ's love. *Aside:* I like this word "enlarged"; it is from St. Paul (*cf.* 2 Cor. 6:11). He keeps on saying to the Corinthians, "[Brethren] be ye also enlarged" (2 Cor. 6:13). *End of aside.* Consequently, the entire struggle in prayer has as its aim the discovery and conquest of the heart. The way towards achieving this is impeded only by vainglory.[5] *Aside:* St. Silouan

says again and again that humility is of the greatest importance, because pride hinders love. *End of aside.*

Powers of cosmic dimensions are ranged against prayer
(*cf.* Eph. 6:12), but so too is the very make-up of fallen man.
When, however, resistance against these destructive forces
deepens, and the gift of prayer from on High is increased, then
dawns also the joy of hope in Christ's supracosmic victory.
But in order for man to attain to the perfection of this kind
of prayer, which Fr. Sophrony defines as the restoration of the
created world from its fall,[6] he is subjected to great tension and
endures multitudinous alternating states. He fluctuates from
states of spiritual euphoria to a sense of inner aridity, and from
an increase to a diminution of his "prayer-strength".[7] These
fluctuations and states, through which the man of prayer must
pass by means of perseverance and with his whole heart, lead
him to the precious knowledge of the mystery of the paths to
salvation. *Aside:* Fr. Sophrony often speaks about the "mystery
of the ways of salvation".[8] That is to say, for each person there
is a unique path towards God, and those who are spiritual
should know this mystery, and dispense for their brethren the
knowledge of these unique paths. *End of aside.* But above all,
these fluctuations and states lead him to the priceless experience of humility.[9] Knowledge and experience exercise man's
mind and heart to enable him to discern those things which are
pleasing to God, and to keep his attention and desire turned
towards them.

In the restoration of the created world from the Fall, which
is brought about by prayer, the transfiguration of the human
body holds a central place. In order to "change" our body humiliated by sin, that it might be "conformed to the Lord's glorious
body" (*cf.* Phil. 3:21), a prolonged struggle of fasting and repentance is required. Made of the dust of the earth, the body exerts
a downward pressure on the spirit, and weighs it down because
of its being subject to corruption and death. In prayer, however,
man's spirit hastens fixedly towards God, and it wills to impart its
upward impetus to the body, so that it too might thirst after the

living God (cf. Phil. 3:21).[10] "My heart and my flesh crieth out for the living God" (Ps. 84:2), says the Psalmist, and "my soul thirsteth for God, for the living God" (Ps. 42:2).

But whence does the human spirit draw its strength to ascend towards God? At every stage of his description of the mystery of the life in Christ, the Staretz, in his own characteristic way, stresses the tremendous importance of repentance for the ascent towards God. This is also the case with prayer, for with equal emphasis, reflecting the common faith of the Fathers who have gone before us, the Staretz underlines that perception of one's sinfulness is the essential prerequisite for Godward prayer. When accompanied by this perception, prayer is offered with repentance and is always acceptable to God our Saviour.[11] As the parable of the Publican and the Pharisee shows, the publican's perception of his sinfulness was the reason why his prayer was acceptable to God. The Pharisee, by contrast, in justifying himself, eliminated all possibility of being heard by God.[12] Repentance, therefore, is the power which raises man's prayer up to heaven, and prayer of repentance is the most acceptable to God.

The chief condition necessary for prayer of repentance is faith in Christ as *God-the-Saviour*, and the observance of His teaching. Faithfulness in Christ's teaching leads to recognition of the divine provenance of the Teacher. *Aside:* That is to say, unless we have faith in Christ as the Absolute God, we cannot really overcome sin or death, and we cannot pray properly. *End of aside.* The eternal significance of this teaching discloses man's spiritual poverty. Perception of this poverty renders him blessed (cf. Matt. 5:3). Man's awareness of the great gulf between him and God becomes more acute and convinces him that the root of all evil and the reason for his subjection to corruption is pride. This leads him to humility; it transfixes him to the invisible Cross of Christ's commandments, and inspires in him lamentation and prayer of repentance.[13]

The second condition necessary for prayer of repentance is "to acknowledge ourselves as wretched sinners".[14] As he seeks discourse with God, man begins by confessing his own sin and by bearing before God the various impassioned states which seize his mind. The acute awareness of his own sin and worthlessness transports man to the plane of the tragedy common to the whole human race. By living the tragedy of his own individual fall, he experiences the tragedy of the fall of each of Adam's descendants, in their universal dimensions through the ages.[15] By confessing this cosmic event in his prayer of repentance, he assumes the only unerring stance of man before God. *Aside:* That is to say, if there is a case when man is infallible, it is when he confesses his sinfulness, because at that moment he is true. When he does that, he attracts the Spirit of Truth, who brings to the surface all of man's hidden and sinful depths, and cleanses him from all unrighteousness, as St. John the Divine says (*cf.* 1 John 1:9). *End of aside.* Henceforth, in a state of profound tension, he endures opposition to sinful passions and sees himself "the worst of all men" (*cf.* 1 Tim. 1:15), and worthy of "outer darkness" (Matt. 8:12; 22:13; 25:30). Living on the "edge" of this ascetic humility summons up within him "the utmost energy of prayer-repentance".[16] *Aside:* By learning the path of St. Silouan's teaching, "*Keep thy mind in hell, and despair not*", man summons up within him "the utmost energy of prayer-repentance". *End of aside.*

Prayer of such intensity, which leads to close examination of all the soul's impulses, is characterized in patristic literature as "watchfulness" (*nepsis*). Watchfulness, brought about by prayer of this kind, preserves man in continuous "standing" before God. At the same time, this standing is also man's judgment by God.[17] The Staretz describes it as standing "before the Last Judgment". Indeed, he underlines the fact that "the more shattering [the soul's] fear of sentence, the more urgent her prayer of repentance".[18] *Aside:* This is linked with what we have said before: the more we experience shame, the greater the strength we derive from the sacrament. *End of aside.* In addition, however, he explains that this takes place by reason of the experience of divine love which preceded it. Contemplation of God's humble and holy love, of which the believer tastes at the beginning of his struggle, astounds him with indescribable regret for his sinful state, but also inspires him with deep veneration for an acceptable standing before God. *Aside:* When God reveals our sinfulness, we have a double vision, a vision at two levels: on the one hand, we see the spotless, blameless Christ, the absolute and indescribable holiness of our Lord; and on the other hand, there is the vision of our utter spiritual poverty and sinfulness. But we do not despair. One vision inspires the other. *End of aside.* The Spirit of God ceaselessly teaches man to condemn himself.[19] Thus, by enduring the judgment of this present life, he prevents the judgment to come (*cf.* 1 Cor. 11:31).

Perfect ascetic watchfulness, which is achieved by means of prayer of repentance, liberates man from every sense of past or future. He is totally absorbed by a single concern: "not to lose *such* a God, and to stop being unworthy of Him".[20] In this way, man's harmonious relationship with God is restored, and the chief place in him is offered to the love of Christ.

From all that has been said, we can see that the great value of prayer is to be found in the cultivation of that humility and love which unite us with Christ. On this point, the Staretz formulates the following spiritual law: "The more we humble ourselves in painful repentance, the more rapidly our prayer reaches God."[21]

Thus, through the practice of prayer, man's life is transferred to or "hidden" in God's Being, while the life of God penetrates and resides in him. *Aside:* We are in Christ and Christ in us. *End of aside.* That is to say, a coinherence of divine and human life takes place in a twofold movement: man raises his spiritual powers towards God, and God descends towards him.[22] The human upsurge is characterised by an irrepressible and agonising urge for repentance, insatiable prayer, and tender love.[23] God's "condescending" revelation is accompanied with the radical transfiguration of man's entire being and the indescribable harmony of love in the heart.[24] Thus, prayer described as an "ever-new creation" is understood in the especial sense of man's collaboration with God "in the Act of creation by Him of immortal gods".[25] Prayer of this kind is a response to the Heavenly Father's call, and becomes the most precious means by which man is deified. Every aspect of the power of human nature that is possessed of Godward prayer becomes supracosmic.

Pure Prayer

Prayer, as inferred in the previous section, is not a natural property of fallen man. *Aside:* That is why we have a commandment to pray. We are commanded by God to do, not natural but supernatural things. We do not have a commandment to sleep, to drink, to eat – these are natural activities – but we have a commandment to pray, because prayer is a supernatural activity. *End of aside.* Prayer is the fruit of the conjoining of man's struggle to fulfil God's commandment with the gift of God, who, in His love for mankind, condescends in order to raise up His creature. As an act that is at once both divine and human, Christian prayer has a supernatural character. The acquisition of prayer is possible only when man is prepared to give his whole being for its sake. In its more perfect manifestations, prayer is a gift of the Holy Spirit, since it is God Himself praying in man (*cf.* Gal. 4:6). This is perfect prayer.

The fluctuations which may be observed in the practice of prayer are due to the instability of the human element. For this reason, prayer always requires both great effort and tension. *Aside:* On this point we differ considerably from the asceticism of the East. They relax in order to contemplate; while when we pray our whole being is in a state of tension, because even our body participates in prayer. *End of aside.* Man gradually becomes braver as perseverance in the work of prayer strengthens his hope. By means of prayer, he acquires a stable equilibrium in his waverings. *Aside:* He acquires stability in instability. *End of aside.* In this way, having been strengthened in his spiritual powers, he is able to continue for longer periods of time in his standing before God, with the mind in the heart. This continuous standing before God, accompanied with the pain of repentance and the humility of spiritual poverty, cleanses the mind and heart of every extraneous element. God and the grace of the new life by which he has been visited become the supplicant's only desire.[26]

Successive visitations of God's grace in time of prayer endow man not only with stability, but also with discernment. He learns the mystery of the ways of salvation, and by means of humility, is made ready for further ascent.[27] As he continues with his mind firmly fixed on God, the moment will come when the eternal Spirit touches his heart. The wondrous "touch of the Holy of holies" lifts man's spirit up to the previously unknown sphere of Uncreated Being.[28]

The created human hypostasis, man, stands before the hypostatic God, the personal God, and the created mind appears before "the first Mind".[29] Through love for God, the mind becomes detached from every created thing and completely forgets the world. The body is not noticed during the time of prayer. Pure prayer comes with a power that lifts man up to the world of the divine Light, in a gentle, peaceful and indescribable way. Once again, the Staretz is in agreement with St. Maximus the Confessor concerning the second state of pure prayer, in those leading the contemplative life (the *theoretikoi*). The man of prayer arrives at this state through divine love, which brings about his total purification. In the upsurge of such prayer, the mind is lifted up to the vision of the divine and infinite Light.[30]

In order to attain to the state of pure prayer, the Christian must first direct his mind and heart entirely towards eternity.[31] The longing to draw near to God consumes the heart, and the prayer which is born of the vision of spiritual poverty and self-hatred concentrates the mind on the Lord whom we seek.[32] Weeping that is brought about by love of God unites and heals the whole man, making him a partaker of the Beloved. *Aside:* Just a few tears of repentance can change the heart. *End of aside.*

The irrepressible urge to weep before the invisible but beloved Lord, which is rekindled by self-loathing, inspires prayer during which the mind does not return to itself.[33] Man's spirit is absorbed in prayer to Christ, who purifies him of the passions and the desire for material things. He straddles the boundaries of the created order and is immersed in the One God.[34] Weeping breaks the bonds of earthly existence and introduces the human spirit into the unfettered spheres of heaven. Then the palpable breath of eternity imparts to man the experience of freedom from passion and the sense of the hallowing of his entire being.[35] *Aside:* Tears are very much appreciated in the ascetic ethos of the Fathers, because when we weep we can only have one thought. If we have two thoughts, we cannot weep. And when we weep in prayer, this means that our entire mind is fixed on God. That is why ascetics appreciate tears so much – not psychological tears, but tears of repentance. *End of aside.*

The extreme tension of repentance is converted into prayer of despair. The terror of eternal perdition transforms the whole person into prayer.[36] Such prayer leads in a natural way to spiritual purity, in which the one praying lives in the luminous reality of the Holy Spirit. In this state, "he stands both before God and before himself in the full nakedness of his being".[37] *Aside:* This reminds us of the Epistle to the Hebrews, where it is said that "the word of God is quick, and powerful, and sharper than any two-edged sword, piercing even to the dividing asunder of soul and spirit, and of the joints and marrow, and is a discerner of the thoughts and intents of the heart" (Heb. 4:12). *End of aside.* On this point, Fr. Sophrony's description of his own experience coincides with the teaching of St. Maximus the Confessor concerning the first exalted state of pure prayer, to which belong those leading the active life (the *praktikoi*). Out of fear of God and with good hope, the *praktikoi* turn the mind's attention away from the things of this world towards the sense of the presence of God, and in standing before Him they practise prayer undistractedly.[38]

Purity of mind, which is a prerequisite for pure prayer, is attained by man when he conforms to the will of God. In the monastic tradition, by practising obedience and cutting off one's own will, the monk is freed from the heavy burden of earthly cares, and enters into the sphere of the divine will. Thereby, he comes to know the priceless gift of the mind's purity in God. The Staretz discerns the first description of pure prayer in the words of the Apostle Paul: "I knew a man in Christ . . . (whether in the body, I cannot tell; or whether out of the body, I cannot tell: God knoweth;) such an one caught up to the third heaven . . . into paradise, and heard unspeakable words, which it is not lawful for a man to utter" (2 Cor. 12:2–4). *Aside:* That is to say, for the Staretz, we can speak of pure prayer when the one praying does not know whether he is in the body or outside the body. *End of aside.* Especially worthy of note in this description are the following: the absence of the sense of one's body, and consequently of the material world; being caught up into the eternity of heaven; and the indescribable character of this spiritual state.

Aside: I will tell you a story. After Fr. Sophrony had been at the monastery of St. Panteleimon for some years, he was given a hut about half an hour's walk from the monastery, so that he could retire there for a couple of days to give himself entirely to prayer, because he had always had this desire. One day he begged St. Silouan, his Master, to go with him and see this place of solitude that he had been given. As they were going to the hut, St. Silouan asked Fr. Sophrony, "And how goes prayer in your place of silence?" Fr. Sophrony answered, "When I pray, I have the feeling that the world is forgotten, but I still have the sense of my body." And Father Silouan replied, "And is our body not the world?" Fr. Sophrony marvelled at the word of St. Silouan, at his understanding of pure prayer. *End of aside.*

The state of pure prayer is defined as the human mind's standing "before the First *Nous* [Mind], divested of all that is visible, that is transient".[39] In this state, the man of prayer transcends earthly categories and the divisions of nature, and becomes "a new creature" in Christ (2 Cor. 5:17, Gal. 6:15; 3:26–28).[40]

Pure prayer is a personal encounter with God and discourse with him *face to Face.* In prayer of this kind, the human mind is included in the mind of God, and receives existential knowledge and understanding of things which cannot be expressed in human language.[41] It becomes concentrated on an invisible centre of living and inward communion within the heart. Prayer becomes an active perception of God as Personal, free from imagination and abstract reasoning, "and the mind becomes all attention and listening".[42] Then man acquires the sure sense that his prayer has been favourably heard by God and that he has been accepted into His eternity. This kind of prayer is a gift from on High, and places man at the frontier of time and eternity. In him "the ends of the world are come" (1 Cor. 10:11), for as long as prayer of this kind is active, he remains outside time and beyond the power of death.

The uncreated divine Light overshadows man. In this state, he is "incapable of any thought" and "can recall nothing". Pure prayer accompanied with the vision of the divine Light is defined by St. Silouan as theology. Theology here is understood as "a sharing of being", or as participation in the divine Light, and not as "gnostic" theological speculation. Conversely, for St. Silouan, the theologian is one who, by means of pure prayer, is made worthy to rise to contemplation of the uncreated divine Light.[43]

Pure prayer, which follows upon genuine prayer of repentance, consigns man to the Spirit. By His life-giving power, man is set free from the constraints of time and space. Man's awareness of the cosmic dimensions of the Fall and repentance for himself and for the whole human race to the limit of his natural capacity, lend limitless depth, height and breadth to his prayer. Prayer of this kind penetrates the vast regions of cosmic being, and like lightning, cutting "from end to end in a single flash", travels timelessly through the ages.[44] *Aside:* Fr. Sophrony used to say that the mind of the spiritual man, in an instant, is able to measure the whole earth. *End of aside.* This most precious gift of God's good pleasure makes the human hypostasis worthy of being endowed with a divine state of being. In pure prayer, man "assumes from Him [Christ] the 'mind and feeling' that is in Him."[45] Just as Christ prayed for the whole Adam, and became "the mediator between God and men" (1 Tim. 2:5) and "will have all men to be saved" (1 Tim. 2:4), thus it is also with whoever unites himself with Him by means or pure prayer, for he too receives prayer like His prayer. This is the grace of prayer for the whole world, which the Staretz defines as "hypostatic prayer".[46] *Aside:* He also identifies liturgical prayer as "hypostatic prayer", because it embraces the whole world. He told us that nowadays there is no more *hesychia,* because there are no more deserts. There is no longer the possibility for mental prayer as we read in our Fathers, but he said that if we serve the Liturgy properly, on the level of prayer, we shall have the same fruits as our Fathers had when they prayed in silence in the desert. He equated the prayer of the Liturgy with pure prayer, and refers to both as "hypostatic prayer".[47] *End of aside.* Hence, hypostatic prayer for the whole Adam comes as the crowning point of pure prayer. *Aside.* Fr. Sophrony even says that the hypostatic prayer of the Liturgy is higher. *End of aside.*

As long as prayer of repentance continues, man remains contrite, with the soul in anguish from pain and the burning thirst for the Holy of holies. But as soon as the miracle is accomplished, and he is overshadowed by the spirit of pure prayer, he becomes sensible of eternity, overcomes the pain, and is illumined by a new vision – he is healed. The Light of the uncreated Sun comforts the grieving soul, brings peace to her, heals and bestows incorruptible life on her.[48] The deathly grief of repentance is transformed into "unendurable bliss".[49] Experience of the Light is imprinted in man's spiritual memory. His spirit is ruled by wonder at the Heavenly Father, while a subtle yearning to return to His House conduces to pure prayer flowing peacefully from his whole being. Nevertheless, if in the course of such prayer, according to the word of St. Silouan, an alien thought intrudes – even the perception of our own body – then that prayer is no longer pure.[50]

In the state of rapture, brought about by the gift of pure prayer, the atmosphere and feeling for the word of the Gospel predominate. *Aside.* Man becomes akin to the word of God in the state of pure prayer. *End of aside.* The body goes about in oblivion, but the spirit remains captivated by the fathomless wisdom of Christ's word. *Aside.* In fact, these are free means God has given us to become "the temple of the living God" (2 Cor. 6:16), to abide in His presence and thereby become a habitation of His Spirit. *End of aside.* In this way, free from the restraints of the material world, it senses the burning from the radiance of the noetic Sun, in a way that is analogous to the body under the midday sun.[51] Even after prayer has drawn to an end, the Lord's words reign in the mind of man.[52] *Aside.* And it is wonderful, when the word of

God reigns in the mind of man! St. Paul says that when the word of God dwells richly in us, it brings all thoughts to the captivity of obedience to Christ (*cf.* 2 Cor. 10:5). *End of aside.*

Occasionally, pure prayer is made without words. The mind, in an especial state, acquires a global apprehension of all things. Rapture of the spirit may come at any moment. "Then the world is forgotten, supplications die away, and in rapt silence the soul simply dwells in God."[53] In its purest form, prayer is the human spirit's rapture before God.[54] The ascetic's return from the wondrous state of the world of truly eternal existence to the materiality of the fleshly perception of this world is experienced as "distancing himself from the Lord".[55] *Aside.* Somewhere he even says that this return is like a fall. So, for people who have had such an experience, this natural state in which we exist is indeed a fallen state.[56] *End of aside.*

Pure prayer initiates man in a revelatory manner into the mystery of God, and bestows on him the greatest possible knowledge of God. The "place" where this initiation into the divine knowledge is carried out is the "deep heart". When, by the power of the Holy Spirit, the mind enters the "deep heart", it discovers that the existence and the destiny of the human race are not alien to him. *Aside.* Remember the Mother of God. *End of aside.* The love of God unites him with all men who become the content of his hypostatic existence. *Aside.* Pure prayer and the Liturgy are named "hypostatic prayer" because of this association. *End of aside.* He sees the dimension of this event as the essential requirement of the second great commandment: "Love thy neighbour as thyself." *Aside.* The second commandment is fulfilled with hypostatic prayer. *End of aside.* St. Silouan, who bore within him this sense of ontological unity of all men, used to say that "our brother is our life".[57] *Aside.* Once, a monk came to confess to me; he was crying and I thought, "Kyrie eleison! What happened to him?" I became afraid. Do you know what he told me? – "I am looking in my heart, searching into it, and one of the brethren is absent, and I am not happy." He was weeping because he had grown a little cold towards one of the brethren. *End of aside.*

Pure prayer teaches first of the mystery of God and then of the mystery of man. In God, the man who prays finds and experiences the whole human race as one man, whom he sees henceforth as God sees him. He is disposed towards him just as God is; he loves him as God loves him; and he prays for all, as is pleasing to God, who inspires him to do so. Forgive me.

QUESTIONS & ANSWERS

Question 1 (Bishop Basil): In the lives of many saints, holy men and women, we hear sometimes of occasions when they are in prayer and they are lifted up off the ground. I often wonder what that was. Has that to do with what you said, that the body weighs down the spirit, but in prayer the spirit is attracted upwards? Does this upward attraction lift the body as the body weighs down the soul?

Answer 1: I have never had such an experience, but it must happen. Fr. Sophrony says that a moment comes in the repentance of man when the upsurge of the soul is such that it gives an upward momentum even to the body.

Question 2 (Bishop Basil): I was wondering, for instance in the life of St. Mary of Egypt, St. Zossima saw her off the ground?

Answer 2: Well, we see it in the life of our Lord, and the lives of the saints are a repetition of the life of our Lord. It is possible. Once I asked Fr. Sophrony about a story in the Desert Fathers, where it is said that a monk went to Alexandria to sell their handiwork. He did not want to go, because he was afraid of falling into a temptation, but his Elder told him, "Go, and I trust that God, through the prayers of my Elder, will protect you." Notice that he did not say, "through *my* prayers". In the spiritual life, we always "blame" our elders, and then we are safe. Therefore, this monk went to Alexandria; he was invited to a house in order to sell his handiwork, and a temptation began while he was there, between the monk and the daughter of the man who had invited him, and with fear he said, "By the prayers of my Father, save me, O Lord." Suddenly he found himself on the way back to the skete. And I asked Fr. Sophrony, "What happened? Was he taken just like that from the door of the house and put at the gate of the skete?" And Fr. Sophrony said, "No! But by invoking the prayers of his Father, in a humble spirit, such a prayer came to him that ravished him, and when he came to his senses he was already before the skete." So, sometimes when we read these accounts we create myths and thrills in our minds. There is something very great, something wondrous in these accounts, but not as we perceive it with our imagination, because we do not have the same experience. But it is very common in the life of monks to suffer a great temptation, even tribulation, and to say, "By the prayers of my spiritual Father", and instantly be delivered. As I have heard concerning temptations, not only when they are awake, but also when they are attacked in their sleep, and in their sleep they say, "By the prayers of my Father", the enemy has no power over them. Because there is humility in saying "by the prayers of my Father", it is only a thin, slender image that goes by and cannot excite any temptation. This is the institution of the Church – all the prostrations we make before priests, before the bishop, and so forth, are to cultivate this humble attitude, and so protect us from temptations. Fr. Sophrony said that in every institution – in the institution of the bishop, of the spiritual father, of the priest in general – there is a potential charism of the Holy Spirit. It is up to us to find it.

Question 3: Could you tell us what kind of prayer life Fr. Sophrony had? He read the Gospels, he said the Jesus Prayer . . .

Answer 3: Yes. Fr. Sophrony told me that when he went to the Monastery of St. Panteleimon, he was a man who had lived in two great capitals of the world, first in Moscow and then in Paris. In addition to that, he was an artist and as many city folk do, he learned to live by night. He could work better during the night, and up to the end of his life he was a man who lived during the night. When he went to the Holy Mountain, he had to learn to sleep at sunset and get up at eleven o' clock, just before midnight, in order to perform his rule, and at midnight to go to the service which lasted until the morning. And he confessed, "I could hardly sleep an hour or two before the service. And for years I was like a drunkard during the services, suffering greatly from lack of sleep." But he told me also that, even when he was still in the monastery, as soon as he went into his cell, he could hardly close the door behind him when he was on the floor, weeping until he was exhausted. He went to the desert, in order not to be restricted by the bell ringing: in the *coenobium,* the bell rings and you have to go to church; the bell rings and you have to go to the refectory . . . You have to follow a timetable, and for him that was difficult. He told me that when he went to the desert, sometimes for weeks he would not rise from the floor to look through the hole of his cave, whether it was day or night, but he was there, on the floor, weeping, soaking a number of towels. When he became exhausted, he would sleep there for two hours, wake up and continue weeping. And this would take place for weeks at a time, without him even looking through the hole of his cave to see whether it was day or night. These people are "great horses of God". I was a little donkey, and I stayed next to such a man. I learned a lot by seeing and hearing him, but my experience is infinitesimal. I am telling you all this, but I do not do it myself. How could I expect that from you? But it is good to see how great our God is in His saints. Each one must find his own measure: one can pray for one hour, another a quarter of an hour, another only ten minutes; but we must find even ten minutes, during which only God and us are upon earth.

Question 4: How should we pray, Father? Should we use the liturgical life of the Church, like the Hours, for example?

Answer 4: We must read the services, but prayer is sweet when we pray also in our own words, using something that God gives us from the Scriptures. We could pray with the words of the Scriptures or of a liturgical text, or with a thought inspired directly by God – then prayer is even sweeter. But just as a novelist first learns the grammar and syntax of his language and afterwards, possessing the language now, develops his own style; in the same way, first of all we must learn the services of the Church, and assimilate them, so that they become the language of our heart, and then we have the freedom to pray in our own words, and we are within the spirit of the services, of the great Church.

Question 5: Father, I remember that back in my early years of being interested in Christianity and learning the Protestant teachings, we were not supposed to condemn ourselves . . . Could you explain, clarify that a little bit?

Answer 5: We know that the devil is an "accuser"; we see it in the *Book of Job.* We should not be afraid of his accusations, but rather put ourselves beneath his accusation, in which case he vanishes. Fr. Sophrony describes the temptation of a deacon on the Holy Mountain, to whom the devil appeared, and said, "I like proud people. You are a proud man, and I have come to take you with me," and the deacon replied, "I am worse than all", and the enemy vanished. Not only did he accept the accusation of the enemy who called him "proud", but he even said, "I am worse than all". I have experienced it myself and I have seen it in others as well, that when we are troubled by a thought, it is more effective to say this before God, "Lord, you see my abomination: I am worse than all, and unworthy of Thy grace . . . *but* have mercy on me." Immediately the heart is touched, and as soon as the heart is touched the thought vanishes, because it has no grip. The question is to find the heart, because if we find the heart, we are strong. If our mind is outside the heart we are like a reed blown about by the wind. We know that the enemy is an "accuser", but the idea is not to be afraid, and to "go down", and when he sees that we are going down, he leaves us alone, because he cannot follow us, since his only desire is to go up and set his throne above God. When we go down, he realizes that we are not of his spirit. We go down to the Head of the "inverted pyramid", Christ, to be united with Him.

Question 6: You mentioned something about the fact that there are no more deserts. I did not understand.

Answer 6: Really, it is very difficult to find a desert because the world has penetrated everywhere. You may build a monastery in a desert, but there will be ten computers with emails and internet. Where is the desert? The world is in the heart of the monastery. I went once to a monastery to see a very good friend of mine, a really good monk and man of prayer. He had a transistor, and I asked him, "Is this a transistor?" He answered, "Yes, sometimes I listen to the Liturgy from the Cathedral of Athens and the sermons of the priest there." I replied, "But don't you think that by opening the radio the world comes into your cell?" "Yes, you are right", he said, and acknowledged that previous to having a radio he would weep every day, and from the moment he began listening to news and even to the Liturgy and the sermons, he lost the energy and the grace to weep in prayer. There are no deserts now. I do not know how we can live without computers. In our Monastery we also have computers; so far, thank God, we do not have the internet or email, but we use computers for our publications, for editing our books in order to reduce our costs. You know all this, you are modern people. The desert is not only a geographical phenomenon.

Question 7: We speak about being tempted, "O, I am good" and saying, "No! I am the worst." What about a false sense of "worst"? In other words, the demon would come and say, "OK, you are the greatest of the repentant people of the world." It is funny, but from a different level I am getting a false sense of repentance.

Answer 7: You will not avoid such thoughts. Fr. Sophrony says that sometimes, when he was weeping, and he felt that he was surrounded by the spirit of God, a thought would come and tell him, "Now you are all right". This is like having a balloon and piercing it. He lost everything. Consequently, every time such a thought came, he learned to turn immediately to God and say, "My assassins have come. Deliver me from my enemies." We cannot avoid such thoughts, but when we go through this, and we learn to overcome it, afterwards we do not even take notice of such thoughts, and, with just a movement of the mind, we can repel them, and our mind remains undisturbed. It comes with time.

Question 8: Father, living in the world, how do we find the desert in ourselves? How do we make a desert?

Answer 8: I am sure that you have a room where you sleep. If you close the door, you are alone with God. This is our desert, no matter where we are. I am with you here, but each one of you has his own mind and heart; he listens to me, but at the same time he can converse with his God. Once I went to Fr. Sophrony and I said, "We have so many people coming to us. How can we keep the prayer?" Do you know what he said? "You cannot keep the prayer because you do not pray for the people. If you prayed for them, your inspiration would be multiplied, and then you will have continuous prayer." This reminds me of a story from a Russian *Gherondicon*. There was an Elder with two disciples, living in a hermitage. In the nearby village there was a priest who died suddenly. The people of that big village remained without a priest and the Elder, out of compassion, said to one of his disciples who was a priest, "Go, and help them for a while until they get a priest." In order not to send him alone, he himself decided to remain alone in the hermitage and sent the priest and the monk together to serve that parish. And he gave a precept to each one of them. To the priest he said: "Let the names of your parishioners be continuously on your lips and in your heart before God." To the monk he said, "Let the name of Jesus be on your lips and in your heart continuously." This shows what the ministry of the priest is, and what the task of the monk is. If the priest loves the people and loves them in the way that God loves them, that is to say, in the perspective of desiring their salvation, he will be rich in prayer. On the Day of Judgment, everything we do to contribute to the salvation of our fellow men will come before us and will justify us. This is no small thing.

Question 9: Father, could you repeat the definition of a pure mind?

Answer 9: St. Silouan says that the mind is pure when there is no alien thought. We speak of a pure mind when the thought of God possesses man's entire being. That is why tears are so much appreciated, because one cannot weep unless one has only one thought, the thought of God. If you have two thoughts, you cannot weep.

Question 10: We have a parish and a family, how can we keep this monastic life as a family, as a refuge?

Answer 10: I do not think you can keep a monastic life. I think it is wrong when some monks impose obedience on people living in the world. Obedience is only for monks, in monasteries, where the whole life is organized in the name of God and for the Liturgy. You cannot expect this from people living in the world. There, there are other rules. But we all have an obligation of obedience to the commandments of God. You have to respect your wife and your wife has to respect you. You have to be open and transparent, having no secret from your wife, and she from you; and you can have a competition between the two of you: who will do the will of the other more? Then life is beautiful. Concerning children, I do not believe that it is through words that children learn and receive the spirit of God. I will tell you a story. I know a priest who had three sons. He never taught them, and all of them are in the Church now, and one of them is a clergyman. What he did was the following: he waited until they went to bed, and when they were asleep, he went and knelt by their bed and prayed for some time, and, in this way, the spirit of the prayer of the father was imparted to his sons. He never instructed them, but he spoke to God, and God spoke to their hearts. Now one son is a deacon and the other two are his chanters in his parish. Sometimes we think that with words we can accomplish something, and it is the same when we try to help people. If we speak to God, on many occasions it will be more effective, and *He* will find ways of speaking to them.

Question 11: We face many difficulties, but the one difficulty that I have is the following: when hearing the confessions of many parishioners, many times I wonder who am I, so young and so inexperienced in life, to be giving spiritual advice to others? I always ask God to guide me in what I say, but the one difficult thing that I have is when people confess certain sins, they really beat themselves up and they let that sin keep them down and away from the Church. You want them to see the seriousness of their sins, but yet at the same time you do not want to let that keep them away from the mysteries of the Church. I was wondering if you could give me any advice on this problem?

Answer 11: It is a struggle. We all have this problem. Well, we always try to say a word to console, to implore, to pray, we are

all the time "machinating" to transmit to them something that
would wake them up. But it is not necessary to give an instruction in confession. If a word really comes from your heart, you
can say it, but it is enough to hear the confession and read the
prayer. I think it is a mistake sometimes to feel that we have to
give a lecture to each person who comes to confess. I think the
more humble we are the better. Just listen humbly. If you have
a word, say it; and, again, if you see a danger, warn the person
concerned. The only question I ask people when they come to
confession is if they attend the Liturgy regularly and if they do
not miss any Sunday Church service. Once I remember a Cypriot
girl who came several times to the monastery. She was a student
in London, and she was having some problems. The first time she
came, I consoled her, I prayed for her. She came again; she wept; I
did the same. When she came the third time, and the same thing
happened, I began to think, "My goodness, after so much effort,
by now, she should have left this problem behind. What is the
matter?" Suddenly in our conversation, I discovered that she was
not attending the Liturgy, and I said to her, "If you do not attend
the Liturgy, even God cannot help you." As we said yesterday,
from the moment Christ perfected the Body of the Church in
history, we cannot be saved unless we enlist ourselves in this Body.
Salvation is a very concrete thing, within this Body, the Church, of
whom He is the Head. There is a rule that if somebody, without
really an extreme need, does not attend the Liturgy for three
weeks, that person has to be excluded from the communion of
the Church. We must not see it as a punishment only, but rather
as a measure telling us how long man can remain spiritually alive
without the Liturgy. I have read the rules many times in order to
see how much deadening each sin brings to the soul of man. If
there is a rule which says that when a certain sin is committed the
person concerned must abstain from Holy Communion for two
years, this means that there is a considerable deadening that takes
place in that soul because of the sin. Of course, no spiritual father
will require two years. But it depends, I have no judgement on
that matter; every case is unique. But at least you know how much

he must take upon himself, and how much effort he must make in order to help this person to accelerate the process of healing. If the person is willing, and if the spiritual father is willing to co-work with the person, things can be accelerated. Even time is a relative factor. But now we touch upon areas where there are no recipes. I do not think that we can have any assurance when we are spiritual fathers; many times we are in the dark, but we put our trust in God. It is a very complicated ministry.

NOTES

* "Prayer as Personal Communion" and "Pure Prayer", were originally sections from Chapter 8 ("Prayer as the Way of Creation") of Archimandrite Zacharias' *Anaphora to the Theology of Staretz Sophrony* (Tolleshunt Knights, Essex, 2000), pp. 313–329 [in Greek], trans. C. Veniamin; and reproduced in a mildly reworked form, in the full English translation of the same work, entitled *Christ, Our Way and Our Life: A Presentation of the Theology of Archimandrite Sophrony*, trans. Sister Magdalen (South Canaan, PA: Saint Tikhon's Seminary Press, 2003), pp. 233–245.

1. Hom. XVI, 9, in *The Homilies of Saint Gregory Palamas, op. cit.*, p. 185.

2. *Cf. On Prayer, op. cit.*, p. 9.

3. *Ibid.*

4. *Ibid.*

5. *Cf. ibid.*, p. 11.

6. *Cf. ibid.*, p. 12.

7. *Cf. ibid.*

8. *We Shall See Him, op. cit.*, p. 85.

9. *Cf. op. cit.*, p. 16.

10. *We Shall See Him, op. cit.*, pp. 150–151.

11. *Cf. ibid.*, p. 42.

12. See Hom. II, 6ff, in *The Homilies of Saint Gregory Palamas, op. cit.*, pp. 11ff.

13. *Cf. On Prayer, op. cit.*, p. 157.

14. *Ibid.*

15. *Cf. ibid.*, pp. 17, 30–31.

16. *Ibid.* p. 162.

17. *Cf.* Step 28:1, in St. John Climacus, *The Ladder, op. cit.,* p. 212: "Prayer is the court, the judgment hall and tribunal of the Lord before the judgment to come."

18. *Cf. op. cit.,* p. 52.

19. *Cf. ibid.,* p. 174.

20. *Cf. ibid.,* p. 21.

21. *Cf. ibid.,* p. 157.

22. *Cf. ibid.,* p. 81.

23. *Cf. We Shall See Him, op. cit.,* p. 145.

24. *Cf. loc. cit.*

25. *We Shall See Him, op. cit.,* p. 101.

26. *Cf. On Prayer, op. cit.,* pp. 14, 15–16, and esp. 72.

27. *Cf. ibid.,* pp. 15–16.

28. *Cf. ibid.,* p. 14.

29. Gk. *Noï tô prôtô,* from the *Kontakion* for the second Sunday of Lent, on which we celebrate the memory of St. Gregory Palamas (*c.* 1296–1359); and *cf. We Shall See Him, op. cit.,* p. 91.

30. *Cf. Centuries on Love* II, 6, in *The Philokalia, op. cit.,* pp. 65–66.

31. *We Shall See Him, op. cit.,* p. 55.

32. *Cf. ibid.,* p. 67.

33. *Cf. ibid.,* pp. 37–38, 45, 184–185.

34. *Cf. ibid.,* p. 179.

35. *Cf. ibid.,* p. 54.

36. *Cf. ibid.,* p. 99.

37. *Ibid.,* p. 32.

38. *Cf. Centuries on Love, loc. cit.*

39. *We Shall See Him, op. cit.,* p. 91; and see also n. 29 above.

40. *Ibid.*

41. *Cf. ibid.,* p. 227.

42. *Saint Silouan, op. cit.,* p. 113. *Cf.* Macarius of Egypt, Hom. XXXIII, 2 (PG 34:741D): "The soul which bears God, or rather is borne by God,

becomes . . . all seeing". See also *idem,* Hom. XVIII, 10 (PG 34:641A): "When the soul draws near to attainment of the perfection of the Spirit . . . then she becomes all light, all seeing, all spirit, all joy, all rest, all rejoicing, all love, all compassion, all goodness and kindness."

43. *Cf. Saint Silouan, op. cit.,* pp. 141–144. *Cf.* Evagrius Ponticus's classic definition: "If you are a theologian, you will pray truly. And if you pray truly, you are a theologian", *On Prayer* 61 (PG 79:1180B).

44. *Cf. We Shall See Him, op. cit.,* pp. 100, 227.

45. *On Prayer, op. cit.,* p. 56.

46. *Ibid.,* p. 56.

47. *Cf. His Life is Mine,* trans. R. Edmonds (Crestwood, NY: St. Vladimir's Seminary Press, 1977), pp. 87–89; and *We Shall See Him, op. cit.,* p. 216.

48. *Cf. We Shall See Him, ibid.,* p. 67.

49. *Ibid.,* p. 100.

50. *Cf. ibid.,* p. 97.

51. *Cf. ibid.,* p. 183.

52. *Cf. ibid.,* p. 184.

53. *Saint Silouan, op. cit.,* p. 49.

54. *Cf. We Shall See Him, op. cit.,* p. 112.

55. *Saint Silouan, op. cit.,* p. 205.

56. *Cf. ibid.,* pp. 205–206.

57. *Cf. ibid.,* p. 47.

ON THE JESUS PRAYER

I N HIS EPISTLE TO THE CORINTHIANS, St. Paul
says the following about the human body, as if it were
common knowledge to all Christians: "Know ye not that
ye are the temple of God, and that the Spirit of God dwelleth
in you?" (1 Cor. 3:16). *Aside:* As I have said before, the most
practical means of becoming the temple of the Holy Spirit is
the invocation of the Name of Christ. It is practical because
it can always be with us. We were visited once by a Catholic
priest, and he saw how we prayed the Jesus Prayer continually at the monastery, and he said to Fr. Sophrony, "I cannot
understand why you have to repeat the same prayer for so long."
Fr. Sophrony, in a very friendly way, answered, "We repeat it
because we are slow to understand it, and once we have understood it, we do not want to abandon it." *End of aside.*

The Jesus Prayer is a great *ascesis* of the mind and heart,
spiritual work *par excellence*, and a means of sanctification not
only for monks but also for all Orthodox Christians. It is a short
invocation, with a single thought, which the faithful repeat ceaselessly, in the name of the Lord Jesus: *Lord, Jesus Christ, Son of God,
have mercy upon me, a sinner.* The first part of the prayer, "Lord,
Jesus Christ, Son of God", contains a confession of faith in the
divinity of Christ, but also in all the Holy Trinity. In the second

part, there is a confession made by the one praying. He acknowledges his fall, both universal and personal, his sinfulness and the need for salvation. These two parts of the prayer, the confession of faith and the repentance of the one praying, give fullness and content to the prayer.

The Name of Jesus was given by revelation from Above. It originates from the energy of the divine Being, out of time, and it is not at all a human device. This revelation is an action of the divinity, and confers universal glory on the Name, which is ontologically linked with Christ, the Person who is named. *Aside:* That is to say, the Name of Christ is inseparable from the Person invoked. *End of aside.* Prayer in this Name has as its cornerstone the words of Christ, which He uttered a short while before ascending Golgotha, "Verily, verily I say unto you, Whatsoever ye shall ask the Father in my name, he will give it you. Hitherto have ye asked nothing in my name: ask, and ye shall receive, that your joy may be full" (John 16:23–24).

These words of Christ are both a commandment and a promise. A worthy invocation of His Name fulfils the divine commandment and quickens His Presence in us. It is a fulfilment of the commandment of the Lord, because in the Gospel of St. Luke Christ exhorts us to pray ceaselessly and not be fainthearted (*cf.* Luke 18:1).[1] *Aside:* Therefore, when we try to keep this continuous invocation we are simply fulfilling the commandment, and whoever strives to fulfil a commandment places himself in the Way of the Lord, and the Way is none other than the Lord Himself (*cf.* John 14:6). *End of aside.* Consequently, by placing himself in the Way of the Lord, the Christian encounters the Lord as a fellow traveller, and joins himself to Him. The Name of Jesus Christ becomes the means and "place" for the union of the believer with God-the-Saviour. When this Name is invoked, in a manner which is fitting to God, it brings with it the goodwill of the Holy Spirit, and man lives for ever before the Face of the Lord.

In the Old Testament, when Solomon finished the construction of the Temple, he dedicated it with a lofty spirit of prayer to the glory of the God of Israel (1 Kgs. 8:22–61, 2 Chr. 6:14–42). *Aside:* Solomon really offered God a hypostatic prayer, a prayer that embraced all the needs and aspects of the life of the people of God in Israel. *End of aside.* After this prayer, the Lord appeared to the king and said, "I have heard thy prayer and thy supplication, that thou has made before me: I have hallowed this house, which thou hast built, to put my name there for ever; and mine eyes and mine heart shall be there perpetually" (1 Kgs. 9:3). Then the promise of God towards Solomon was fulfilled, "And I will dwell among the children of Israel, and will not forsake my people Israel" (1 Kgs. 6:13). In other words, when the Name of the Lord was placed in the temple, this added a special honour to it, which drew there the gentle gaze and good favour of God's heart. The sealing of the temple with the divine Name established it as a precious place for the charismatic presence of the Spirit of the Lord: "And the glory of the Lord filled the house of the Lord" (2 Chr. 7:1, *cf.* 1 Kgs. 8:11).

In the New Testament, however, all things were made new and incomparably more tangible. God no longer dwells in temples made with hands (*cf.* Mark 14:58, 2 Cor. 5:1), but His Body is the temple, in which dwells "all the fullness of the Godhead bodily" (Col. 2:9). The Lord perfected this temple for our sake. In addition, the sacrament of Holy Baptism imparts to us the gift of putting on the divinity of the Lord (*cf.* Gal. 3:27), and becoming ourselves the "temple of God", so that the Spirit of the Lord dwells in us (*cf.* 1 Cor. 3:16, 2 Cor. 6:16). Entrance into the grace of Holy Baptism, however, comes through faith in the Name of Jesus Christ. This Name, in the history of the revelation of divine Names, is the one which is new, holy, all-powerful, more excellent, above every other Name (*cf.* Phil. 2:9, Heb. 1:4).

Now the calling of the new Israel is for obedience to the faith for His Name, says St. Paul in the *Epistle to the Romans* (*cf.* Rom. 1:5). The mission of the Lord's chosen consists in bearing this Name (*cf.* Acts 9:15), suffering for this Name, regarding shame for it as a privilege (*cf.* Acts 5:41), and being ready to die for the Name of the Lord Jesus (*cf.* Acts 21:13). *Aside:* Do you remember when the prophets in Caesarea tried to prevent St. Paul from going up to Jerusalem, because they knew that there he would be arrested and killed? The Apostle was very upset and admonished them, "What are you doing? I am ready to die for this name. I do not consider my soul of any value" (*cf.* Acts 21:8–14). *End of aside.*

Members of the Body of Christ are those over whom His Name has been invoked, and who themselves can call upon the Name of Jesus Christ. In a word, the Name of Jesus Christ seals the believer and works him into a temple of divinity, a place for the charismatic presence of the Holy Spirit. The Name of Jesus Christ is ontologically linked with the Person of the Lord Jesus Himself. Holding on to it, the believer bears God Himself within him, but only as regards His energy, since His substance is beyond appellation and participation.

In order that the practice of prayer bares fruit, the union of mind and heart is pursued. It is impossible to attain this union by technical means. Technical methods may only help the mind's attention in finding the entrance to the heart, but not in dwelling there. However, in the case of beginners and inexperienced ascetics, there is a great danger in over-appreciating these methods, and this can even lead to a distortion of the spiritual life.

In exercising oneself in the Jesus Prayer two factors are indispensable. The first is the faithful effort made by man to focus his attention in his heart, and humbly predispose his spirit. The second, and incomparably more important, is the grace of the Holy Spirit, without which nothing can succeed, no word and no act is accomplished.

All the gifts of the Holy Spirit came into the world through the descent of the only-begotten Son of God to earth and to the nethermost parts of the earth and, subsequently, through His ascension. Man repeats this "way" to a certain extent; he lowers his mind into the depths of his heart, and there discovers and meets God-the-Saviour. Once the mind has been strengthened by grace, it rules over the heart, that is to say, over man's whole being, and directs all his existence Godward. *Aside:* This is the third movement, about which we talked previously. The first movement is outwards, because of the fall into sin and the passions. The second movement is when we "go down" and discover our heart.

When the mind rules over the heart, that is, over man's entire being, and directs all his existence towards God, that is the third movement. This is the "cyclical movement of the mind", about which we read in the treatises of St. Gregory Palamas on the Holy Hesychasts.[2] *End of aside.* When the mind is united to the heart all the powers of the human soul function harmoniously. However, in order for the mind to manage this descent into the heart and be united there with it, the grace of God is needed. It does not descend by technical methods, as for example by bodily posture or through controlling one's breathing – these are secondary. The mind that has been polluted by the fall of Lucifer and left to its own devices is not in a position to "go down". Only when it has been crucified by the wisdom of the crucified Lord in the struggle to keep the Gospel commandments can it descend. *Aside:* That is to say, the mind finds the heart when the mind conforms to the word and commandments of Christ. *End of aside.* Then man knows in his heart the power of God, and is able to keep his mind there with prayerful attention, invoking the divine Name. Moreover, according to contemporary hesychastic experience, it is stressed that the foundation of each spiritual ascent is repentance – "the way of descent" that presupposes faith in the divinity of Christ and acknowledgement of man's sinfulness.

In the light of this method – of finding and possessing the heart – it can be seen that monastic obedience is an inestimably precious and valuable gift, for it is here that it finds its true value. The aim of "the single thought-prayer of Jesus" is that the believer remains in the living Presence of God. This presence is extremely beneficial and healing. It is a power that files off the rust brought by the Fall, consumes the spirit of wickedness, and heals the mind and heart of man. This Presence of God integrates and unifies man's whole existence, and in this state he only has one thought, one direction of spirit, one desire as he struggles to worship in spirit and truth the One God in the Holy Trinity. The secret that makes the Jesus Prayer efficacious is humility and the extreme attention of the mind, both of which are found by the one who prays through tears of repentance.

During the course of the struggle for unceasing prayer of a single thought we acquire knowledge of many aspects of the mystical life in Christ. Firstly, the energy of the Divinity is transmitted to the soul and body, due to the ontological link which exists between the Name and the Person of Jesus, which we invoke. The whole man is progressively freed from a carnal mind and from the domination of sin, and becomes the object of the Lord's visitation. The hypostatic principle begins to be actualized in him. Secondly, by trying to keep the mind in the heart and centering his attention exclusively on the thought of God, he slowly learns how to ignore the suggestions coming from Satan, which violently try to intrude upon and hinder the holy work of prayer. Thirdly, prayer becomes a positive way of training the ascetic to receive from God those thoughts which open the heart and captivate every thought to the obedience of Christ. Then, all things work together in such a way as to contribute to the process of sanctification through love in the Spirit: from one fullness of divine love to a greater fullness of divine love. *Aside:* Everything contributes to the good for those who love the Lord, says the Apostle (*cf.* Rom. 8:28). *End of aside.* Fourthly, vigilance of mind is accomplished naturally, "because greater is he that is in your heart, than he that is in the world" (1 John 4:4). *Aside:* That is to say, when watchfulness or vigilance (*nepsis*) becomes natural. *End of aside.*

The whole work of mental prayer is infinitely creative. Before the beginning of the world, the Spirit of God was hovering above the abyss, and at a given moment, there was an explosion from which all of creation was hatched. *Aside:* This is the modern theory in astronomy of the "Big Bang". Astronomers have come to believe that the starting point of creation was a big explosion, from which emerged all the galaxies and all creation. I happened to be once in a dentist's waiting-room, and from a magazine there I read a popularized version of the "Big Bang" theory. The good thing about this theory is that at least they agree that the world came into being in a single moment from non-being, just by one explosion. But who provoked the explosion, they cannot say. The Bible, though, speaks of this explosion: "Let there be light: and there was light" (Gen. 1:3). That is the "Big Bang", described in the first lines of the Bible. *End of aside.* In a similar manner, the godly disciple fixes his mind in the heart during mental prayer, and the Name of the Lord Jesus broods over its abyss. The divine energy of this Name is transmitted to the heart, which becomes able to control its every movement, observe its enemies when they approach from without, and chase them away through the power of the Name of Christ. *Aside:* When the mind descends into the heart, then those who pray are able to see intrusive thoughts (*logismoi*) approaching from without, and feel their energy, even before they have seen of what kind they are. They close the door to an intrusive thought, and do not even try to find out whether it is a thought of vainglory, or a thought of the flesh, or a thought of pride, or of any other passion. Those who have united the mind to the heart have closed the door to every thought, but they can feel the energy of an approaching thought. It is like a king sitting on his throne in a castle, who can see his enemies outside the castle, but is safe from them, and cannot be touched by them. *End of aside.*

Through such inner vigilance, sin is reduced to the minimum possible. When, finally, the moment of God's good pleasure arrives, and the energy of prayer has reached its fullness, the awesome opening of the heart takes place – the "Big Bang" of the heart – and man receives the experience of eternity. *Aside:* That is to say, the energy of the spirit has to accumulate in the heart in order to make this opening up of the heart; and this is the true new birth in the Spirit. There are degrees of rebirth in the Spirit. *End of aside.* Therein God enters and dwells, working out the true renewal of man on the ontological level of His divine love.

The practice of the Jesus Prayer is rich in the variants of sensations and changes of the heart, which are essentially events on the plane of the Spirit. *Aside:* The one who really prays with his heart constantly experiences changes in his heart; as we read in the Psalms of Vespers, his heart is all the time stretching upwards (*cf.* Ps. 84:5 Lxx). *End of aside.* According to God's revelation, man is a "deep heart" (*cf.* Ps. 64:6 Lxx), endowed with a mental and divine sensation. That is to say, he is inspired by the beneficial alternations proceeding from the Spirit, and is made worthy of God's care and attention until he comes to stand before God with his whole being, possessed of pure prayer and fulfilling the law of the commandments of love. Thereby, his pre-eternal destiny is also fulfilled. He becomes a king of all creation, and brings before God every creature in intercession.

However, despite being surrounded by God's rich mercy and care, this path of *ascesis* is also accompanied by a superhuman struggle against visible and invisible powers of *cosmic* dimensions. This struggle precedes rapture and illumination by the Uncreated Light, an event which itself is a victory of *supracosmic* dimensions. Prolonged and unceasing invocation of the divine Name of Jesus, and inner guarding of the mind, aim at fortifying an unceasing movement towards prayer of repentance. In this way, prayer becomes a natural mode of being for man, the garment of his soul, and an immediate instinct of his heart for every phenomenon of the spiritual world. This spiritual state is very important at the hour of death. *Aside:* Because at the hour of death, says Fr. Sophrony, everything disintegrates, but this habit of prayer remains with the soul and goes along with it.[3] *End of aside.*

The ascetic practice of mental prayer becomes a training and preparation for the end of this earthly sojourn, so that the birth of the believer into heavenly life may occur as safely and painlessly as possible. At the Divine Liturgy all corruptible and temporal existence is remembered before God, and exchanged for the incorruptible and heavenly life of His Son. Similarly, during unceasing prayer, the believer participates continually in the uncreated energy and grace of Christ, and lives the indescribable enlargement which comes from the Holy Spirit. He becomes a participant in the universality of the New Adam and recalls before God all creation. *Aside:* That is a great moment. *End of aside.* He constitutes the binding principal between God and the rest of creation. *Aside:* He becomes a priest of the whole creation. This is the solution of the environmental crisis. *End of aside.* He becomes a servant of the greatest miracle of our existence, man's union with God.

In other words, the Jesus Prayer is offered as the most suitable precondition for the acquisition of prayer for the world, which is the intercession of the saints. The word of God uncovers before us both ourselves and the whole of creation. Thus, unceasing invocation of the Name of Jesus makes us transparent in His presence, and capable of taking part in the hymn that all creation offers up to God: "The heavens declare the glory of God; and the firmament showeth his handiwork" (Ps. 19:1).

In this excellent ascetic cultivation of the Prayer of Jesus, there is one great danger among many others, and that is pride. In order for the Christian to attain to the highest form of this prayer, and finally inherit in an inexpressible manner the majestic and heavenly life in eternity, he needs a spiritual mentor and an angel. *Aside:* "A faithful guide", as we pray in the Liturgy. *End of aside.* Moreover, he does not cease to reproach himself in all things as being unworthy of God.

Nowadays, we often encounter a certain confusion, and even delusion, in the inexperienced, which results in the mistaken association of the Jesus Prayer with the practice of Yoga, of Buddhism, transcendental meditation, and other such progeny of the East. The similarity, though, which is said to be between them, is, if anything, solely external and on a very low level. The radical difference between Christianity and other beliefs is that the Jesus Prayer is founded on the revelation of the living and personal God, the Holy Trinity. In following other paths, it is not possible to cultivate a personal relationship between God and him who prays. Oriental asceticism propounds the asceticism of mental divesture from everything that is relative and transient, so that man can be united to an impersonal Absolute, with which it is believed he is of the same nature, but has undergone degradation and corruption through entering the multiform and changing life of the present world. This asceticism is egocentric and based on man's own will. *Aside:* In these traditions it is man who sets the programme, a programme that is bound to work and must be followed; and nowhere is it even mentioned, in the *Upanishads,* for example, that pride is an obstacle, or that humility is a virtue. *End of aside.* Oriental asceticism has more of an intellectual character and is not at all connected with the heart.

In these ascetical traditions, man struggles to return to the anonymous, suprapersonal Absolute, and be fused into it. He desires to extinguish his human hypostasis, his human personhood, in the anonymous ocean of this pure being. However, this contemplation is not a vision of God, but the contemplation of man's own self. It does not transcend the limits of created being, neither does it touch upon the primordial Being of the "living God" of revelation. This kind of asceticism may provide a degree of repose and sharpen the psychic and intellectual functions of man, but the fact remains true that, "that which is born of the flesh is flesh" (John 3:6), and cannot please God. *Aside:* But this is the "old man"; they strengthen the "old man" (*cf.* Eph. 4:22–23, Col. 3:9–10). *End of aside.*

The most perfect "divesting" of the mind from every passionate attachment to the visible and transient elements of this world is accomplished naturally, through the fervour of repentance. Pain of the heart, which is born of the grace of repentance, not only detaches the mind from things corruptible, but rather attaches it to that which is unseen and eternal. *Aside:* We are not only detached but attached; we are not only divesting but investing. Even in its best form, Buddhism is only half of the matter, and concerns only the human factor. *End of aside.* In this respect, divesture alone remains but partial and imperfect, relating as it does merely to the human factor on the created level of being. In Christianity there is, however, a further clothing of the soul with the grace of God which must necessarily follow, and this is the fullness of life immortal. Many admire Buddha and compare him to Christ. They say that Buddha had compassion and felt pity for human suffering, and with beautiful words taught both the possibility and the manner by which man may detach himself from sufferings, and remain calm. However, the only-begotten Son of God, Christ, through His Passion, Cross and Resurrection, voluntarily and without sin, took pain upon Himself and transformed it into a means of expressing His perfect love. With this love He healed His creature from the great wound caused by the sin of our forefather and made him into a new creation. This is why pain is so precious in the practice of the prayer, and its presence is a sign that the ascetic is not far from the true and holy Way. Without experiencing pain, the Christian cannot know the depths of being, and remains a stranger to the love that conquers sin and death.

Immediately after Christ's Resurrection and the establishing of the Church, those distinguished as Christians were those who "called upon the name" of Christ. And the new "election" of God was identified with the struggle of "bearing his name" (Acts 9:14–15). Just as the Lord had said that we cannot live for ever except we eat of the Flesh of the Son of man and drink His Blood (cf. John 6:51–54), so also do the witnesses of His resurrection confirm, from the very first, that "there is none other name under heaven given among men, whereby we must be saved" (Acts 4:12). Thus, the invocation of the Name of the Lord Jesus Christ and communion in His Body and Blood have become the two fundamental paths of life, effecting the salvation of the new people of God, who were bought by His "suffering of death" (Heb. 2:9).

QUESTIONS & ANSWERS

Question 1: Is there ever a variation of the Jesus Prayer, instead of saying, "Have mercy upon me *a* sinner", saying, "Have mercy upon me *the* sinner", with the definite article? Is that proper?

Answer 1: Yes, I think so. It depends on what you want to emphasize. Sometimes people put the emphasis on the word, "*Lord* Jesus Christ, have mercy upon me a sinner," whereas at other times they would say, "Lord *Jesus* Christ, have mercy . . .", and again at other times they might say, "Lord Jesus *Christ*, have mercy . . ."; it depends on the state of the soul.

Question 2 (Bishop Basil): I was thinking more of the prayer before Holy Communion: "I believe, O Lord, and I confess that Thou art truly the Christ, the Son of the living God, who came into the world *to save sinners of whom I am chief.*"

Answer 2: Yes. I am sorry. Because English is not my language I sometimes cannot feel the fine differences, but I understand what you mean.

Question 3: Father, I have heard that there could be dangers associated with certain breathing techniques in the practice of the Jesus Prayer?

Answer 3: The danger is that if man is not experienced and he does not know what to look for, he can be deluded, because he may attach too much importance to those things. He will mistake some phenomena, which are secondary, for the real end of the prayer. But those who are experienced in prayer can use breathing techniques without being in danger. It is dangerous especially for beginners, however even those who are experienced do not use these breathing techniques very much, but only at small intervals, because if this is done with arrogance it can even do harm. But when one has wept in repentance, the mind becomes so light and moves so fast that the prayer finds its own rhythm naturally. In these cases, the mind has such a reverence before God, that breathing itself becomes more timid before His Presence. It is not that we deliberately restrain our breath, but naturally, the mind stands before God in awe and reverence and invokes His Name. That is why St. Theophan the Recluse in one of his letters to a nun says that before you sit on your stool and begin the invocation of the Name, it is good to weep for a time for your sins, because that weeping cleanses and makes light both the heart and the mind, and the mind easily finds the heart and the rhythm of the prayer, naturally, without any artificial method.

Question 4: Father, I am sorry I had to leave the room for a while and I wanted to know if you have said again anything about the emotions.

Answer 4: Several people have asked me to explain in a little more detail the transformation of psychological states into spiritual states. Let us say that I live in the monastery and one of the brothers, Fr. John who is from Cyprus and who is a man of the heart, who has simplicity but wisdom as well, let us say that he said a hard word to me, and I received the "kick" of his word like a sword in my heart. This is hypothetical, such a thing has never happened between the two of us. But let us assume that he said this hard word that offended me, and I felt it like a sharp knife in my heart. I cannot avoid this pain; the pain is real. There are two ways of reacting. The psychological way would be to say the following: "Father John, I have done so much for you. I have prayed so much for you. I have received you with so much love into our community, and I have always cared for you. How ungrateful! You are not a good man." This is a bitter reaction, but that is how we react in the world. This kind of reaction destroys me. The best way is to realize that although the pain is real and I can do nothing about it, I can change the thought immediately and converse with God. I can lift my mind up to God and say, "Lord, you have seen me in the sleep of despondency, in the sleep of death and negligence, and you have sent your angel to wake me up. Have mercy upon him and upon me, and forgive me all my sins." Like that, I begin to pray for the forgiveness of my sins, and after praying for a while in such a manner the pain in the heart turns into such great comfort that by the end of the prayer I feel so refreshed that I even forget how the prayer began.

In the world, people establish a ladder to spiritual accomplishment according to human criteria, and they say, "If I have read one service a day, I am on the first step of the ladder. If I have read two services, I am on the second step. If I have read all the services, I am good and perfect." This is a psychological calculation and it is not real at all. St. John of the Ladder gives us another ladder to spiritual perfection, more real and infallible. What is our reaction when we are insulted? If we are insulted and we constrain our heart not to answer back, then we have put our feet on the first step of the ladder. If we not only do not answer back, but also pray for the one who has offended us, then we have taken the second step of divine ascent. If we not only pray for that person but also feel sorry that he suffered harm to his soul for doing that to us, and are full of compassion for him, then we are on the third step. And if we rejoice that we have been humiliated for the Lord's sake, then we are on an even higher step on the ladder of the way to perfection. You see, he gives us a system of classifying spiritual states that is infallible. The moment we take offence, we reveal where we stand. If we get angry and irritated, and we react, that means that we have not yet even set a single foot on this ladder. The Fathers knew that unless we learn to transform our state, we will never be able to ascend the ladder that leads to divine perfection.

Question 5: Father, it seems to me that in the beginning you are going to walk down a little bit before you start to come back up. I am talking about setting your mind into hell, without despair.

Answer 5: Yes, it is like when we are diving, we go to the bottom, we hit it, and we surface very quickly. It is very quick if we hit the bottom with our feet. Those who have done diving in their youth know this. Yes, it does help to go down first.

Question 6: You said something very briefly about pain being necessary. What do you mean by that? Could you elaborate on that a little bit?

Answer 6: Pain is a way of showing concretely that we have love. As Christ showed His love by suffering for us, so we also, when we endure pain, show our gratitude to Him, and put ourselves on the Way of the Lord. Pain has the following beneficial aspect: for example, if now I break my finger, my whole mind is there, because it is painful, my finger burns with pain. I broke the bone of my finger and my mind is concentrated there. If my heart is broken with pain, my mind will go there naturally; and that state is very beneficial. Weeping, fasting, vigilance, accepting offence, all these things have one purpose: to unravel the "deep heart", to help the mind find the "deep heart". That is why humility finds the heart, while pride buries it. Someone who is proud cannot feel his heart, he has no heart. Vainglory covers the heart completely. So we have to go through the pain of humiliation in order to find the heart, because the heart is not only the physical centre of the human being, or the psychological one, but also the spiritual centre of personhood. The whole Bible speaks about the heart as the place where the choice is taken for God, as the place where man meets God and where God speaks to him. What is precious in the eyes of God, says St. Peter, is the "hidden man of the heart" (1 Pet. 3:4). Pain helps us to find the deep man of the heart.

Question 7: Father, could you go over the four steps that you mentioned just now?

Answer 7: If you are insulted and you force yourself not to answer back, and you exercise control over yourself – that is the first step, says St. John of the Ladder. If you have not only not answered back, but managed to find some strength to pray for the one who insulted you, which is the best way to restore your own peace, then you are on the second step. The third step is if you feel compassion for the harm that the other person's soul suffered by insulting you. And the fourth is what we are taught by the Book of Acts: to rejoice when we are offended for the sake of the Lord.

Question 8: Going back to pain, when you used the image of physical and spiritual pain, when the physical pain is such that it is very consuming, how can that not be a distraction?

Answer 8: Yes, I know. This matter is not easy and sometimes when the pain caused by weeping and repentance becomes too great, it can drown you completely. Then you have to relax a little bit, to be able to live. But the criterion is this: if prayer flows, that means that there is no harm; that means that God is in control of everything. But if the pain does not go away, it would be better to stop and examine the matter again. As a general principle in ascetical life, if you force yourself and things get better, that means it is good to keep forcing yourself; but if you force yourself and things do not get better, then stop, because there may be an organic problem.

Question 9: My question was rather when someone suffers from a disease such as mine: I suffer from an illness that causes constant pain in my body, like now the absolute agony of my neck, and it is very difficult to focus on anything, how can one pass through that physical pain to find the pain of the soul, so that one can cry out to God from the depths of one's being?

Answer 9: Yes, it is very difficult when you have this physical pain, which does not allow you to concentrate and stay your mind in the heart, but the pain can become a sacrifice to God if at that moment of pain you say, "Glory be to Thee O Lord, glory be to Thee, O Lord." Just release this little cry from time to time, "Glory be to Thee O Lord, glory be to Thee, O Lord." The pain will remain, but you will be given grace that overshadows the pain.

I knew a sixty year old Cypriot lady who had cancer. She came to the monastery, and told me, "I have cancer. The doctors told me that in six months I shall die." I said to her, "Androula, then go for the meeting with the Lord, hold on to His word: whether we die or live we are the Lord's (cf. Rom. 14:8), and prepare for this meeting. You have six months. Wonderful! It is the greatest moment of your life." She was a woman of prayer. I never console people, "Ah, you will live, it will pass." I say rather, "Prepare for the meeting", even if they live afterwards. The woman accepted it, and started saying, "Glory be to Thee, O Lord", all the time. One day she said to me, "I want you to promise me just one thing: when I will not be able to come to the monastery any more, that you will come to see me once in the hospital, before I die." I agreed, and before she died I went twice. The first time I went she was in a pretty bad state, but very peaceful, and I asked her how she was. She said, "Thanks to God, I am well", even though she was not well – she was dying. She kept saying, "Glory be to Thee, O Lord", and she was saying another prayer that I had asked her to say, "Lord, I am Thine, save me" (cf. Ps. 119:94). "Just surrender to the Lord with this prayer", I said to her, "you do not need any other prayers." After a while, I went to see her again. Her situation had worsened. They phoned me, and I left for the hospital taking Holy Communion with me, although I was not sure if she would be able to partake. I arrived and I saw her: her tummy was like a balloon, from the cancer. The only part of her body that was free from cancer was from the throat up. I asked her, "How are you, Androula?" Her face was pale but luminous. She started crying. I was thinking, "Oh, my God, I hope she is not fainthearted." I said, "Why are you crying?" Do you know what she told me? "Am I worthy to be given such a grace to bear this monstrous thing? Who am I? Glory be to the Lord!" She was in such deep humility.

She could not thank God worthily for the grace that she had been given to bear that terrible cancer. She added, "My relatives come here thinking to console me, and they disturb my prayer, and do not understand it. And the Lord is there – she pointed to the corner of the room – waiting for me." And her soul departed like that, like lightning. After that, I returned to the monastery, and the next day celebrated the Liturgy. During the Liturgy, these words were sounding in my heart: "She is saved." "She is saved." "She is saved." I could hear these words sounding in my heart. And I was crying and could not control myself. I normally control myself, because it is not proper for a monk to cry before others. Fr. Symeon, who is the oldest priest of our monastery, asked me, "What is the matter with you today?" I said, "I just cannot control myself." I had such joy, and the only thing that was sounding in my heart was, "She is saved." "She is saved." "She is saved." It was such a beautiful Liturgy, and I thanked God who informed my heart that she was received as a saint in the kingdom. I have seen many people, who had cancer, who came to have a similarly glorious end, after accepting their cancer in accordance with the word of St. Paul, who said that whether we live or die we make it our purpose to be pleasing to God (cf. Rom. 14:8).

Question 10: Are you saying that when one has such a pain, which we sometimes cannot even find the words to describe, it is right to give in to it and not to fight it, but to accept it? That is what I have done, I just gave up fighting and accepted it, simply saying, "Thanks be to God." That was my question. Is it alright just to give in to it?

Answer 10: I know your pain, because I had it with my back for several years. It is not "giving in". When we have such a pain, we are being led as a sheep to the slaughter, but what can we do? We just remain speechless before the shearer, and we say, "Glory be to Thee, O Lord."

Question 11: Can you comment on two things? One is the use of self-flagellation that has been known at least in the West. The other thing is that we live in a culture that says utterly the opposite of what you are suggesting; we are told over and over again that we must fight against the pain. The medical disciplines of our culture say, "You fight against it." The language of the medical discipline is the language of war against pain, war against suffering, and we are bombarded with this whole sort of thing, television and so forth, the whole culture is built this way now.

Answer 11: Yes, but this is the way of the world, and the world is at enmity with God. We know this is the case, and whoever loves the world cannot please God. Well, these things are done slowly, slowly, by experience. Forgive me, I will tell you something. I made a small experiment in the following way for myself. I knew from the writings of the Fathers that three things are most pleasing before God. The first, they say, is pure prayer, and to do all our works purely. The second is monastic obedience, because that is a total sacrifice. In monastic obedience, freedom, which is the most precious thing that a man has, is laid at the feet of Christ. The third is giving thanks in illness and tribulations. And once I went to hospital to have an operation, and I thought I would try what the Fathers say. In the week after the operation I was convalescing in the hospital, and all the time I was there I said no other prayer but, "Glory be to Thee, O Lord. I thank Thee, O Lord, for all things." And it was so beautiful there that at the end of the week I did not want to leave the hospital. So, we have to try these things: "Taste and see that the Lord is good" (Ps. 34:8).

We can perform our own experiments. In physics, for instance, we see that an able scientist first forms an hypothesis, then he or another scientist carries out experiments to verify this hypothesis, and if it is verified then it is formulated and recognized as a law that governs the relationship of physical phenomena. That is how we have obtained all the laws of physics. In our faith, all the revelation of God is given to us in a hypothetical form. Do you know why? Because God is kind, and does not want to constrict our freedom, to impose anything on us, and He says, "If you accept my teaching, you will know whence it comes" (*cf.* John 7:16–17), that is to say, whether it is from a human being or from God; and if it is from God, it will engender newness of life. And you will notice that the commandments of the Lord, and all His words, are given as hypotheses. For example, "Be still, and know that I am God" (Ps. 46:10). If you try stillness, if you make your own experiment, then you will know. "Blessed are they that mourn: for they shall be comforted" (Matt. 5:4). If we mourn, then we shall receive the comfort of the Comforter. Although I have not prepared verses specifically on this subject, I have already mentioned one: "If you receive my teaching, you will know whence this teaching comes" (cf. John 7:17). All the revelation of God – the word of God – is given to us as a hypothesis, which we can analyse in its hypothetical form, not because it is not true, but because God is kind and wants *us* to carry out the experiment, and prove it to ourselves, and establish it as a law of our life. That is how the commandment of God becomes a law of our life. We make our experiment, we see that it works, and therefore His word becomes absolute for us. That is why it is wrong to classify theology as a theoretical science; it is a positive science. It follows the method of the positive sciences exactly, and even more so than the science of medicine.

Question 12: You talked about repentance, sorrow and weeping for sins, but with everything you say I see joy in you – I see great joy.

Answer 12: And I am not a good monk. Myself, I am a very bad monk. But Fr. Sophrony told us that when he was on the Holy Mountain if the fathers saw a monk to be sullen – depressed – they would say, "He has not wept in the night. That is why he is sad. If he had wept in the night he would have joy; he would have squared his account with God; he would have received the testimony of His forgiveness in his heart." So the fathers say that if you have not found joy or fire after your prayer that means that you have prayed in an external way, not to say in a Pharisaic way. This is what they say in the *Philokalia.* And this is what we sing: "Through the Cross joy has come into the world."[4] That was the main concern of St. Paul. He did not try to teach his disciples to perform miracles; he only wanted to teach them "Jesus Christ, and him crucified" (cf. 1 Cor. 2:2), because he knew that if they accepted Christ and Him crucified, they would certainly know the power of His Resurrection as well, in a natural way.

Question 13: You talked about the four stages or steps of forgiving when somebody insults us. If we are not able to do the first step, to pray for them, does that come from pride, from vainglory?

Answer 13: Yes, mainly from pride, because pride, as St. Silouan says, is the only obstacle to love and forgiveness.

Question 14 (Bishop Basil): Father Zacharias, when I returned from visiting your monastery last year, it was several days before we had our annual retreat, and I shared with the fathers and brothers some experiences of my visit to your monastery, and there were some questions. Perhaps you might enlighten us or at least share something with them about the uniqueness of the place of the Jesus Prayer in the Community of Saint John the Baptist. I tried to explain to them – also telling them that it is not automatically "exportable" – how Elder Sophrony had instituted at St. John's that which was common among the hermits on the Holy Mountain.

Answer 14: You know, that came by necessity, like all the forms of life that we have at the monastery: the double community and everything else. It was not planned; it just happened naturally, by Providence, I would say. In the beginning they had no books; they were seven people and seven different nationalities, seven different languages. So praying with the Jesus Prayer was the most convenient way. Fifty years ago, when they started the community in France, they had no translations into English, even of liturgical books.

Do you know how our monastery started? When Fr. Sophrony left the Holy Mountain, he went to France in order to publish his book on St. Silouan with the idea of going back to the Holy Mountain afterwards. He knew that in France there were many Russians who had printing presses, theological schools, many parishes and so on – the Russian immigration was then flourishing. Many of course, afterwards, left Europe and came to the New World, and the Russian immigration diminished considerably. But after the Revolution two million Russians went to France. So, Fr. Sophrony went to France to edit the book on St. Silouan. The first edition was roneo-typed: he hand-typed it, and bound it – he did everything himself. Because he worked so hard, under very difficult conditions, he fell ill with a bad ulcer of the stomach, a terrible haemorrhage; and the doctors had to cut out almost all of his stomach and join the oesophagus with the intestine. Because of this, he could not take much food for many years. He would eat very little, several times a day.

So, after having suffered this operation in France, he could not go back to the Holy Mountain, so he remained captive in a Russian Home for elderly people in a suburb of Paris, at Sainte-Geneviève-des-Bois. As soon as he had recovered a little, since there was a chapel in the Home, he started having services there – he was a monk. And the old people joined him, because they had nothing else to do. They had the staff of the Home there to serve them, and so they had three hours of prayer in the morning and three hours in the evening. Fr. Sophrony told them to pray the Jesus Prayer, and many of these old men and women became monks and nuns, and they established a mixed community in the Home. And since they had nothing to do all day, they sat at a round table and Fr. Sophrony would teach them, spending time in church and around the table. In this way, a mixed community emerged in the Home. But once his book had been printed some young people learned about it, and they also began to come to him. The first three monks – Fr. Iriney, Fr. Symeon and Fr. Procopy – looked around near the Home and found a stable, and they made some rooms there, where they could sleep whilst spending the day in the Home. One of those three was the reader of the Chapel of the Home, because he was a Russian and could sing beautifully. They ate from the leftovers of the elderly people, and spent their time with Fr. Sophrony, at the services and in the Home.

After a while though, the young people that had gathered around, both men and women, did not want to continue their whole life, there, in the Home – they were too young, in their twenties. So they began to urge Fr. Sophrony to fount a monastery for them. This was impossible in France, because there the State is separated from the Church. The French State tolerates some monasteries as charity organisations, but not as monasteries. In any case, it was difficult; they probably could have done it if it were God's will. When they started looking into the matter, several friends of Fr. Sophrony began to look in their own countries, some in Sweden, some in Holland, some in Ireland, some in England. But the lady who was looking for a place for a monastery in England was the more able. She was the lady who translated the books of Fr. Sophrony into English, Rosemary Edmonds. She was a secretary in one of the Ministries, and the personal translator of de Gaulle during the war. She met Fr. Sophrony when he was in the hospital having his operation, and became connected with him. She became Orthodox and was the person who found a place for him to go to England.

When Fr. Sophrony applied to go to England, he was interviewed at the British Embassy in France, and the Consul there asked him, "How can you contribute to our life in England?" Fr. Sophrony answered, "We will be useless to you; we cannot produce anything, but we are looking for a quiet place to have our Liturgy." And the Consul said, "Strange people!" But they submitted their application for a visa to go to England, and the case of Fr. Sophrony was discussed in Parliament. It was a critical moment, as it was becoming very difficult for foreigners to come to England. I do not remember all the details, although I have read the story somewhere. But the matter was debated in the House of Commons, and there were some there who were determined not to let them come to England, because Fr. Sophrony made a petition to come with his *synodia*, with his company. We have the Government paper with the Minutes of the debate; we keep the document in the Archives of the monastery. At a moment when the mood of the debate was definitely inclining towards a refusal, one Member of Parliament stood up and said, "You do not wish to allow the Archimandrite to come, because they cannot contribute to our economy and to our life; so if the twelve Apostles came to Dover, you would only take Judas, because he had the money!" At that moment, the Home Secretary, Butler, signed the forms and said, "Give the Archimandrite whatever he wants." So he received permission in this miraculous way, went back to the mixed community and told them that they could all come with him to England, if they wanted. But the elderly people, who were secure with a pension in France and had their Church services there, could not migrate to England and start a new adventure, without knowing the language, the way of life, and so on. So, they preferred to stay in France, and Fr. Sophrony left a Hieromonk for them, Fr. Silouan, who continued the services there until his death, in 1991. The younger group, together with two elderly nuns, went to England, to the house which Rosemary Edmonds had found for them. They divided it into two halves. The nuns used the one half, and the other half was taken by the three young monks and Fr. Sophrony. There they lived very quietly and in extreme poverty. Their basic diet was potatoes and nettles. I am ashamed to mention this, because we eat so well now at the monastery; but we say this to show how wonderful is the Providence of God.

The first couple of years were very quiet, nobody knew them, so they had the luxury of having more time for prayer and study. They lived a real hesychastic life. Then they were discovered by the Cypriots, who began coming in coaches, because they found out that here was a holy old man who could confess them – Fr. Sophrony. So with their arrival the silence of the monastery came to an end. Fr. Sophrony received them gladly; he was very happy, but felt that their life would now change. They needed a place to receive visitors, so they had to begin building, which was difficult because the monastery is located in a "green belt" and, although the authorities were extremely clement, it was not easy to get permission. They would not give English people permission to build there, but to us they did give permission, and we are very grateful for that. The Providence of God was wonderful, people were coming in great numbers, and Fr. Sophrony from morning until night was receiving them in confession. People were very happy, many lives were restored, and Fr. Sophrony realized that the two old nuns were doing great work by taking care of the women and children; so he was completely free from care to receive the people in confession. But when the two nuns became too old, he had to take one or two younger nuns to take care of the old ones, because the monks could not look after them, and so slowly, without realizing it, a double community was formed. There was no plan, it just happened like that. The four sisters soon became seven, and the house was overfull. But prayer was much stronger in those days than now, even though they were very poor: they had only one meal a day and afternoon tea. Now we have three meals a day.

At that moment, God provided for us to build a place for the sisters, so the house called the Old Rectory was left for the fathers, and the sisters would come there for meals, on the ground floor, where the refectory and chapel were situated. Then, as people began to come in greater numbers, more sisters joined our community, because there was enough room to accommodate them in their new house. Then came another impasse, and God opened another door. We put up the refectory building where the library is now, and we began to breathe again. But after some years things were impossible, we thought we could not manage. Then at that moment God gave us the means to buy the farm opposite, and now we are organizing life in a better way. The sisters will be in the farm across the road, and all the old property will remain for the fathers. "When we bought the farm, we bought our lungs", Fr. Sophrony used to say. "We can breathe now." And he would say, "Let's imagine that the road is the river Nile. On one side of the river are the sisters, on the other will be the brothers." Now, at this moment, we are building the cells for the sisters. Some of the sisters have moved already, because there is a house there which can accommodate six. Some are still in the house on the old property, and there are three others in one of our guesthouses in the village: we have two guesthouses in the village, for women guests.

So, I have told you all this to show that there are no plans in the spiritual life. Providence imposes the plan, and that is the best way, because then you have courage. I remember one day when we were flooded by people and we did not have room to accommodate them. (This was a time when we were afraid that we would not get the permission to build the hall.) That day I was the cook in the old kitchen, and that old kitchen had eight doors. People were entering from every door, and at the same time I had to cook, answer the phone, and give drinks to the guests who had just arrived. I said to the Hegoumen, "I am sure we will get the permission for a new building because, look, it is impossible. I am sure that God will make a way for us." The following week permission was granted.

When we go along with the Providence of God, we have courage to struggle, because the choice was not ours. God put us there; He will provide. The Apostle Paul says that "the spirits of the prophets are subject to the prophets" (1 Cor. 14:32). That is to say, if we were truly prophetic, we would not show any of our inner activity, of our inner life; it is more humble not to show anything, in order to preserve humility, which is precious, and so as not to provoke the conscience of our fellows. This is the culture and ethos of the Church. In the Church, we avoid doing anything that might provoke attention. For instance, the way we read in the Church is in a neutral tone, so that the people of God who are present can hear it if they want, and they can disengage if they want to follow their own rhythm of inner prayer. This is the culture of the Church. If I spent the whole night in prayer, and have a different rhythm within me, I am not forced to follow another one: I have my own rhythm, and I do not provoke anyone. Therefore, we do everything in order to protect our humility, and to protect the consciences of our fellows. That is why, in the Orthodox Church, truly charismatic people do not make a show of their gifts and graces. In the West – may God forgive me for what I say, I do not want to criticize – I think charismatic people are not free from the lust for power, and sometimes they air their graces and their gifts in order to dominate their fellows. Forgive me for that. That is madness and destruction, as the Lord said to the mother of the sons of Zebedee (Matt. 20:20–28). Forgive me Bishop, I have said too much.

NOTES

1. See also *e.g.* Rom. 12:12, Eph. 6:18, Col. 4:2, and 1 Thess. 5:17.

2. See *The Triads: Gregory Palamas, loc. cit.,* and pp. 77–78 above.

3. *Cf. On Prayer, op. cit.,* p. 150.

4. *Cf.* Resurrection Ode, which follows upon the Ikos of the Canon for Easter, and immediately after the Gospel reading in Sunday Matins. It is also said secretly by the Deacon as he holds the Paten over the Chalice following Holy Communion.

SPIRITUAL FATHERHOOD
AS A MINISTRY OF RECONCILIATION
BETWEEN MAN AND GOD*

I N ARCHIMANDRITE SOPHRONY'S ascetic theology and practice, spiritual fatherhood is linked with the mystery of the word of God, which is begotten in the heart of man through prayer.[1] The Prophet Isaiah says that when a word "proceeds from the mouth of God, it does not find rest or return to void unless it has first accomplished its work" (cf. Isa. 55:11). He also says that it is a fiery coal, which purifies and sanctifies those whom it touches (cf. Isa. 6:6–7). *Aside:* We also repeat these words after we have received Communion: "Lo, this hath touched thy lips; and thine iniquity is taken away, and thy sin purged." *End of aside.* This prophetic ministry of the word of God is the service of the spiritual fathers of Christ's Church. Spiritual fathers are those who, in the fear of God, remain "unwavering in the pre-eternal current of the will of God",[2] and who are vouchsafed to hear the "still small voice" of Christ (1 Kgs. 19:12), and to obey it with humility and discernment, overcoming their own "psychological" inclination, even when this speaks against what Christ inspires.

Aside: This may need some explanation. Do you remember the Prophet Jonah? He was a true prophet. His psychological understanding was against the word he received from God, nevertheless he had the discernment to obey God and utter His prophecy. Therefore, if we are truly spiritual people, we must always discern the word of God, even if it is contrary to our "psychology", to our understanding. *End of aside.* Spiritual fathers become bearers of the word of God, and they transmit it for the edification of the people, and "minister grace unto the hearts of the hearers" (*cf.* Eph. 4:29). This living word accomplishes the spiritual regeneration of the faithful.

Christ was prophetically announced in the Old Testament as "the Father of the world to come" (Isa. 9:6 Lxx). By His ineffable "generation" (Isa. 53:8). *Aside:* Who can utter His generation, not only His heavenly generation, but even His earthly generation? *End of aside.* By His ineffable "generation", He came and spoke to us of the creative and life-giving words of His Father (*cf.* John 6:63). Even more, "He was led as a sheep to the slaughter" (Isa. 53:7 Lxx, Acts 8:32), and in His Blood He "purified unto himself" a new "peculiar people" (*cf.* Titus 2:14). The dread dispensation of His humble descent, below all creation, and His ascent "above the heavens", has "filled all things" with the deifying power of His Presence (*cf.* Eph. 4:10). Nothing in the created world remained "not manifest in his sight" (Heb. 4:13). His living word sowed an "incorruptible seed" (1 Pet. 1:23), and by the grace of His Spirit He gave to man the gift of "adoption of sons" (Gal. 4:5); that is, He begot the Church and made the faithful into "children of the resurrection" (Luke 20:36), and "a kind of firstfruits of his creatures" (Jas. 1:18). The completion of His way and work set Christ forth as head and father of a new race, which "awaits" Him (*cf.* Phil. 3:20), as "Saviour of all men, specially of those that believe" (1 Tim. 4:10).

To redress the injustice of inequality, which penetrated human life after the Fall, Christ overturned the pyramid of cosmic being, and placed Himself as the head of the now inverted pyramid.[3] He bore the sin and infirmity of the whole world, and restored true justice as an inalienable claim for the spirit and consciousness of man. He gave every man equal value, because He gave the same commandments to all, and also His own unique example, which denied to no one "the ascent to the top rung" of perfection.[4] *Aside:* We are all equal before God because we have all received the same commandments.[5] *End of aside.*

As mentioned above, the great value of monasticism lies in the path of humility, which follows the downward way to the summit of the inverted pyramid. In the measure in which the monk approaches Christ in His descent, he also will become a partaker of Christ's spiritual fatherhood. *Aside:* But this is the case not only for monks, but for every minister and for every Christian. *End of aside.*

Monasticism is pre-eminently a spiritual gift of humility, which is cultivated by the ascetic effort of obedience. Obedience principally concerns the heart of man, and its characteristic is to disclose the "deep heart", wherein lies the principle and centre of his hypostasis. This is the "place" where the "incorruptible seed" of God's word is sown (*cf.* 1 Pet. 1:23), bringing forth fruit in the apprenticeship of the commandments of Christ. As Fr. Sophrony affirms, God is generally good to every "contrite heart" (*cf.* Ps. 51:17).[6] This goodness transmits to them the "knowledge of the mysteries of the kingdom of heaven" (*cf.* Matt. 13:11).[7] Such knowledge is necessary for a spiritual father in order to give him clear discernment between created things and the uncreated gifts of God, so that in the light of these gifts he may weigh up with wisdom and exactitude every phenomenon in life, and raise it to the spiritual plane. *Aside:* That is, to make this change from the psychological state to the spiritual one. *End of aside.* It is also beneficial for this knowledge to be as full as possible, covering the whole range of spiritual states about which he ventures to teach others.[8]

Fr. Sophrony, expressing with inspiration his admiration for the work of the spiritual father, says that it is "both a dread and a fascinating one. Painful but inspiring".[9] It is a vocation and a gift of incomparable value, serving a supreme creative purpose: the spiritual father becomes "a collaborator of God in the creation of immortal gods",[10] who can be led into "eternity in the uncreated Light".[11]

The spiritual father has his heart stripped by repentance and continuous standing before God. At the same time, his intellect travels the length, depth and height of the Lord. A "world of indescribable magnitude is disclosed to the spirit of man through prayer. Prayer unfolds both the dark depths of hell and the luminous heavenly spheres".[12] The knowledge of this way gives his life stability and deep peace. However in order to be in a position to "sense the rhythm of the interior world of each and every man who turns to him",[13] it benefits him to take continual refuge in God with a painful heart, to seek fervently to learn God's will and to be given an appropriate word to express it for the benefit and inspiration of his brethren. Even during his conversations with people, he has the "hearing" of his intellect alert in his heart so as to "detect God's thinking",[14] the first thought which is born there.

The spiritual father's prophetic word, staying on the path of God's will through the prayer of repentance and announcing it to his brethren, comports many difficulties. A word which comes through prayer is given from on high. It "opens up to us the eternal spheres of the unoriginate Spirit",[15] which are in essence beyond description. Such a word is laden with the grace of the Holy Spirit, yet it must be addressed to "psychological" human beings, who reject the "things of the Spirit of God" and consider them as "foolishness" (1 Cor. 2:14). If the word of God is to bring about the regeneration of man, and not "grind him to powder" (Matt. 21:44), then one must be ready to make sacrifices. This word is a gift of God's love and the call to the acquisition of such love. But this love begets within man "a whole gamut of different torments for the spirit".[16] The spiritual martyrdom is metaphysical and extends into eternity. Because of this, when the spiritual father realizes that the disciple is operating on a psychological level and has not the resolution or the self-denial for struggle, he may not seek a direct word of God through prayer, but instead he condescends and speaks from his human experience. Out of pity for the person, he thereby avoids leading him into the grave sin of fighting against God.[17]

Bishop Basil interjects: Father Zacharias, are you saying that the spiritual father *should* do that or that he just does it?

Fr. Zacharias: Fr. Sophrony said that he did so when he saw that people were psychological human beings (*psychikoi anthropoi*), and resisted the things of the Spirit. In such cases, he would not ask for a word directly from God, but would simply say something from his mind, or from his experience, so as not to set man against God.

Even when the faithful show confidence in their spiritual father and "receive him as a prophet in the name of a prophet" (Matt. 10:41), his ministry is not straightforward. He cannot rely on his previously acquired successes or knowledge. The spiritual father is pre-eminently a dispenser of the word of God, and the word given from Above is "not after man" (Gal. 1:11). *Aside:* The Gospel of Christ in general is not "after man", nor given by man. The word of God goes beyond man's measure, and thus appears "hard" (John 6:60). I think here in the West a book appeared not so long ago with the title, *The Hard Sayings of Jesus*,[18] which is an indication of how they understand the Gospel. *End of aside.* It is revealed in the sphere of eternal light, yet at the same time it bestows perfect self-knowledge. This word provokes a prophetic "earthquake" (1 Kgs. 19:11), and, as the Gospel says, "splits man in two" (Matt. 10:35) by "the sword of the Spirit" (Eph. 6:17). It causes his heart to break with unbearable shame over its own poverty, yet it also inspires man thereafter to sense "everything in us that resists Christ's word"[19] as the presence of death within him. If he resolutely and patiently bears the consequences and sufferings of this spiritual struggle and becomes cleansed of all the corruption of the "old man", then the presence of God within him increases, becoming like the "voice of a light breeze" (1 Kgs. 19:12 Lxx), without the possibility of being observed (*cf.* Luke 17:20). This breeze is the humble love of Christ, which redeems fallen humans and opens to them the kingdom of the Heavenly Father.

A spiritual father strives to bring the word of God to those who turn to him. This word is the seed of eternal life. When it is accepted, as we noted above, it cleaves the heart like a sword and gives no rest; and yet it regenerates the whole man, and renders him fit for the kingdom of heaven. This dividing asunder and tension created by the word of God must in no way be calmed or diminished by the spiritual father. *Aside:* I remember that once Fr. Sophrony was very displeased when he heard that one of us had tried to console someone, and reduced the tension that person had had for repentance. He said that we should increase that tension, not diminish it. *End of aside.* On the contrary, according to Fr. Sophrony's understanding, it is profitable for him rather to intensify these effects to the highest possible degree, and to guide his disciple as if to "the threshold of death",[20] so that he puts to death the "old man", corrupt and sinful. *Aside:* This is a very difficult art. The spiritual fathers of old used to artificially lead their disciples to the threshold of death, in order to mortify the passions in them, and to mortify the "old man". This requires much discernment: nowadays nobody does it. *End of aside.* This fearful and risky enterprise is undertaken by the spiritual father according to the measure of his discernment, his experience and the power of the prayer he offers for his disciples. *Aside:* I say this because I have a friend who is a spiritual father and who told me that he prayed more for the people he rebuked than for those whom he had never rebuked, because he did not want them to fall into despair. *End of aside.*

For this task, the spiritual father employs two methods: one positive and the other negative. By using the negative method, he tries with wisdom and *finesse* to preserve the disciple from vanity about the spiritual gifts he happens to have, because vainglory hardens the depths of the heart, the "place of spiritual prayer".[21] He points out the insufficiencies and the negative elements in the conduct of the disciple. Thus the disciple's intellect and heart are humbled, while the desire for more profound spiritual knowledge is rekindled.[22] Of course, what is significant is the power of grace which accompanies the spiritual father's suggestions, and not his expertise or eloquence. If the word of the spiritual father is to transmit spiritual gifts, it must come from a burning heart, full of love for the people, and praying for them out of deep compassion. All the prophets applied this negative method, especially St. John the Baptist. He called those who came to him a "generation of vipers", and yet the evangelist affirms that it was with such words, "in his exhortation", that "he preached unto the people" (Luke 3:7–18). *Aside:* That is to say, he called them "children of vipers" and with those words he consoled them. Why? Because he crushed the arrogance of their mind, brought contrition to them, contrition brought humility, humility brought grace, and in that there was incorruptible comfort. *End of aside*. The same method lies behind St. Paul's words when he says, "Who is he then that maketh me glad, but the same which is made sorry by me?" (2 Cor. 2:2). The "hard words" of the Lord Jesus and all the spiritual fathers who partake in Him have the purpose of breaking down the strongholds that man's arrogance erects, and of preparing in the faithful a humble disposition to learn from the "meek and lowly" Lord (*cf.* Matt. 11:29).

The positive method is on a higher level and is even more difficult, more creative. It presupposes that the spiritual father knows not only the practice but also the "theory" of ascetic life. This theory is the fruit of the "greater love" of Christ, which His servant has assimilated, and into which he strives to initiate his disciples; the theory which is informed by this love guarantees that everything be done for the glory of God and the good of man. *Aside:* In simple terms, the spiritual father tries to indicate to the disciple, when he is in affliction, difficulty and tribulation the blessing in disguise under those circumstances. *End of aside*.

The spiritual father, having accomplished in his personal repentance the descent to the apex of the inverted pyramid, becomes one with Christ and a communicant in His state. In His life in the flesh, Christ "lived at one and the same time the fulness – unattainable for us – both of suffering and of triumphant victory: both death and Divine glory".[23] In the same way, too, the servant of Christ becomes in his time capable of "rejoicing with them that rejoice, and weeping with them that weep" (*cf.* Rom. 12:15). *Aside:* The one who lives in repentance has this energy in his heart, and this energy can turn into joy, or it can turn into sadness; he can rejoice with them that rejoice and be sad with them that are sad. It is the *ethos* of the New Testament. Otherwise, as Fr. Sophrony used to say, the spiritual father would have to set a timetable for hearing confessions: "Today, from eight to ten, I receive people who are in affliction, and from ten to twelve, people who are rejoicing." The spiritual father who has this energy in his heart is able, at the same time, both to rejoice and to weep with those in affliction.[24] *End of aside*. Christ took upon Himself the death of man, and swallowed it up in His divine life (*cf.* 1 Cor. 15:54). In an analogical way, the spiritual father, too, firmly established in communion with the grace of Christ, takes on the death in his brethren, and raises them up to divine life (*cf.* 2 Cor. 4:12),[25] in which he has become a "partaker" (2 Pet. 1:4). *Aside:* St. Paul says to the Corinthians, "death worketh in us, but life in you" (2 Cor. 4:12). That is, the Apostle was taking upon himself the death of his disciples, and transmitting his life to them. *End of aside.*

Because the spiritual father knows the path to the lowest point of the inverted pyramid, he crosses over from old views, which Lucifer invented "in the paroxysm of his pride",[26] into the new "inverse" approach, which is the perspective of the Gospel. The Lord inaugurated the theory of this vision by His example and His word, which exalts the humble (*cf.* Luke 14:11; 18:14), and abominates what is "highly esteemed among men" (Luke 16:15). In this theological vision, Christ is to be found at the centre of all created being, and brings to it the fullness of the Godhead. Just as in the case of the inverted perspective in iconography, the face or the event portrayed emerges from the centre towards which everything turns, so also in this theory Christ becomes the point towards which all the meanings and desires of man are directed. *Aside:* That is to say, the spiritual father tries to establish in his disciple the same perspective, so that Christ becomes the centre, that He may be increased always. *End of aside.* In the light of this theory, it is easy to understand that "the last shall be first, and the first last" (Matt. 20:16); that "he that hateth his life in this world shall keep it unto life eternal" (John 12:25); and also, that physical death does not touch the soul.

In his ministry, the spiritual father strives to transmit to the faithful the theory of the inverted pyramid, which is the only one capable of inspiring the heart to repentance and transformation according to the same Spirit, active at the point of the inverted pyramid. Then the faithful travel resolutely "downwards", and Christ becomes the reference point of their lives. Just as in Orthodox iconography the painter remains anonymous, so also the spiritual father, while showing all godly zeal to "betroth souls and present them pure to Christ" (*cf.* 2 Cor. 11:2), must remain anonymous. Released from the passion of lust for power, he rejoices, like St. John the Baptist, to see Christ "increase, while he decreases" (*cf.* John 3:30). *Aside:* Unfortunately, nowadays we see a sad tendency in some spiritual fathers to want to create their own kingdom, and that is really a distortion of the Gospel. *End of aside.*

In essence, the spiritual father accomplishes an apostolic work. He imitates the Apostle Paul and preaches exclusively "Christ, and him crucified" (1 Cor. 2:2; *cf.* 1:23, Gal. 3:1), that men might know that He is also "the power of God, and the wisdom of God" (1 Cor. 1:24). Christians are inspired by the vision of the "crucified God", of Christ the "lamb without blemish and without spot" (1 Pet. 1:19), who carries the weight of the upturned pyramid, and they, too, prefer "rather to take wrong" (1 Cor. 6:7), because to "suffer" wrongfully "in the behalf of Christ" (*cf.* Phil. 1:29), is a "thankworthy" gift from God (1 Pet. 2:19–20).

Aside: All the scandals in the history of the Church are because no one wants to bear injustice. We all want to uphold our own dignity and justice; no one wants to take the blame or to suffer a bit of injustice, whereas the Lord tells us not to resist the evil one, and to prefer rather to suffer injustice, as St. Paul exhorts the Corinthians, than to go to civil courts (*cf.* 1 Cor. 6:7). *End of aside.*

The spiritual father, propounding continually to his disciples the "theory" of the inverted perspective of the Gospel, ignites in them the effect of God's grace. He brings them to the blessed honour of bearing in their bodies the "marks of the Lord Jesus" (Gal. 6:17), and of suffering wrong for the sake of Him who "first loved us" and "gave himself for us" (1 John 4:19). This "theory", held by the confessor, can lead his spiritual children to perfect labour and inspiration, according to which their life's aim becomes the desire that Christ be magnified "whether by life or by death" (Phil. 1:20).

In other words, Fr. Sophrony affirms that in the perspective of the inverted pyramid, true victory, which remains inviolable for all eternity, is the victory won by the "bruises" (*cf.* Isa. 53:5) of the good Shepherd.[27] Those who follow in His footsteps, and in their sufferings remain faithful to His love, become participants and heirs of this victory. Upon them "the spirit of glory and of God resteth", as St. Peter says (1 Pet. 4:14), and they bear unfading fruitfulness.[28]

The life of the spiritual father, who abides in the protracted grief of repentance, is rich in its fluctuations between joy and pain. Following Christ, who embraced "in one eternal act heaven and earth and the nether regions",[29] so too His servant, with his repeated cycles of falls and rises, brings both "heaven and hell"[30] stably and uninterruptedly into his heart. His perception is refined, and his heart, as Fr. Sophrony habitually put it, becomes like a radar which detects all at once the whole earth, like lightning going from one end of the earth to the other. Fr. Sophrony actually saw in this an "indication of . . . approaching to likeness to Christ".[31]

The spiritual father, being in the same state as Christ, becomes for the faithful at every contact an opening to eternal life. As the Almighty Lord spoke "the words of man", but through them opened up the eternal dimension of His Absolute Being,[32] so also His minister pronounces common words, but transmits grace and becomes the means of regeneration for his brethren.

A spiritual father knows both the Way of Christ, and the various temptations that are met with on this way before divine love is acquired; and he can thus be a wellspring of inspiration for his disciples. Possessing an integral spiritual vision, he upholds the faithful and encourages them to become partakers of Christ's sufferings, and thereby to learn "existentially" how eminent is "Divine providence for us".[33] *Aside:* Divine providence is known in suffering and great need. *End of aside.* The confessor, by his word, his prayer and his example, strives to introduce every man into the sphere of Christ's peace.[34] With patience and love, he cares for those whom the providence of the Most High has entrusted to him, in order that the image of Christ, darkened by the Fall, be formed and established in them. He bears their weaknesses and identifies with their lives. As one who is himself "compassed with infirmity" (Heb. 5:2), he offers repentance on behalf of himself and others. In this repentance he becomes like Christ, who took upon himself the sin of the whole world. In the present age, which is antipathetic to the humble Spirit of Christ, this service is burdensome, and never attains the desired result. Hence, Fr. Sophrony's observation that without continual and intensive heartfelt prayer, which seeks out a word from God and His divine blessing, this spiritual service is in vain. It becomes transformed into a "half-blind" worldly activity.[35] *Aside:* That is to say, if the word that the spiritual father says is not seasoned with grace, nor proceeds from a heart which is warmed by the love of Christ, it becomes like the work of psychologists or counsellors – a "half-blind" worldly activity. The word of the spiritual father must bear the seal of grace, the seasoning of grace. *End of aside.*

A spiritual father bears in himself the blessedness flowing from the knowledge of Christ's way, and he thus becomes the means of leading the life of men out of the hell they have created (by the negative effect of their passions),[36] and into pure Christian life and spiritual freedom. He is ground down by the death which has wounded them. Even more, he endures tribulations which are a consequence of the spiritual colour-blindness of passions and human distortions.[37] He is constrained by only one thought: how the person can be healed.[38] He tries to diagnose the cause and the intensity of the passions, and the measure of spiritual death due to ignorance of God, so that with hope in Him, the sufferings and misfortunes of life may be overshadowed with divine grace and be reduced to second place.[39] In the heart of the spiritual father, the tribulations of the whole earth are heaped up, giving rise to fervent, tearful prayers, in which the petitions of every weak and suffering man are brought before God. When he feels – once again, in his heart – that the tribulation has been changed into repose and joy, he accepts this as a sure sign that his prayer has reached the ears of the Lord of Sabaoth, and that it will have a beneficial effect.[40] *Aside:* Fr. Sophrony used to say that when the spiritual father prays for his children, as soon as he pronounces their names, he feels in his heart their state, whether they are in a good state or in a bad state, in comfort or in despair. *End of aside.* The father confessor offers this sacred service on behalf of the "little ones", the unfortunate ones who are themselves completely indifferent. He does not plot against their freedom, but instead considers exclusively his future reward.[41] *Aside:* That is to say, he must remain selfless, only consider God's reward, and not expect to be rewarded by anyone or anything in this world. *End of aside.*

The spiritual father is the image of the "good Shepherd" who has "greater love", and "lays down his life for his sheep" (John 10:11). To acquire this love, however, and to accomplish his work in a manner pleasing to God, it helps the spiritual father if he has passed through the spiritual furnace of fear of God and the path of repentance "unto the breaking of his bones".[42] Only then will divine love dwell in his soul and, with it, the divine fear which belongs to the perfect. This love is the "precious pearl", priceless and of incomparable value. A man trembles lest he lose this treasure. This fear preserves this love, and this love increases to the point of fullness. When the great love of Christ visits the heart and enlightens the intellect, man's spirit is enlarged, and encompasses "all creation in compassionate love".[43] This state demonstrates beyond any doubt that a man is united with the God of love.

The prayer of repentance, accompanied by self-hatred, detaches man's spirit from everything created, and transports it "into light-bearing infinity, into indescribable depths", where "all is transformed into love of God".[44] His soul would prefer to remain in this festal joy of divine love, but this love for Christ is linked inseparably with love for one's fellow man. Furthermore, it was love for man that caused the self-emptying of the Son of God. Hence, the spiritual father, in his turn also, has to remain in a state of grace – but not in so extreme a way as to be unable to engage with this world as it is – and to take into his heart the difficulties and sufferings of his brethren.[45] *Aside:* Fr. Sophrony used to say that there are twelve degrees of grace, and in order to function in this world one has to descend at least to the eighth degree. *End of aside.* He patiently endures apostolic *kenosis*, and as St. Paul describes, he is "spent" for the souls of the Christian faithful (*cf.* 2 Cor. 12:15). He finds himself in continual conflict and antagonism between the desire to be given over to the love of

God and the need to collaborate with other people for the sake of their benefit and progress.

The father confessor knows better than anyone that there is nothing more precious in the world than the knowledge of the true God, which is acquired by repentance and by training in sacred inner prayer and silence. But he cannot forget, either, the Lord's commandment: "Go, and teach all nations . . ." (*cf.* Matt. 28:19). He is absolutely persuaded that "one thing is needful" (Luke 10:42), but from love for his people his soul does not cease to be anxious to "help but a single soul to salvation".[46] Both aspects of life are necessary if he is to fulfil God's plan; on the one hand, for him to preserve safely the treasure of the mystery of divine love, and on the other, for him to "commit it to faithful men, who shall be able to teach others also" (*cf.* 2 Tim. 2:2).

As in our consideration of monasticism, and more particularly in the ascetic effort of obedience, the monk learns gradually to bear within himself the life of all the brotherhood, and eventually the life of the whole world. *Aside:* Fr. Sophrony used to tell us that life in the monastic community is an exercise that enables us to become universal. If each one in the community learns to bear the rest of the community in his heart, then slowly, slowly, he will come to bear the whole world in his heart. It is an exercise that enlarges the heart to attain the universality of Christ. *End of aside.* In a similar manner the spiritual father, too, in fulfilling his ministry, is led to the hypostatic form of existence. He ceases to live only for himself; he is concerned for all mankind and prays for them, and his prayer covers all the possible states of life, positive and negative. He adopts the tragedy of the world, and "is overwhelmed by the breath of death that strikes the human race".[47] In his struggle to free the weak from their passions he is himself attacked by those passions, and lives them as his own personal passions, even though in many cases he had not known them previously. *Aside:* Sometimes spiritual fathers are suddenly attacked by a passion, and they do not know why, because they have never had such an experience before. It is because of this effort, and communion they have with people – the effort they make to help the people. *End of aside.* He offers repentance for himself and for all the sins of those whom God has entrusted to him. His prayer increases and takes on cosmic dimensions, and his repentance resembles the sacrifice offered by Christ for the sins of the world.[48]

The spiritual father's hypostatic repentance and prayer confronts the whole drama of human sin: how it began in paradise, and how it is blotted out by the grace of repentance, given by Christ after His resurrection. Sin, says Fr. Sophrony, began with the pusillanimity of Eve and the brazenness of Adam. It continues to be manifested in fratricide, in the splitting apart of mankind's whole nature. It was finally overcome by "the smiting of the Shepherd" (*cf.* Matt. 26:31, Zech. 13:7).[49]

With the break-up of human nature caused by sin, men ceased to see themselves in other human beings, and they did not recognize "our common unity of life".[50] A spiritual father who prays for people receives in his heart a sensation, "information", about the soul or spiritual state of those for whom he supplicates before God. He experiences the spiritual joy "of the few" and the desolation of the souls of "the many" (Matt. 7:13–14). By the painful experience of the states and misfortunes of the people he serves, he becomes extended, so as to encompass the whole of mankind throughout the ages. At the time of his repentance, he becomes a participant in Christ's state, and at the same time he is made aware of, and inspired by, the primordial idea of the Creator concerning man. *Aside:* It is when Christ is formed in the heart of man that he sees the primordial plan of God for him, and understands what it means to be a human being. *End of aside.* Later, however, during his ministry, the dramatic and striking contrast between this divine plan and fallen man with his passions – beyond his power of resistance – is revealed to him. He is overwhelmed by a critical dilemma: whether to confront this tragic vision psychologically, using his natural reasoning like therapists of this world, and as a result to survive without being totally broken by the tension of universal pain; or, as Fr. Sophrony expresses it, to "continue further".[51] *Aside:* That is to say, when the

spiritual father faces the drama of the Fall of man, he is confronted
with a dilemma: to fight for the reducing of that tragedy, or to
face it on a merely psychological level, so as not to be crushed.
Physicians, in order to survive, do not engage themselves in the
sufferings of their patients, at least not much; otherwise they
could not bear it. So, the spiritual father has to adjust the dose of
his participation in the suffering of the people according to his
spiritual strength, in order not to be crushed. I remember when
I first became a spiritual father, I was so stupid: I thought that I
could meet any problem, and I wanted to cope with any difficulty
and help every situation. I remember that by the evening I had
so much pain in my heart that I could not even read the prayer
of absolution. And Fr. Sophrony said to me, "Ah! You will not last
long. You must moderate the dose, and learn to be a bit like the
doctors, otherwise you will not survive." And I learned, because
otherwise it is impossible. *End of aside.*

However, this "going further" – that is, assuming the tragedy
– is inaccessible to man unless he has been previously strengthened by fullness of faith and the grace of repentance. *Aside:*
There is a measure to what man can undertake, and each one has
to find his measure. *End of aside.* According to the same conception, "continuing further" means that the spiritual father follows
Christ into the garden of Gethsemane. He goes up with Him to
Golgotha, "to live with Him, by His strength, the tragedy of the
world as his own *personal* tragedy",[52] or, as Fr. Sophrony put it on
several other occasions, to drink the "cup of Christ",[53] so that his
spiritual service becomes identified with the Lord's redeeming
work of reconciling the world with God.

Consequently, as he accomplishes his service, the spiritual
father breaks the closed circle of his own "individualism"; his
being is expanded, and he bears within himself the life of the
whole human race, and all the history of men's relations with
God. Fr. Sophrony noted that he enters "into the wide expanses
of 'hypostatic' forms of being, conquering death and participating
in divine infinity".[54] *Aside:* This is something that the Church has.
We may not be bearers of this, but the Church possesses this, in

some of Her members – maybe only a few in each generation – but this reality *does* exist in the bosom of the Church. *End of aside.*

Spiritual paternity, because it is a path towards the marvellous hypostatic form of being, entails superhuman effort. Without the might of God, man is small, and as he follows Jesus in the ascent to Golgotha, he feels "dazzled" and "fearful". His service as a spiritual father is made more difficult by the mass apostasy of our times, which Fr. Sophrony identifies with "the hour and the power of darkness" (Luke 22:53).[55] In a father confessor's ministry, his bodily constitution also resists; the body becomes exhausted, and according to its instinct of self-preservation, it wants to close its eyes to the vision of the pain and innumerable calamities of mankind, his fellow-sufferers. *Aside:* But whoever has become a partaker of the Spirit of Christ cannot avoid meeting the ocean of human misfortune.[56] *End of aside.* Just as in his repentance it was revealed to him that he belongs to that great body which is the totality of mankind, and is inseparably bound up with its lot, so now also, in order to "continue further", he is opened up to greater spiritual sufferings, and with a deeper agony of prayer he embraces all of suffering mankind. He shares the Lord's Gethsemane prayer, which was given to us as an example. *Aside:* Fr. Sophrony called these three prayers "hypostatic prayers": "liturgical prayer", because the Liturgy is a prayer for the salvation of the whole world; "pure prayer", and "the prayer of the Lord at Gethsemane", because the latter was a prayer for the whole world. *End of aside.*

As he sheds intense tears, his soul "suddenly, unexpectedly, unwittingly"[57] becomes widened, and he enters ontologically into the essence of sin, that is to say, separation from the light of the Face of God. His soul takes on supernatural dimensions. He also experiences his personal sin as the sin of the whole human race, and as a repetition of Adam's sin.[58] In the prayer of total repentance "energy will appear, of another order, not of this world".[59]

The effect of this energy is that "the horizons of [the spiritual father's] individual life are immeasurably widened",[60] and individualistic limits are surpassed. In other words, "death

[the voluntary death of repentance] overcomes death [the involuntary death caused by sin], and the power of the Resurrection
prevails",[61] which is the prize gained by the hypostatic spirits. By
a "lowly downward movement" of repentance he overcomes the
"all-destroying passion of pride", and "the blessing of Christ-like
humility descends on man, making us children of the Heavenly
Father".[62] Forgive me.

QUESTIONS & ANSWERS

Question 1: You said you learned to reduce the pain that people
bring. How did you do that?

Answer 1: By being able to listen to them prayerfully, to listen
with prayer. Give them a word of consolation, and indicate to
them that their pain and suffering is a sign of God's grace.

Question 2: I was thinking of *your* pain, the pain that *you*, a
spiritual father, feel.

Answer 2: You do that by being humble and not trying to
do more than you are able to do. Just be humble and know that
"unto us a Saviour is born" (*cf.* Isa. 9:6); we are not the saviours of
the world, but Christ is the Saviour of the world. Be humble and
know your limitations. But if you are proud and you try to cope
with every circumstance, thinking that you are a great prophet,
then you might not be able to bear it. The best thing is to have in
mind that Christ is our Saviour, while you are just a poor instru-
ment, a poor servant: you go as far as you are able to, you do what
you can, and you leave the rest to God. This was the principle
of the Desert Fathers, the rule they had in their life: to do that
which they were able to do, without the anxiety of being bound
by rules. By dying for us, God has freed us from the slavery of
the law, yet we create laws and make ourselves slaves to them. If
we make ourselves slaves to rules, when we fulfil those rules we
become proud that we have done so, and when we do not fulfil
them, we are tormented and do not feel satisfied. Neither the one,
nor the other is necessary. We must do what we can, and, with
faith and gratitude, leave the rest to God. This was the rule of the

first ascetics of the Desert, and I think a spiritual father should have it as well: to do what he is able to do. We can all function beneficially if we know our place and our measure, and do not try to exceed it. We are precious stones with which the heavenly Architect builds up the temple of God. But if we try to go beyond our measure, then we spoil everything.

Question 3: Parish priests are not spiritual fathers. Explain to us the role of parish priests, and knowing our limits as parish priests.

Answer 3: I know parish priests in Greece who are wonderful spiritual fathers. They are married priests, with six or eight children, but really prophetic in their ministry; they have a great following, and they help many people. But every priest can be a spiritual father, in the sense that he is the one who presides over the Eucharistic assembly. He is the one who dispenses the word of God. You do not need to play the role of the prophet, but you can receive the person who comes to you sympathetically, and listen and read the prayer of absolution. What more is required? You have the backing of the whole Church, of your bishop and, through him, of the universal Orthodox Church. You do not need to utter prophetic words or teach lofty matters. You are still the father. We all come from different families. Some have bright and educated parents, and some have completely illiterate parents, but they still do their work, and this does not hinder them from becoming educated.

Question 4: How would you inspire or encourage individuals when they come for confession, and you know that they are simply "going through the mechanics": they just want the prayer of absolution, and they are not making a fervent or genuine confession?

Answer 4: It is very difficult, and it is a great art to stir up in them a deeper consciousness of the matter. You hear ten sins, and some even very grievous ones, but the nature of those sins is such that you cannot make any comment. Suddenly, they say something, and then you see that they have a proud approach. You step on it, trying to crush a little bit the arrogance of their mind, but with measure, so that they get slightly bitten in the heart, and receive some awareness of why things are as they are with them. But this is not an easy matter. As for myself, I do not even try this nowadays, I just humble myself and pray, and may God accomplish that in them.

Question 5: I found interesting the comment you made in the beginning about someone receiving the word on a psychological level, versus someone receiving the word on a spiritual level. What I observed is that if you do not notice that, and you give a spiritual word to someone who is receiving it on a psychological level, it can actually do much damage, and it gets processed wrongly, it gets caught up with all that psychological dysfunction. I am learning that there is a lot of discernment in this, because people take a spiritual word, and it gets mixed up with a lot of psychological nonsense.

Answer 5: You are right, even the Lord told us not to throw the holy things to the dogs, or the pearls to the swine (*cf.* Matt. 7:6). We must not just readily give that which we have received with great fear and agony, with a lot of prayer and repentance. We must entrust what we have received to people who can appreciate it, and who can take it.

Question 6: This is the question that flows out of that: Do you think that there is a role for psychology to bring people to being able spiritually to receive something, to help them work through the dysfunction, so that then they can receive the word?

Answer 6: I think sometimes it can be profitable. For example, I had someone who was suffering from agoraphobia. I was trying to help that young man and I could not, because he would not admit it. I have a wonderful friend who is a psychologist, but a devout Christian as well. He listens to the people he receives with a rosary in his pocket and praying at the same time. He is a top psychologist, invited to places all over the world. He goes to America to lecture, to Russia, to Australia even. He is a Cypriot, a specialist in Jung, based in London, at the Tavistock Clinic – a very prestigious place. I asked this young man to go to him, because I thought that just the idea that he needs to go to a psychologist will bring a little humility to his heart, and give him a start. But even there I did not succeed; neither I, nor my friend the psychologist, because it was a very complicated case. Nevertheless, I think that my thought was correct: even the idea that somebody needs to go and see a psychologist can bring a bit of humility, and this is beneficial.

Question 7 (Bishop Basil): In our country we put our priests in a different situation than other Orthodox priests from many other countries: all of them are put in the position of being confessors, instead of making some *pneumatikoi*, spiritual fathers, and others not. But even those who know in their hearts that they are not *pneumatikoi* need to be encouraged. I grew up with a priest who hardly knew my language; he struggled with all his heart to learn our language, and to pray in our language, that is, English, rather than in Arabic. Because he prayed in such broken English, we did not understand the English, and those who did not know English, the elderly people who desired Arabic, certainly did not understand what was going on. So the situation was not edifying as regards the intelligibility of the language, but what was edifying was that he did that out of love for us young people. And what was edifying for the elders, was that he did that all out of love for their children and grandchildren. He never preached a sermon for twenty-five years; he just read sermons that other people had written, those simple things published many years ago by the Carpatho-Russian Diocese, a series of Sunday sermons. And we got some in very broken English, but again what was edifying was that he did it out of love for us. He even humiliated himself to make all of these mispronunciations. He used to sit with me when I was thirteen years old – he, a senior priest from Syria – before every Liturgy, to read the Gospel to me, and then to write in Arabic phonetics the words that he could not pronounce just by reading. My point is: he was not gifted in conveying in language the depths of what was in his heart, but he did it by his actions. And the same is true for confession. He never heard a confession for twenty five years; all he did was to pray on our heads; and we, who are seminary educated, or literates, or who read a lot of books, we deprecate that people want us just to pray on their heads. But for some of us, that is all we can do. And for twenty-five years that is all that he did. But when he prayed on my head, he really prayed. The repentance was left to me; that was my job. The priest's job is to pray for me. Another example is Fr. A. E. from Detroit, a married man with thirteen children, a man of this world, working hard in order to bring up his family. To listen to him, to talk to him, you would not know the things he did. That is the beauty of it! If you were an elderly person or a sick person in our parish, and it snowed, you would get up in the morning and your sidewalk would be shovelled. You had no idea who did it. If you were an old person, and in spring it was time for your garden to be tilled, you would get up in the morning and your garden would be tilled. In the middle of the summer you would wake up and the lawn would be mown. It was our priest. That was his sermon. So if we are not, and I freely admit that I am not, graced to give words, then we can at least strive to be like Fr. A. E., and while we might not be a *Gheron*, an Elder, we can still lead people to the kingdom, and we can still "live homilies" and incarnate the Gospel.

Answer 7: I am glad you said that, because it is what I think as well. If we know our measure, we can be useful; we can do our work. But if we try to exceed our measure, without being able to do it, then we destroy even the little we could normally do.

Question 8: I get people coming that are so depressed and despondent because they are trying to do too much, they cannot see their families any more, they are workaholics, they have gone crazy in their lives. It is because they are not capable; they have bitten off too much – God didn't give them that. They just need to recognize what it is that God has given to them, and let the rest be God's.

Answer 8: Forgive me, I am losing my mind now. I speak with you, and you are a priest, and you are much better than I am – I am sure about that. But the Liturgy, really, surpasses all of us. Who can be up to the measure of the Liturgy? Who can grasp the dimensions of the spirit of the Liturgy? And yet, we can all celebrate the Liturgy, if we are conscious of the fact that we are unworthy, that it is Christ who does so, and that we are simply poor instruments. If we have that awareness, we can all celebrate the Liturgy, and we shall all receive a blessing. But to celebrate the Liturgy properly is another thing. One of our saints – I think it was St. Ephraim the Syrian – celebrated the Liturgy once, and he did not celebrate again: once was sufficient for him, because he *lived* the mystery in the power of the Spirit. Like Christ, He celebrated it once only, and it remains unto all ages. A saint might do it, but then it is enough for him. What he uttered, he uttered once in the Spirit, and that remains for ever. We, however, are not like that. I am the first to say that I am not like that. But if we have the awareness that we are but poor instruments, and that Christ is the King and the Priest, we can all celebrate the Liturgy, and we all receive a benefit, to a greater or lesser degree.

Question 9: I have always understood that there is a difference between a confessor and a spiritual father, while in your presentation you were talking about both at the same time. This morning you answered Fr. John's question by saying that as a confessor you just read the prayer of absolution. You also said that Fr. Sophrony made you a spiritual father after some years. I am far from that, but in this country to be spiritual fathers and counsellors and confessors and janitors, and everything else at the same time . . .

Answer 9: But even the same spiritual father has a different approach with different people. I have a friend who is a wonderful spiritual father; now he has become a Metropolitan in Greece, and he said to me, "With some of the people who confess to me I am just a priest, with some others I am a confessor, with some others I am a spiritual father, and even with some I am a *Gheron.*" You have to adjust yourself, as Fr. Sophrony said, to the interior rhythm of everybody who approaches you. You must judge this. Some only require a priest, and I offer myself to them as a priest. Why impose on them as a spiritual father? Some come and they want just a confessor, so I offer myself as a confessor. Some come with greater trust, and I can be a spiritual father. The same priest has to take a different attitude with different people.

Question 10 (Bishop Basil): Can I just make a suggestion? We have made, for the sake of convenience, for the sake of discussion, a distinction between a confessor and a spiritual father; but technically the language of the Church is not "father confessor". The service is *For the Making of a Spiritual Father*. This is what is said in the *Euchologion* (*The Great Prayer Book*), and this means that you are allowed to hear confessions. But for us, in this country, we have done it for the sake of discussion, otherwise it is interchangeable. But I think that Fr. Paul's question has to do with people who see themselves as clairvoyant Elders, like a *Gheron*. So let us forget this dichotomy, made just for the sake of discussion, and use the language of the Church, in which spiritual father and father confessor are almost synonymous; but without setting ourselves up to be some clairvoyant *Gheron*.

Answer 10: May I say something? I was made spiritual father by the Archbishop of Cyprus; Fr. Raphael by the Archbishop of Thyateira and Great Britain – each one of the priests of our Monastery was made spiritual father by a different bishop. Of course, I went to Cyprus to be ordained with the blessing of our Patriarch (Bartholemew). When I came back from the ordination, Fr. Sophrony sent us to the local Archbishop, who was at first Methodios, and then when he left, to Archbishop Gregory, to tell him the following: "We are confessing your people. Please give us a guideline. What do you want us to have in mind when we confess your flock?" Fr. Sophrony did not advise us how to confess them, but he sent us to ask the local bishop, because, in any case, the priesthood is of the bishop: we function as priests by delegation. I remember when we went to see Archbishop Gregory and spoke the words Fr. Sophrony advised us to say, he was very kind to us, and said, "You know, Cypriot immigrants here in London live under difficult conditions. They do not live as they would normally do in their own country, in Cyprus or in Greece, so I beg you to be more indulgent with them than you would be if you were in Cyprus or in Greece. I do not mean that you must not be strict sometimes, but have this as a basic principle: to be more indulgent to them, because they live under more difficult conditions." That was the only guideline he gave us, which was really very reasonable, very wise, and, in fact, even Archbishop Methodios, Archbishop Gregory's predecessor, told us more or less the same thing. Fr. Sophrony, who had such experience, and who could have done this in the most prophetic manner, did not tell us how to confess the people. Of course, we discussed things, and we learned from him, but nevertheless he sent us to the local Archbishop to receive some guidelines, and to have in mind that we are performing in the name of the Church, with the backing of the Church, of the Archbishop, and of the whole universal Orthodox Church. We are one body.

Question 11: There are people who are only used to having the prayer of absolution read over their heads. Where did this practice come from? I was trying to find out the history of this practice. But I have started to do the following for the older people: to read the absolution prayer, because they have never learned confession in the way we are talking about it. They do not know any other way of confessing their sins.

Answer 11: You do well! Just obey the people, do what they ask you. I do the same. In Paris there were two priests. One was taking his time; he let the people speak, and each confession lasted for quite some time. The other was very quick, because he received a tip for every confession, and he would even boast about it afterwards, "Father such-and-such takes half an hour for each person; myself, in one hour, I freed two hundred!" And I remember that in my village, when we went to the priest to have the prayer read over us, we had to have a few pennies to put in his hand at the end of the prayer. Maybe it came from that, I do not know.

Question 12 (Bishop Basil): There are priests who do not have the faculty to hear confessions. As I said earlier, in many countries not every priest is expected to hear confessions, but that does not mean that the people do not need absolution for their sins before they come to the Chalice. In our tradition, there is a prayer that is read *For the Making of a Spiritual Father.*

Answer 12: I will tell you something, Your Grace. In London, Archbishop Gregory, through an Encyclical, demanded from his priests, before they come out with the Chalice, to come out and read the prayer of absolution for all the Church, so that those who had prepared for Communion could receive the absolution.

Bishop Basil: I think there is a way, though, which we can find, to make somebody admit that they have sinned, especially people who come rather nonchalantly, and just want the prayer read over their head. We are allowed to ask them some questions. These are not prying questions: "Do you keep the fast?" Some people will say, "No". "Do you have a prayer rule?" Some will say, "No". The ones who says, "Yes", you will ask if they have been faithful to it every day since the last confession. Some people are going to say, "No". If they have answered, "Yes", you ask again, "Is there anyone whom you have not forgiven, not that you hate necessarily, but who has hurt you, and for whom you have *a little hard spot* on your heart?" Some of the people will still say "Yes". And if they still answer "Yes" to all of the above, then the next question, which is the last, has to "get" them, "Is there somebody that you have to ask forgiveness of: your wife, your husband, your neighbour, your boss?" There are ways of getting them at least to admit that they are not perfect; and that is a beginning. I do not think we should let them walk away without saying that they have done something for which they are sorry. They might not say that they are sorry, but just admit "Yes" to one of those questions. Then the rest is up to you: "Are you sorry that you have not kept the fast?" You are not asking what happened behind closed doors. You are not prying into what they consider their "private life". You are just asking simple questions. I think that would be enough. And pray! You know, the prayer is conditional anyway, for the sins for which they have repented. It is not magic. If they repent, they are forgiven.

Question 13: In this country, we hear from time to time that priests and confessors are giving directions to people on whether they should buy a different car or a new television set, and things like this.

Answer 13: This is absolutely a distortion of the Gospel. Sometimes in the world people are taught by some spiritual fathers to ask for a blessing for every little thing they do in their lives: whether they should buy a car, or a new TV set, or if they should go on holiday (vacation). I do not allow people to ask me this kind of question. If they come and say to me, "Do I have the blessing to go on holiday?" I tell them, "Discuss it with your wife and consult your pocket." It is a wrong transfer of the monastic life into the world, and afterwards the world enters the monastery with vengeance. If we do not respect the freedom of the people in the world, then the world will take its revenge, by coming to the monastery and taking *our* spiritual freedom. I do not interfere, and I do not wish to control the lives of people who are not of the monastery, and who simply happen to come to confession, first of all, because I wish to safeguard my own freedom. It is wrong to try and control people in such matters. In the monastery we ask a blessing for everything, but even in the monastery we only do that in the beginning; it cannot go on for very long, just until we learn. We do this in the monastery, because there everything is done *in the name of God,* everything is done *around the Liturgy.* It is a different way of life. In the world, if you go to the factory to work, you have to conform to the discipline of the rules of the work there. God has nothing to do with that. I don't mean absolutely nothing, of course, but what can one say about that? Forgive me, you understand what I mean.

Question 14: Some people come to me and confess about "hard feelings" in their heart. They will not come to Communion because they have these feelings, and I ask them, "Do you want to have these emotions against others?" They will say, "No, but I still feel them." And I tell them – I hope I don't do damage – that our emotions come under the control of the *nous* only very late, and they should go to Communion, praying for God to soften their feelings, because their will is to forgive. Is that safe?

Answer 14: I think so, Father, but I think that there is no recipe for these things. You have to judge each case separately – there is no recipe.

NOTES

* First published in English in *Christ, Our Way and Our Life, op. cit.,* pp. 142–156.

1. *Cf. On Prayer, op. cit.,* p. 89.

2. *Prayer for Spiritual Fathers*. English translation not yet published.

3. *Cf. Saint Silouan, op. cit.*, pp. 237–239.

4. *On Prayer, op. cit.*, p. 98.

5. *Ibid.*

6. *We Shall See Him, op. cit.*, p. 178.

7. *Cf. ibid.*, p. 178.

8. *Cf. On Prayer, op. cit.*, p. 89.

9. *Ibid.*, p. 88.

10. *Prayer for Spiritual Fathers*, see note 2 above.

11. *On Prayer, loc. cit.*

12. *We Shall See Him, op. cit.*, pp. 78–79.

13. *On Prayer, op. cit.*, p. 88.

14. *Ibid.*, p. 90.

15. *Ibid.*, p. 93.

16. *We Shall See Him, op. cit.*, p. 88.

17. *Cf. ibid.*, p. 93.

18. F. F. Bruce, *The Hard Sayings of Jesus* (London: Hodder and Stoughton, 1983).

19. *On Prayer, op. cit.*, p. 93.

20. *Ibid.*, p. 101.

21. *Ibid.*, p. 11.

22. *Cf. ibid.*, p. 87.

23. *Ibid.*, p. 100.

24. *Cf. ibid.*, p. 99.

25. *Cf. ibid.*, p. 96–97.

26. *We Shall See Him, op. cit.*, p. 78.

27. *Cf. On Prayer, op. cit.*, p. 112.

28. *Cf. ibid.*

29. *We Shall See Him, op. cit.*, pp. 60–61.

30. *On Prayer, op. cit.*, pp. 99–100.

31. *Ibid.*

32. *Ibid.*, p. 111.

33. *Ibid.*, p. 100.

34. *Cf. ibid.*, p. 109.

35. *Cf. ibid.*, pp. 108–109.

36. *Cf. ibid.*, p. 90.

37. *Cf. ibid.*, p. 91.

38. *Cf. ibid.*, p. 95.

39. *Cf. ibid.*, p. 94.

40. *Cf. ibid.*, p. 95.

41. *Cf. ibid.*, p. 112.

42. *Prayer for Spiritual Fathers,* see note 2 above.

43. *On Prayer, op. cit.,* p. 103.

44. *Ibid.*

45. *Cf. ibid.*, p. 104.

46. *Saint Silouan, op. cit.,* p. 341.

47. *On Prayer, op. cit.,* p. 109.

48. *Cf. ibid.*, pp. 109–110.

49. *Ibid.*, pp. 109–112.

50. *Ibid.*, p. 111.

51. *Ibid.*, p. 114.

52. *Ibid.*

53. *Saint Silouan, op. cit.,* pp. 47, 240; *We Shall See Him, op. cit.,* pp. 31, 41, 200; *On Prayer, op. cit.,* pp. 28, 41.

54. *On Prayer, op. cit.,* p. 116.

55. *Ibid.*, p. 112.

56. *Cf. His Life is Mine, op. cit.,* p. 87.

57. *Op. cit.,* p. 114.

58. *Cf. ibid.*, pp. 109–110, 115.

59. *Ibid.*, p. 116.

60. *Ibid.*

61. *Ibid.*, p. 117.

62. *Ibid.*, p. 114.

THE PRESENTATION OF CHRIST THAT JUSTIFIED GOD AND MAN*

WE HEARD IN TODAY'S GOSPEL (Matt. 26:7–13) how the woman who brought precious ointment to Christ was praised by Him for her act of love. The people, with their carnal mind, judged her for being wasteful, but the Lord, who saw in the alabaster box all the love that this woman had in her heart, praised her. Today is the leave-taking of a feast of love. Today the Lord is presented in the Temple, and the word "presented" is loaded with meaning. Formerly, as a layman, I would pray before the Liturgy to be counted worthy to partake of the holy body and blood of Christ. From the moment God gave me, unworthy though I am, the grace of priesthood, I have never prayed to be made worthy of the communion of the Body and Blood of Christ, but I have always prayed that He grant me a holy *presentation* before His holy altar, and Holy Communion is contained therein.

Christ came to be presented in the Temple of God, in the City of God. His presentation is a perfect presentation. As in the Liturgy, "presentation" reminds us of a sacrifice, and the Holy Apostle Paul says clearly that we should present our bodies as a living sacrifice (*cf.* Rom. 12:1), not conforming to this world, but seeking for that holy and perfect will of God, and conforming to it, because in *that* will there is life eternal in abundance (*cf.* John 10:10), whereas this world is but fleeting, passing away. Today is the beginning of the Presentation of our Lord, the beginning of His sacrifice, the beginning of the showing of His great Love. The Presentation of the Lord was perfect and very pleasing to God the Father, because He was a pure thanksgiving (*cf.* Eph. 5:2). Our presentation is not a pure thanksgiving, which is why in the Liturgy we give thanks *and we supplicate,* we give thanks *and we make entreaty.* We give thanks for all the things God has done for us – and there are so many to be numbered, and such great things! But we also make supplication, because we are still not free from sin; whereas the Lord, sinless as He was, was a pure thanksgiving to God (*cf.* Heb. 7:26–27). With His presentation, in a single act, He embraced heaven and earth and the infernal regions (*cf.* Eph. 4:9–10).

By this perfect presentation, the Lord justified both God and man. He justified God, because He showed the infinite love of God for the salvation of the world. "God so loved the world, that he gave his only begotten Son" for its salvation (*cf.* John 3:16). The Son so loved the world that He accepted, for our sakes, to become a lamb led to the slaughter (*cf.* Acts 8:32, Isa. 53:7). The Holy Spirit, also with love, witnessed to this act of our Lord, because the Lord's presentation, in which He embraced heaven and earth and all the created world, was done in the power of the eternal Spirit. With this presentation, He filled the whole of the created world with His creative and saving energy, so that we might be able to meet the Lord *wherever we may be:* whether in joy or in the hell of our difficulties, He is present, because He has filled the entire universe with His divine energy and life. He filled the waters by being baptized in the Jordan; He illumined the infernal regions by His descent into Hades. When He was ascended into heaven, as it is said in the Gospel, He went up slowly, slowly (*cf.* Luke 24:50–51), in order to sanctify all the air and all the skies. Therefore, *the entire life of our Lord was but a single presentation before God,* and this presentation was perfect and holy, and justified God for His great love.

But He also justified man, because He showed us a perfect example of obedience. He so loved God the Father and all mankind that He did not spare his life, and He did all this without anybody being able to reprove Him of sin. He did all this in a sinless manner, in a perfect way, and showed us a perfect example. Thereby, whoever walks in the steps of our Lord is accepted by God, because in His presentation He embraces us as well. The life of each one of us, and especially the life of priests, is a presentation before God. The presentation of our Lord was perfect because of His love. Our presentation is acceptable and agreeable to God when we have love, when we respond to Him in love. In love He revealed His person to us, love "unto the end" (*cf.* John 13:1), because He said: "Greater love hath no man than this, that a man lay down his life for his friends" (John 15:13). Man becomes truthful before God when he responds with love, the love according to the commandment of God, love to self-hatred, because then he is also a true image of God.

I must say that these days I have been very moved to be with you, to live with you, and see the love and simplicity from, first of all, our deeply respected and greatly beloved Bishop, to the last of the priests; to see the love you have among you, and the simplicity, provoking one another with love, exhorting one another, assembling together in love, awaiting that great and notable day of our Lord. As Simeon, who was just and devout, and the Prophetess Anna, who, because of her love for God, was continually in the Temple, were able to recognize and receive the Giver of Life, Christ, so also this conversation and this "paroxysm" of love that is inspired in our assemblies is the best preparation to receive the Lord, who is come and shall come again. Love, the Apostle says, never faileth (*cf.* 1 Cor. 13:8). He who has love, the servant of love, cannot be separated from the God of love (*cf.* Rom. 8:35–39), because love is immortal, love is God Himself (*cf.* 1 John 4:8; 4:16). Therefore for our presentation to be worthy and agreeable to God we must always bear in mind that this is the sign of the servant of God: love. "Where I am, there shall also my servant be", says the Lord (John 12:26);

and if He is a God of love, and of love "unto the end", and if "Greater love hath no man than this", thus must His servant be. He must be a servant of love. Because I was so comforted by the love you showed me over these past few days, though I am unworthy and last of all, I dare to pray that God may bless this remnant here, all of you, and bless all your work in this country, and make out of you "leaven", which will leaven the whole lump of America (cf. 1 Cor. 5:6, Gal. 5:9). This is my prayer, and with this prayer I proceed to the Liturgy, with the blessing of our Bishop. May God bless this remnant. May God make it leaven to leaven the whole lump of America. And may God bless all those who bless this remnant. Amen.

NOTES

* Homily given for the Leave-taking of the Feast of the Meeting of Our Lord and God and Saviour Jesus Christ, on the last day of the Retreat, February 9.

Appendix

On Monasticism I*

FOR US CHRISTIANS there is nothing beyond Christ. He is for us the absolute God and the perfect man. As He said, "I am the way, the truth, and the life" (John 14:6), and so it is very important for us to know this Way, Truth and Life. The Way is Christ Himself, and if we know the way, and put ourselves on the way, He becomes our fellow traveller, our companion, because He is the way, binding Himself to us, as He joined Luke and Cleopas on the way to Emmaus (*cf.* Luke 24:15). He is Truth itself, both divine and human, and when we know this truth we become truthful in two ways. In the first place, we know the Truth which is Christ Himself, whom we worship in Spirit and truth (*cf.* John 4:24); and, at the same time, we begin to know the truth about ourselves, the truth of our total poverty, thus we stand before Him in awe and reverence, and we perform our service to Him. He is also Life itself (John 11:25; 14:6), and without knowing this gift of the life that He brought upon earth we remain desolate; as He said, we "die in our sins" (*cf.* John 8:24). Nevertheless, if we know His gift, then we know that it is the gift of life, and indeed of life in abundance (*cf.* John 10:10). So, Christ is the Way, and it is vital for us to know this Way.

How did Christ reveal this way upon earth? He revealed it by coming down from heaven to earth, and even more so, by going down to the nethermost parts of the earth (*cf.* Eph. 4:10). That is to say, His way is a humble way. He is a humble God (*cf.* Matt. 11:29), and He knows how to "lay down his life for his friends" (John 15:13), because as God He has power to take it up again.

You know, we have all been created "in the image and likeness" of God (Gen. 1:26). God instilled in us the capacity of knowing Him, and of knowing Him fully. He gave us the ability to receive the evangelical revelation, which was to come in His only-begotten Son. From the very beginning, He implanted in us that capacity, by creating us in His image and likeness. But, of course, we know the tragic event that took place, man's falling away from the living presence of God. But God did not abandon man, and man, within his very being, never forgot that his origins were in God: he has always possessed the innate desire for justice, for equality, for freedom of spirit. Yet, through the tragic event of the Fall, we see in our empirical being that there is no justice, there is no equality, there is no freedom of spirit.

And this monstrous empirical being, which is our world, has the appearance of a pyramid. We have the powerful of the earth sitting at the top of the pyramid on the shoulders of those beneath them; there is no equality, and the strong exercise dominion over the weak. But this is not the idea of God. God wanted us all to be equal, and that is why He gave us all the same commandments. That is the sign of our equality before God; and each one of us must apply them to his own life, but He gave the *same* commandments to us all. So, we are faced with this monstrous pyramid of the empirical being of this world, the powerful of the earth exercising authority, as the Lord says (*cf.* Matt. 20:25), and they are even called benefactors. But He said to the twelve, "If any man desire to be first, the same shall be last of all, and servant of all" (Mark 9:35). So the Lord, in order to heal this distortion of the world, as Fr. Sophrony says, inverted the pyramid, and at the head of it He put Himself. He went down to the bottom of it, that is to say, He went to the abyss of the fall of man, and took upon Himself the "burden" of the whole world, the entire weight of the pyramid.[1]

From that moment on, who could stand in judgment before Him? He justified God, but He also justified man. He justified God by showing His love – love "unto the end" (John 13:1), that "greater love" that no one has as He does, as the Lord says in the Gospel (John 15:13). He justified God by showing His love to the end, and in obedience to the commandment of God the Father He laid down His life for the world (1 John 3:16). Who can enter into judgment with God from that time forward? He did not spare His only-begotten Son, but gave Him for us. Will He not give everything to us together with Him, says the Apostle? (*cf.* Rom. 8:32).

But He also justified man, because He traced a path for us; He showed us a way upon earth, the Way, of which the prophets spoke, and could only dream of. The way He revealed upon earth, by putting Himself at the bottom of the inverted pyramid, is the way of "going down", the way of descent. He showed this to be the Way, and in doing so He justified man, He gave him an example. If man follows His way, then God the Father will receive him as His son, and God will repeat to every person the same words He spoke to His own Son, "Thou art my Son, to day have I begotten thee" (Heb. 5:5), and "This is my beloved Son, in whom I am well pleased" (Matt. 3:17; 17:5). He says the same to all of us who follow the path of Christ, "going down" to meet Him at the bottom of the inverted pyramid. God showed His love to man by disclosing the Way of His Son upon earth; and man, in his turn, shows his love to God when he follows this Way, which is the way of humility.

This Way was prefigured in the Old Testament. We all remember the three youths in Babylon, who were thrown into the furnace by King Nebuchadnezzar, because they did not join the apostasy of the rest of the people of Israel in Babylon, but remained steadfast in the faith of their forefathers, in the true "God of Abraham, the God of Isaac, and the God of Jacob" (Exod. 3:6), the "God of the living" (Mark 12:27). They were thrown into the furnace, and Nebuchadnezzar the king sat on a very elevated throne watching the spectacle. He saw this great furnace, so great that it devoured his servants who poured oil into it. Such was the magnitude of this fire. And the king, watching this spectacle, said in amazement, "Did not we cast three men bound into the midst of the fire? . . . Lo, I see four men loose, walking in the midst of the fire, and they have no hurt; and the form of the fourth is like the Son of God" (Dan. 3:24–25). And indeed, He was the Son of God, the Word of God, but not yet incarnate. He was without flesh then, like an angel, "the Angel of Great Counsel", as the Old Testament calls Him (Isa. 9:6 Lxx). So, Christ came down to keep them company, to join these three youths in the furnace. But it is necessary to look more closely at what was taking place in the furnace, which could attract the second Person of the Holy Trinity, the Son of God, "by whom all things were made".[2] What was it that attracted Him to come down and join the three youths in the furnace? We can examine what happened by reading the prayer of the three youths as it was recorded by Daniel the Prophet. The three youths in the flame did not lift up their hands to God, and say, "O God Almighty, we are not like the heathen around us, and because we have kept the true faith Thou hast kept us harmless in the flame, and we thank Thee because Thou hast done such a great wonder for us". Instead, they lowered their head, and even more so, their mind, and they said, "We have sinned, we have committed iniquity": they took upon themselves the sin of their people. "We have sinned, we have transgressed, we have committed iniquity, and Thou hast rightly brought upon us the judgment of this furnace, *but*" – then comes *the but of faith,* having "gone down" first with the "*but*" of faith – "do not abandon us to the end, O God of our Fathers." If you read this prayer you will find it is one of the most beautiful (*cf.* S. of III Children 1–67).[3] That is to say, prophetically, the three youths put themselves in the Way of our Lord, in the way of "going down". And because they put themselves prophetically in the way of going down, they found Him who is *the* Way as their companion. He joined them in the flames, and saved them.

I will give you another example about the way of the Lord, nearer to His incarnation, which has to do with His Mother, the

Most Holy Virgin Mary. She was dedicated to the temple of God from a very young age, and in that temple the Mother of God lived in prayer and under instruction in the Law and the Prophets of the Old Testament. And the Mother of God made two discoveries in the temple. In praying, she suddenly discovered her "deep heart", as we learn from holy Tradition. This, however, may also be seen in the verses of the New Testament. According to the definition of the Old Testament, "man is a deep heart" (*cf.* Ps. 64:6). And this deep heart of man, as King Solomon says, requires a divine and noetic sensation, the sensation of God (*cf.* Prov. 15:14 Lxx). So, the Mother of God found the "deep heart" through her humble prayer. In fact, when she found her "deep heart", there she met God, because God is met in the depths of our heart.

Then she discovered a second thing: her unity with the rest of mankind, and she began to intercede for the whole world in the Holy of Holies at a very young age.[4] While she was instructed in the Prophets by the priests of the temple, she read the text of Isaiah which says, "Behold, a virgin shall conceive, and bear a son, and shall call his name Immanuel", God with us (Isa. 7:14), the passage we read every year at Christmas; and, by the grace of God, her whole being was ignited by those words, and she began praying from that moment in this way: "Oh God of my Fathers, make me worthy to be the servant of that woman who will bring Immanuel to the world." And in the fervency of this humble prayer, to become the servant of the mother of Immanuel, the Archangel Gabriel appears and says to her, "Not the servant, but the mother." That is why she says that God "hath regarded the low estate of his handmaiden" (Luke 1:48). So, why did that happen? Because the Mother of God, prophetically, put herself in the Way of the Lord, and fulfilled, prophetically, the law which her Son was to give – that "those who will humble themselves shall be exalted" (*cf.* Matt. 23:12) – she was exalted most highly, above the Cherubim and Seraphim. Because she placed herself prophetically in the Way of the Lord – and the Way *is* the Lord – the Lord was united with her, and became her Son. So we see how important it is to know the Way of the Lord.

I have begun my talk with the importance of the Way of the Lord because I am going to say something very proud, and I want to be tolerated. Fr. Paul asked me to explain how monasticism is beneficial to the Church. And this could be seen as pride on our part, to speak of ourselves as being beneficial to the Church, since the Church, being Christ Himself, the Body of Christ, has no need of anyone. But we are all given a gift in this Body, and we cannot in fact be members of this Body unless we have received a gift from the Holy Spirit. And each of us, says St. Paul, has a special gift in the building up of this Body (cf. Rom. 12:5–8). So, I say all this as an introduction, in order to justify what I am now going to say about monasticism, in order to be tolerated, and not simply regarded as proud. If there is anything about monasticism that is beneficial to the Church, it is precisely that it preserves upon earth this great science of God, which initiates man into the Way of the Lord, the way by which one learns to "go down". All monastic life is organized in such a way so as to impart unto us the spirit of this way of "going down".

I remember that when I became priest and spiritual father, Fr. Sophrony, our father founder, said to me, "Don't be afraid to encourage young people to learn to 'go down', because it is the only way for them to overcome their passions". We have to learn this way otherwise we cannot become passionless, we cannot fulfil the commandment of God, who said, "Be ye perfect, even as your Father which is in Heaven is perfect" (Matt. 5:48). We have to learn this perfection in order to mirror, to reflect upon earth, the perfection of our Heavenly Father. This perfection was manifested in the flesh of our Lord Jesus Christ, but we are all called to be imitators of our Lord. And if monasticism is justified, it is justified in this way: that it is a science that teaches people the way of "going down".

You may ask, what is the difference between monks and lay Christians? There is no difference. The difference lies in the way we go about it. St. Paul, when he speaks of celibacy and non-celibacy, says that neither celibacy nor married life avails, but the fulfilling of the commandment of God (cf. 1 Cor. 7:7–9, 17–19). So monasticism is justified in teaching us the way of going down, and there are many ways of doing that. But before I continue, I should like to say little more about the gift of each member of the Body of Christ. St. Paul says that "when he [Christ] ascended up on high, he led captivity captive, and gave gifts unto men" (Eph. 4:8). "Captivity" means freedom. Christ, then, gave us freedom and the gifts of the Holy Spirit. And suddenly, with wonder, the Apostle exclaims, "Now that he ascended, what is it but that he also descended first into the lower parts of the earth" (Eph. 4:9), giving freedom to all, and "He that descended is the same also that ascended up far above all heavens, that he might fill all things" (Eph. 4:10). He filled the whole universe with His divine energy, so that we human beings can meet Christ under any condition, in any circumstances in this life. Whether in joy or in the hell of our afflictions He is there. Having come down to the earth, He sanctified the waters of the river Jordan, and when we go down into the water of baptism, we die in Christ. We die in Christ, that is to say, we die to sin. Having made the decision to be dead unto sin, we "go down" into the water in His name, in the name of the Father, and of the Son, and of the Holy Spirit. And we come up "in newness of life" (Rom. 6:4), having "put on Christ" (Gal. 3:27). We put on the new humanity of the new Adam, Christ, and in that humanity dwells the fullness of the Godhead. So, by going down to the nethermost parts of the earth, and then ascending and sitting on the right hand of the Father, Christ gave us true freedom, He led captivity captive and gave gifts to men, the gifts of the Holy Spirit. And in monasticism we learn that way of going down, in order to acquire the gifts of Christ.

However, we do not always want to accept the Gospel in the true way. The Gospel continuously speaks about death; that if we wish to truly live we must die. St. Paul says, "For if ye live after the flesh, ye shall die: but if ye through the Spirit do mortify the deeds of the body, ye shall live" (Rom. 8:13). The Gospel speaks about shame. If we bear shame and reproach for His sake, we shall be partakers of His glory (cf. Heb. 11:26, 2 Tim. 1:8–10). The Gospel speaks about the Cross of Christ, that if we take up this cross, and come to love Him, and follow Him to the point of hatred of one's own soul (*cf.* Matt. 16:24–25), then we are truly His disciples (*cf.* John 13:34–35). All this is hard. To us it is proposed to learn to die if we wish to live. And we have to make the choice, either we live in order to die, or we learn to die in order to live; because it is impossible to be a Christian and to live.[5] That is why St. Paul says, "I die daily" (1 Cor. 15:31). The Apostle says again that God does not judge twice. If we judge ourselves now, in the light of His commandments, we shall not be judged then (1 Cor. 11:31). So, there is a way of anticipating that glorious end.

I shall now make a parenthesis on the Desert Fathers of the fourth century. That century was the most luminous century in the history of monasticism, because suddenly, in the desert of Egypt, a divine perfection was revealed. One of those holy Fathers said that if man wants, from morning until evening, he can attain to divine perfection. And if the Fathers say so, it is possible, for this is the fruit of their own experience. But the hard thing about this is how to maintain the desire for perfection every day. The way to keep it up every day is given to us by St. Paul. Every time he speaks about the sublimity of the Way of Christ, of the way of the new life in Christ, he refers immediately to the Second Coming of the Lord. That is to say, the only way to maintain our inspiration and "newness of life" is to put ourselves before the dread judgment-seat of Christ. And if we judge ourselves now, we shall not be judged then (1 Cor. 11:31). Even the Lord Himself says that when people, persecutors, bring you to judgment before a court, not to premeditate what to say. In that hour, says the Lord, "I will give you a mouth and wisdom, which all your adversaries shall not be able to gainsay nor resist" (Luke 21:15). But we are not always persecuted. Thanks to God, nowadays the Church in many parts of the world enjoys great peace. But the word of the Lord is true for always, "abideth for ever" (*cf.* 1 Pet. 1:23, 25). How true this is today in America, where even if we are just a little Christian we are praised and helped!

By putting ourselves voluntarily before the judgment of God, that is to say, by examining ourselves strictly in the light of His commandments (that is our judgment) He gives us "a mouth and wisdom". He puts in our mouth, rather in our heart, the prayer of repentance, which justifies us. St. John the Divine says that there is a way for man to become infallible – the only way upon earth that man can be infallible – is when he acknowledges his sinfulness. He says, "If we say that we have no sin, we deceive ourselves, and the truth is not in us. If we confess our sins, He is faithful and just to forgive our sins, and to cleanse us from all unrighteousness" (1 John 1:8–9). Therefore, the only time we are infallible is when we confess our sinfulness, because we confess a universal truth, our own personal fall, and the Fall of the whole Adam, of all mankind. And because we confess a truth, we become truthful, and by becoming truthful we attract the Spirit of Truth that works in us the true prayer that justifies us, the true prayer that makes us "children of God" (John 11:52, Rom. 8:21; 9:8, Gal. 3:26), "children of light" (John 12:36, 1 Thess. 5:5). You know, it is the Spirit of God the Father that cries in our hearts, "Abba, Father!" (cf. Gal. 4:6).

In monasticism, we aim to acquire this art. There lies the benefit of monasticism: to teach its people the way of "going down", the way of bearing shame in order to wash away shame by shame. Because if we bear shame in this life, in confessing our Heavenly Father, says the Lord, then we shall have no shame before Him at the Second Coming. When He comes in glory He will acknowledge us before all the angels and all the saints (cf. Mark 8:38).

So by shame we extinguish shame. That is why the sacrament of confession is so powerful and so regenerating. We bear a little shame on earth for the sake of the Lord, and He gives us such grace, so as to be able to overcome our sins and receive healing for our brokenness. Therefore, because He Himself, in His way down, bore the "cross of shame" (cf. Heb. 12:2), the more shame we bear the better, the more grace we shall receive for our healing and for a glorious salvation, "a better resurrection", as St. Paul says (Heb. 11:35). And so it is unavoidable for us, too, to bear a little shame, if we wish to follow Him. He bore shame for our salvation, the cross of shame, and when we share that shame for His sake, according to His commandment, and in order to reconcile ourselves to Him, He considers that a response of gratitude, and He measures out His gifts to us.

Furthermore, our Saviour bore shame in suffering "without the gate" (Heb. 13:12), outside the gate, that is to say, completely cast out. He came to this earth and was rejected by the Synagogue, which was founded in His name. He is cast out from it; He has no place in the House of God upon earth, though He is eaten up by the zeal of the House of His Father (*cf.* Ps. 69:10 Lxx, John 2:17). In a similar manner, the monk bears shame: he has no dignity, not even ecclesiastical dignity. His is a very humble estate. As priests, we have glory. We preside over an assembly and dispense the word of God. This is blessed, of course. This ministry is given to us for the building up of the Body of the Church. But it is a *temporary* thing. In the World to Come, there will be no such ministries. Then there shall only be love – the love of the Master. In the same way that Christ came to earth and was rejected, and even suffered, being cast outside the gate, outside the camp of this world, so also do monks try to imitate this way. They go outside of this world, outside the camp of this world, to meet Christ. This lends an eschatological perspective to the way of the monks. That is to say, they vigilantly await the Bridegroom; they stand ready to receive Him. As was mentioned earlier, this is the only way not to slumber in this "awaiting", before the Coming of our Lord. It is the only way to maintain our inspiration for salvation.

And now I come to a more specific point. But before I do so, I should like to demonstrate a little more this way of accepting the shame of the Lord and receiving the grace of His salvation. Remember when the Lord was going through Jericho to Jerusalem for His Holy Passion, a very noble and notable man of Jericho, Zacchaeus, desired to see the Lord, but was unable to do so, because he was "little of stature", as the Gospel tells us (Luke 19:3). So he made himself a laughing stock, and climbed up a sycamore tree in order to be able to see the Lord. He suffered shame because of his desire to see the Lord, and the Lord noticed him. And not only did He notice him, but He spoke to him saying, "Zacchaeus, make haste, and come down; for to day I must abide at thy house" (Luke 19:5). The Lord visited his house, because He saw Zacchaeus' suffering of shame as a "kinship" with Him. Zacchaeus put himself in the Way of the Lord, voluntarily suffering shame, and so it was unavoidable that he should meet the Lord; and, as we know, the Lord joined Zacchaeus. And do you remember what happened? Christ visited Zacchaeus, and from the moment of the Lord's visitation, his heart was enlarged and he was restored to spiritual health, and straightway desired to restore every injustice he had committed. He said, "If I have taken any thing from any man by false accusation, I restore him fourfold" (Luke 19:8). This "fourfold" is very significant, for it indicates the four dimensions of the mystery of the Cross and Resurrection of Christ: "the breadth, and length, and depth, and height" (Eph. 3:18), which became the source of every grace, the source of every gift. The depth of this great mystery is "the way down", to the nethermost parts; its height is "His rising up", above the Heavens; and its breadth and length is seen in the grace of His Cross reaching all nations: "And I, if I be lifted up from the earth, will draw all men unto me," says the Lord (John 12:32).

Zacchaeus, by putting himself in the Way of the Lord, and bearing a little shame for His sake, found the Lord a companion, a guest in his house, *and therefore his heart was enlarged to embrace all people.* So, when we put ourselves in the Way of our Lord, and we learn to "go down", we become partakers of His gift, and this gift *enlarges the heart,* and then man finds his true destiny. Because each one of us, if we are to be in the image of the new Adam, Christ, should bear in his heart the rest of humanity. Therefore, whoever puts himself in the Way of the Lord receives this enlargement of the Cross and Resurrection of the Lord, and this enlargement makes him universal. We cannot become universal with technology, with computers and mobile phones, and such things. True universality comes when we put ourselves in the Way of the Lord. That is why St. Paul says to the Corinthians, "Brethren, be ye also enlarged!" (2 Cor. 6:13). He wanted them to know the power of the Cross and Resurrection of Christ, and thereby become "enlarged". When we read our Fathers,

St. Silouan for example, we see that the monk's calling is fulfilled
when he becomes an intercessor for the whole world.[6] And we see
this phenomenon clearly in the case of the Apostles, who said, "It
is not expedient that we should leave the preaching of the word of
God, and be spent in serving tables, the widows and the poor. Let
us choose seven people for this ministry." And they chose seven
deacons to help in these matters (cf. Acts 6:1–6). Man truly fulfils his
destiny, his purpose – he fulfils God's will for him – when he becomes
an intercessor in his prayers, bares in his heart the whole world,
and humbly brings every creature before God in fervent supplication. This is impossible, humanly speaking. It is only possible if the
state of the new Adam is transmitted to us. Just as God desires all
mankind to be saved (cf. 1 Tim. 2:4), so He imparts to us the same
mind and the same heart which was in Christ Jesus, as says St. Paul
to the Philippians (cf. Phil. 2:5).

In the monastery we learn this very concretely. We are a
small community – let us say twenty to twenty-five people – and
every time we stand before God, immediately, together with our
standing before God, we bring before Him at least these twenty-
five fellows, with whom we form *that* body in *that* place. And we
learn to widen our existence. Every time I stand before God, in my
heart there are at least twenty-five people. And if I am a priest, I
stand and bear in my heart my parishioners. This is an exercise for
monks and priests. Slowly but surely the day will come when the
Lord will see this spirit in them, and "He that is faithful in that
which is least will be made faithful also in much", says the Lord
(cf. Luke 16:10), and then He will impart to them His Spirit, which
embraces the whole world. So, the monastery is a place where we
exercise ourselves daily to acquire the universality of Christ.

Now, having said all this, I want to be even more daring, and
ask for your forgiveness and tolerance for what I am about to say.
We monks are strange people. St. Paul says that we have to become
mad first, before acquiring a little bit of a mind (cf. 1 Cor. 3:18). Let
us put it in a different way. In the history of monasticism, every
time God gave some great word to a monk, announcing through
that word the deep judgments of His will for the world, the

monks of that monastery, for generations and generations, would repeat the word of this holy monk, and in doing so they served their fellow people, and worked out their own salvation. In our case, in our monastic family, the Lord gave a word to our Father in God, St. Silouan, who was recently canonized, and the word he was given was the following: *"Keep thy mind in hell, and despair not!"* In his writings, where St. Silouan speaks in great simplicity, but with apostolic authority, not a single word is a human word: all that he says is given by the Holy Spirit. If you read him, you will immediately understand this. In his writings, he says that the word which God gave him – *"Keep thy mind in hell, and despair not!"* – is a noble and great science. It was the Lord Himself who gave him this commandment at a very tragic moment in his life, when he was really in the hell of despair. The Lord sounded this word in his heart, and, together with his word, He imparted to him the state of His grace, which liberated him from every impurity and captivity of mind. For to *"keep thy mind in hell"* means to be placed in the Way of the Lord, and bear shame for the Lord, and stand in the judgment of the Lord, and to judge one's self as worthy of the worst punishment – that is, that we are worthy *even of hell.* But, this is not done in a morbid way. Far from it! For this is done out of love for the Lord, and in faith, without despairing, because He is also able to pull us out of the depths of hell. St. Silouan was living his hell, and it was as if the Lord had said to him, "Well, remain as you are, be humble, and accept that you are worthy of that, *but* do not despair." And strange wonder, the Lord offered him hell, and his spirit emerged in triumph. From that moment on, his mind was cleansed, and his enemies – the devils which kept appearing to him – disappeared.[7] When we put ourselves in the Way of our Lord, "going down", the enemy cannot follow us, because this is a humble way. The enemy cannot "go down". Lucifer wants to set his throne above the throne of God, and the entire world is poisoned by his spirit. But when we accept the injunction of the Lord, and we learn to judge ourselves, and we learn to go down, we are delivered, because the enemy cannot follow us. And when we are delivered, then we come up again with the strength of the

Lord. We "go down" in order to "go up", but we must first go down. And we say, "Lord, I am the worst of all." Remember how in the Gospel, when the Apostles came to the Lord, and said to Him, "Lord, Increase our faith!" (Luke 17:5). The Lord gave them a teaching, and at the end says to them, "When ye shall have done all those things which are commanded you, say, We are unprofitable servants: we have done that which was our duty to do" (Luke 17:10). So this – to consider ourselves worse than all – is the summit of ascetical humility.

But there is yet another kind of humility, says St. Silouan, which is indescribable – the humility of Christ.[8] He says that when we see the Lord – he himself was accounted worthy of seeing Him – at the moment of the vision, man acquires this indescribable humility of Christ, and *so much* does he desire that the Lord be magnified, that he himself is willing to be decreased *even to hell,* provided that the Lord is magnified.[9] So great is the love that is imparted! This is what we find in the Book of Revelation, where we read that the saints loved God "unto death" (Rev. 12:11). Only when it overcomes death is love strong. When we are threatened by death, and yet believe in Christ and follow Him "whithersoever he goeth" (Rev. 14:4), even to "the nethermost parts" (*cf.* Eph. 4:10), is our faith and love for the Lord stronger than death, conquering death.[10] "In thy light shall we see light" (Ps. 36:9), says the Psalmist, and when we see the Lord in His Light, we see two things: on one hand, we see the spotless and indescribable holiness of our Saviour; and on the other, we see our terrible and wretched ugliness. We hate the latter, and we ardently desire the former, even "unto death". We condemn ourselves to hell, because of the darkness and distortion that we bear within us, but we have a longing for the holiness of the Lord, which is stronger even than death. *"Keep thy mind in hell, and despair not!"*

Having seen the state that our fall has condemned us to, we count ourselves as worthy of hell, but of course we do not despair: we are helped by the Holy Spirit. I am not speaking here about a psychological activity; this is the mystery of our faith. As soon as we place ourselves under that judgment, the Spirit co-works within us, testifying to the truth of the activity of the exercise. When we condemn ourselves even unto death, to the worst condemnation, how can we be shaken by any other misfortune in this life? By insults, by hatred, by illness? By voluntarily putting ourselves beneath every creature, we humble ourselves so that we have the strength to bear things of lesser difficulty. That is why the Prophet Micah says, "I will bear the indignation of the Lord, because I have sinned against him" (cf. Mic. 7:9). I hate my sinfulness, therefore I am ready to bear the chastening of the Lord. And by continually doing so, standing before God, we see that this exercise, which the saint was taught by the Lord Himself, contains all the features of the Way of the Lord: shame – we bear the shame of our spiritual poverty at that moment; judgment – we stand before God, and we give glory and justice to Him, and are ready to accept the "shame of the face" upon us, as the Prophet Daniel says, "To Thee, O Lord, all justice and to us the shame of the face" (cf. Dan. 9:8 Lxx). Moreover, we take on pain, that part of the Way of the Lord, which is the Cross. When we strive to follow this way, we are pierced by a terrible pain on all levels of our being; and that pain becomes salutary, because it gathers all our spirit into one, in our heart. And by this concentration, we fulfil the commandment of God, because we are commanded to love God with all our heart and mind (cf. Deut. 6:5, Matt. 22:37). But in our ordinary fallen state, our mind is divided into a thousand pieces. We have one thing in our mind, another in our senses, and yet another in our heart: we are completely dispersed and divided. This activity, however, concentrates the mind in the heart, and once the mind is joined to the heart and exercises dominion over all the nature of man, it turns the whole being of man to God. Then man fulfils properly the first commandment – to love God with all his heart, with all his mind, with all his being (cf. Matt. 22:37). When you love Him in that way, you will receive His Spirit. You will receive the enlargement of His Spirit and embrace the whole world in your intercession, thus fulfilling the second commandment, to love your neighbour as yourself (cf. Lev. 19:18, Matt. 22:39), because your neighbour becomes the content of your heart.

We never cease to wonder when we see the example of our Lord. Going alone to Golgotha; and before Golgotha, He prayed in the garden of Gethsemane with bloody sweat. Christ sweated blood in His prayer for the whole world (*cf.* Luke 22:44). From the Gospel of St. John, we learn that He was addressing his prayer to God the Father, "O righteous Father, the world hath not known thee" (John 17:25). That is to say, in His heart at that moment there was only one thought. He did not care who was coming to arrest Him, whether they were Romans or Jews. He said, "The cup which my Father hath given me, shall I not drink it?" (John 18:11). He was conversing with the Father, and He accepted the Cup of His Father, because He willed that the world be saved. He was praying for the salvation of this world, which "knew not" the Heavenly Father. Therefore, in Gethsemane He bore in his heart and prayed for the whole world. He ascended Golgotha alone, bearing in His heart the whole world. He was crucified with the whole world in His heart. He went down to the nether regions of the earth, and was buried with the same content in his heart. But because His death was sinless and voluntary, He was raised the third day, having tasted just enough of death in order to destroy it for our sake. He was risen the third day with the same content in His heart. All that died with Him, was risen again with Him. And it is the same with us: if we die completely before the Lord, with what we die we rise up again; and if we have embraced the whole world in our prayer, or if we have brought the whole world before the Lord in our priestly service and offered a reasonable bloodless sacrifice for the whole world, that means we are spreading the blessing of God in return upon all creation.

That is man's calling, and that is how monks live it more concretely in the act of repentance; because repentance and monasticism in our tradition are designated by the same word. When we say "my repentance" in Greek, it means "my monastery". "I return to my repentance tomorrow", let's say, means "I return to my monastery". So, there it becomes more specific. It is the same gift of life, the same gift of grace, the same gift of the Holy Spirit. The same promise is given to all of us, but monks organize their lives, "artificially", in such a way as to be able not to fail in acquiring this gift.

But this Way does not apply only to monks. If you carefully read, for example, the prayers before Holy Communion, you will notice that they are divided into two parts. In the first part, there is a downward movement; and in the second part, there is an upward, Godward movement. In the first part, for example, when we say, "O Lord of heaven and earth, though I am unworthy of heaven and earth, and even of this transitory life, and have sinned more than any other", and so on, we are making a very daring movement downward, judging ourselves and putting all the blame upon ourselves. And having done that, coming to the middle of the prayer we say, "But, O Lord, despise not Thy servant: come to my help, and give me the grace to partake without condemnation", and so on. Therefore, we have one movement downwards, and then, having reached the bottom, the *but* of faith comes. This is the spirit of the Church expressed in Her prayers. When diving, to use an analogy, we go down, and once our feet hit the bottom we begin to surface. In the same way, when we have gone down in spirit, having crushed the arrogance of our mind and the insensitivity and hardness of our heart, and the heart is "bitten" with contrition – contrition being the beginning of humility, which attracts grace (Jas. 4:6)[11] – once we have made this movement and found grace . . . we go up! And then with boldness we stand before God, and present Him all our petitions.

This is the great science. I have said only a few words, and I do not know if I have said all that I wanted to say, but this is the benefit of monasticism: it cultivates and preserves upon earth the Way of the Lord, the way of the great science. This science unifies the whole being of man through repentance, which makes him able to receive the enlargement of the Spirit, and embrace the whole world with his spirit, with his heart. And in so doing, man justifies the purpose of his creation. Forgive me, father.

Father Paul's Afterword: Thank you, Father, for this vision of the monastic life in Christ that you have opened up before us. There is much to assimilate, much to try to comprehend. I would

like to open the floor this time for your questions, if you have
a question for Fr. Zacharias concerning anything related to his
presentation on monasticism.

QUESTIONS & ANSWERS

Question 1: I didn't hear clearly what you said about the Mother
of God's first discovery in the Holy of Holies. Would you repeat
that, please?

Answer 1: Yes: the first discovery that the Mother of God made
was that of her "deep heart" (*cf.* Ps. 64:6 Lxx). Then in the deep heart
she was united with all mankind, because there she found God and all
mankind. And we called that her second discovery, but in actual fact
the experience was really only a single event: sometimes we systematize for pedagogical purposes, for the sake of clarity and to transmit
certain truths. And you see, we need to find our heart. Salvation is
in the heart. St. Paul says, "Do not torment yourselves thinking who
shall go up to Heaven and bring Christ down, and who shall go down
to hell to bring Christ up? Do not torment yourselves thinking; you
will not solve your problems by thinking, but rather believe and
confess, and then you will know with your heart" (*cf.* Rom. 10:6–10).
And one of St. Silouan's teachings is this: that we need to find the
"deep heart", and we find it only with humility, because pride buries
the heart. Pride hinders love. Whoever is proud cannot love. Our
father founder, Fr. Sophrony, the disciple of St. Silouan, once went
to St. Silouan and said, "What a pity! I am always ill, and always busy
with different activities in the monastery, and I am not able to study
the Fathers and learn their theology." And the holy Staretz, after
remaining silent for a moment, replied, "And do you esteem that a
great thing? Do you think that is important? It is a great thing to
humble ourselves, because pride prevents love".

Question 2: In your theory of the inverted pyramid, you
mentioned how there is no equality in this world, and the strong
exercise dominion over the weak, but that this is not the idea
of God; that God wanted us all to be equal. But what about the
people who now exercise authority over us – like the President of

the United States – who make decisions for us, and so on. Is that the way it's supposed to be?

Answer 2: That is blessed by God. That is by economy. It is not what God wants. What He wants, He says, is that we all be equal, and not in need of any other to exercise authority over us, or even teach us, because we shall all know God, and be taught directly by God. That is the state in Paradise. We are not against those who exercise dominion over us, because we vote for them and we elect them. St. Paul says that the truly spiritual man must pray for them – he never turns against authority (*cf.* 1 Tim. 2:1–2). The only way for the spiritual man is to "go down". You see, I said that although the monk has no place in the Church, he does have the task to repent. Although he has no ecclesiastical dignity, yet he is the one – may God forgive me because I am myself so poor – who gives spiritual content to the institution of the Church. Just as the Lord, who, cast out of the Synagogue, was the fullness of the Law and the Prophets, the expectation of all nations, and eaten up by the zeal for the House of His Father (*cf.* John 2:17), so too with the monk, who with no ecclesiastical dignity is consumed with zeal for that holy institution, the Church. The spiritual man never turns against authority. We love our bishops not only when they are as nice as yours here in Wichita, but even when they are cruel. We humble ourselves before them in order to preserve the vessel that contains all the gifts of the Holy Spirit. And the sign of the spiritual man who is born again of the Holy Spirit is this: when you humble yourself before him, he humbles himself even more. There is only one way for spiritual people: to make their way through humility, that is to "go down", to submit themselves to the mighty hand of the Providence of God in this temporary life until He will exalt them "in due time", as St. Peter says (1 Pet. 5:6).

Question 3: Even though you did not mention Fools for Christ, Zacchaeus is a model of a fool for Christ.

Answer 3: Wonderful! Thank you very much! You have touched the heart of the matter. St. Paul says that if you want to be wise, you must first become mad (*cf.* 1 Cor. 3:18–19), and we see the essence of the matter in the "fool for Christ", because he makes himself foolish for the sake of the Lord, in order to avoid vainglory and hide the gift of God, and perhaps even increase it. When you are despised by everybody, kicked by everybody, you have pain in the heart; and if you are wise, you use that pain as energy for godly ascent. We spoke about this in the conference with my dear fellow ministers and brothers;[12] about how to change psychological states into spiritual states, and in this category of saints we see this happening very, very clearly. They use the psychological energy of the "kicks" of their fellows – they use their pain – and they install a transformer within their hearts that turns that psychological energy into spiritual energy for divine ascent. Thank you very much for your question. I intended to speak about madness and wisdom, not in specific connection with Fools for Christ, but with shame . . . and I omitted it.

Question 4: When you are "going down", when you are humbling yourself to the "bottom", how do you prevent yourself from being proud in doing that?

Answer 4: At first it will be difficult. In the beginning you will have intrusive thoughts; but you try again, and then again, and gradually you learn to discern them, because when they come they say, "Ah, now you are doing the right thing. Ah, now you are all right." But you learn by experience, and as soon as you see them approaching, you will say to yourself, "Now my assassins are coming", and take no notice of them at all, but simply continue your work, and the Spirit will come to your aid. It is the Spirit that "bites" the heart and attracts the mind to it, and once the heart is bitten by the Spirit, and the mind descends, intrusive thoughts vanish. That is the beauty of tears, of spiritual tears – not psychological tears that wither man's life. Spiritual tears have this beauty: that when you weep with the thought of God, your mind and your heart are one, they are united. You cannot weep unless you have only one thought. Sometimes people weep from hatred, because they have but one thought with which they hate, or they have one thought of pitying themselves – and this destroys them. But when you have but one thought for God, and you weep, that brings healing and unification of one's entire being, and raises man to such a level, as we have said, as to be able to love God with all his heart, with all his mind, with his whole being.

Question 5: You spoke of the word of St. Silouan, *"Keep your mind in hell, and despair not!"* How can I keep my mind in hell and experience that I am worthy of hell, experience my condemnation before God, without becoming a prisoner of guilt and shame and condemnation, so that it crushes me?

Answer 5: All the things you mention are a matter of faith. But I am grateful that Father Paul has asked this question. I was under the impression that I would be addressing monks today, but never mind, I am addressing fellow Christians – it is the same. The word given to St. Silouan and the activity that it proposes is not for everyone. One has to be really psychologically sound to be able to do this. One would crack otherwise, because when we do this we place ourselves under the utmost tension. And you know, how else can you keep the Spirit of God unless you exert yourself to the maximum? This is not for everybody, not even for all monks. I remember once, when I first became a spiritual father, Fr. Sophrony rebuked me for trying to teach this way to a nun who was not able to take it. He said to me, "You are stupid, you do not realize that you will crush her. She is not for that. She will be saved by doing her work humbly, and by following the normal pattern of the monastic life, fulfilling all of her duties." But, even if this activity is not for everyone, we try a little dose, in order to maintain a humble spirit before God, and to say, "Lord, I thank Thee for all the things that Thou hast done for me, of which I know and of which I know not, whether manifest or hid, I thank Thee for all that Thou hast done for me . . . though I am unworthy". And this is a very light form of the same thing, but if we continue giving thanks to God in this way, remembering that He always treats us with goodness, even though we are unworthy, slowly, slowly, grace will accumulate in our soul, it will heal our spirit, and then, perhaps, we shall even be able to practise the Way revealed to St. Silouan, each of us according to his own measure and strength.

Question 6: You mentioned the four dimensions of the Cross, and you mentioned its "height" and depth", and the "breadth" of the mystery of the Cross, reaching unto the utmost parts of the earth, but what does the "length" of the Cross signify?

Answer 6: The "length" of the Way of Christ begins from the bosom of the Divinity and reaches to the end of time. The length is the length of the Way, that Way for which He is the beginning and the end, that Way for which He is the *Alpha* and the *Omega*. That is why we are so happy in our life in the Church. We do not have any rules to fulfil in our monastery. Fr. Sophrony had an "allergy" against rules. He said, "Christ liberated us from all rules, why enslave ourselves to rules that we make ourselves." We follow one rule that the Fathers of the Golden Age of monasticism gave: we do our best, what we can, and we leave the rest to God. And therein lies humility. *As long as we put ourselves in the Way of the Lord, He will meet us.* And the Way of the Lord is always the same. He is the beginning – let us put ourselves even at the beginning! – and He is the end. He is the same. That is why He says that the worker of the eleventh hour receives the same wages as the worker of the first hour (Matt. 20:9–16). Thus He is the beginning and the end, and the "length" of that Way.

NOTES

* This first talk on Monasticism was delivered extemporaneously.

1. For more details on Fr. Sophrony's theory of the "inverted pyramid", see *Saint Silouan, op. cit.,* pp. 237–239; and pp. 69–70, 130, 165–166, and 170–172 above.

2. *The Nicene-Constantinopolitan Creed.*

3. *The Song of the Three Holy Children* is included among the Old Testament Apocrypha in most English editions of the Bible. See also Dan. 3:26–30.

4. See esp. St. Gregory Palamas, Homily LIII, 49 and 53, *On the Entry into the Holy of Holies of Our Exceedingly Pure Lady, Mother of God and Ever-Virgin Mary, and Her Divine Manner of Life There,* in *Mary the Mother of God, loc. cit.;* and pp. 33–34, 47–48, and 51 above.

5. *Cf. Saint Silouan, op. cit.,* p. 241.

6. *Cf. ibid.*, p. 407.

7. *Cf. ibid.*, p. 431.

8. *Cf. ibid.*, pp. 300, 308, 310.

9. *Cf. ibid.*, p. 310.

10. *Cf. We Shall See Him, op. cit.*, p. 72.

11. "God resisteth the proud, but giveth grace unto the humble."

12. See pp. 109–112, 149–151, and 166 above.

ON MONASTICISM II*

THE SUBJECT OF THIS SECOND PRESENTATION on monasticism is "Fidelity to the Monastic Vows as a Means of Healing the Estrangement Brought About by Original Sin" – how we are healed by fulfilling the monastic vows. Monasticism is a gift of grace. By receiving this charism, man becomes capable of following the example of the Lord, and of imitating the angelic way of life. The "extreme humility", which Christ's Face inspires, and the unbridled desire for God, which monastic life cultivates, attract divine grace towards man. This grace frees him from passions, and makes him in the likeness of Christ – supra-cosmic. *Aside:* This is what the Lord says, "Be of good cheer; I have overcome the world" (John 16:33). *End of aside.*

In paradise man was in communion with God, and God was life and security for him. Disobedience and the fall into sin disrupted this life-giving unity with God, and death entered man's life with all its devastating consequences. Thus, man lost the security and support he had from God, the Giver of life, and out of fear and the struggle for survival, he conceived his own way of life, based thenceforward on his natural, created powers. Previously, he had kept the commandments of God and enjoyed every good thing, and lived in incorruption. After the transgression, though, seeking protection from the threat of death, he took refuge in the following three substitutes or pseudo-supports, which were to alienate him from the life of God (*cf.* Eph. 4:18). The first pseudo-support is his self-will and the persuasiveness of his logical reasoning. The second is the pleasure (*hedonê*) of the senses and the desires naturally associated with reproduction; and the third pseudo-support is the possession of material goods. These are the three substitutes that man turned to for survival, having lost the true security and life of God.

By relying on the persuasiveness of his own logical judgement and will, man undergoes the first alienation and falls into the Luciferian delusion of self-deification, raising a wall between himself and God. In succumbing to the lure of progeny and the pleasure of the senses, he puts on the "garments of skin" (Gen. 3:21), and undergoes the second alienation. The first alienation occurred through the arrogance of his mind, the second took place by putting his trust in the pleasure of the senses, and in the desire for progeny. His life is thus preserved, but it is changed into a "living death", that is, into a life of self-love combined with spiritual death – a prolongation of life in death. Finally, so as to feel secure he makes efforts to acquire "much goods for many years" (*cf.* Luke 12:19), as "the fool hath said in his heart" (Ps. 14:1), and so he brings upon himself the third alienation, which completely darkens his intellect and hardens his heart. He is now given over to the vanities of this world and the folly of idolatry.

The fall into the whirlpool of these three alienations disposes the conscience of man negatively with regard to God, to his neighbour, and to the material world. In his relationship with God, he gives preference to himself; in his relationship with his neighbour, he is led by the passionate desire to dominate – lust for power; in his relationship to the material world, he is given over to the frenzy of acquisitiveness.

Monasticism aims to remove these three alienations, and to restore man to a genuine hypostatic form of existence. *Aside:* To the true universality, which is the fulfilment of the purpose of man's creation. *End of aside.* The aim is realized by the accomplishment of the three monastic vows: obedience, virginity or chastity, and poverty or non-acquisitiveness. Obedience, however, is of particular importance, because the other two vows draw their power from it, as a natural corollary.

The Vow of Obedience

Obedience (Gk. *hypakoë*) is the first condition of the monastic life and its basis. Obedience is cultivated by human ascetic effort, but also, and primarily, it is a gift of God.[1] According to Fr. Sophrony, our father founder, obedience is a "sacred mystery" in two senses: it is a "secret" revealed only by the energy of the Holy Spirit, and it is a "sacrament" of the Church. For the life to which it elevates man is indescribable and incomprehensible.[2]

It is Christ who first showed us the model and example of perfect obedience. He came into the world "in the Father's name" and not "in His own name" (*cf.* John 12:50), which would have betrayed a Luciferian tendency to self-divinization.[3] He taught us that His Father's commandment is eternal life. He voluntarily (*cf.* Heb. 10:7, John 5:30) accepted this commandment and fulfilled it without sin (*cf.* John 14:30–31). In addition, as the only-begotten Son, He was unceasingly and constantly the bearer of the good pleasure of the Father and the power of the Holy Spirit and, therefore, in order to save us He demonstrated perfect and exact obedience to the will of His Father, even unto death and the shame of the Cross (*cf.* Phil. 2:8, Heb. 12:2). But the righteous God did not let His child Jesus "see corruption" in the tomb (*cf.* Ps. 16:10, Acts 2:27; 13:35). He raised Him up and exalted Him to be a Prince and Saviour of the world (*cf.* Acts 3:15; 5:31, Heb. 2:10). By His obedience Christ, the new Adam, initiated a new law of life, becoming the healthy root of the "new humanity" (Eph. 2:15; 4:24).

In fulfilling his obedience, the monk imitates Christ, setting himself on the path of the Lord's will. Only a psychologically healthy soul can undertake obedience. Psychological health is manifested by the monk's consciousness that he himself is insufficient for immediate knowledge of the great and perfect will of God. He follows the wise exhortation of Holy Scripture: "Ask thy father, and he will show thee; thine elders and they will tell thee" (Deut. 32:7). He holds to the general rule of monastic *ascesis*: "Do not trust in yourself." He thus has recourse to his spiritual father, confident that to him it has been given to know God's will more clearly. In this way, he recognizes that the true God is the "God of our Fathers" (Exod. 3:15–16), and thus overcomes the disorder of double-minded fallen man, who cannot discover the sure path of life. "A double minded man," says the Apostle James, "is unstable in all his ways" (Jas. 1:8); it is through obedience that he finds stability. Having this humble predisposition, the monk becomes fit to put his hand to the salutary plough of obedience (cf. Luke 9:62).

When the monk seeks the will of God with this disposition, as a lowly disciple, he is prepared to accept the first word of his spiritual father as coming from the mouth of the Lord, in whose name, too, he has asked advice. *Aside:* This is a matter of faith. *End of aside.* He gradually obtains knowledge of the divine will, and becomes capable of discerning the machinations of the enemy. "We are not ignorant of his devices", says St. Paul (2 Cor. 2:11). This discernment is necessary so as to refute every delusory suggestion, because the will of God in this world is manifested in the same relative outward forms in which the natural human will and the demonic will present themselves to the human mind. *Aside:* We have to learn to discern the thoughts (*logismoi*), of which there are three kinds: thoughts from God, natural thoughts, and demonic thoughts. *End of aside.*

It is worth emphasising at this point that obedience, like every other Christian virtue, must be a free and voluntary act in order to have eternal value before God. *Aside:* "If any man serve me, let him follow me", says the Lord (John 12:26). Whatever we do without freedom has no eternal value, only that which we do voluntarily and freely has eternal value before God. *End of aside.* Obedience means free denial of a man's will and opinion, a giving over of his logical judgement to the authority of another person, his Elder or father confessor. Notwithstanding man's creation as a free being in God's likeness, when sin intervened in his life his will was distorted and his intellect darkened. Instead of desiring to think on things Above, he wants to set his mind on things here below, and is attached to objects and values of this world, which are "unprofitable" for the soul (Heb. 13:17).

The free will of man, together with his reason, are the most precious of his natural gifts; and when obedience is at work, it offers these two faculties, the will and the reason, as the most pleasing sacrifice to God. *Aside:* When man becomes a "fool" for the commandment of the Lord, and cuts off his will for the sake of the Lord, it is the most pleasing sacrifice to God, because he has offered to God that which he holds most precious in himself. *End of aside.* Then, as recompense from God, the monk receives the supernatural gift of knowing the good and perfect divine will.

Aside: In the Church an exchange takes place between man and God. We present and offer our life to God, as far as we are able, and in return, God offers His life to us. This exchange of lives takes place in the Church, and even more so in the Liturgy. There is an exchange of life in the bread and wine we offer to God when we say, "Thine own, of thine own, we offer unto thee in all and for all"; and God says to us, "The holy things unto the holy". We put all our life in that bread and wine, all our prayers, all our expectations, everything that our conscience embraces, and we offer it to God. He accepts it, and puts His Life into the bread and wine – the Holy Spirit. He infuses them with His life, and returns them to us in order that we may eat and live, saying to us, "The holy things unto the holy". This takes place *par excellence* in the Divine Liturgy, but it happens also every time we fulfil a commandment. We make a little effort and, in return, we receive an incorruptible gift from God. The exchange is unequal, because our God is bountiful and loving-kind. We offer a corruptible and sinful life to God, and He offers back to us His limitless, incorruptible and eternal Life. And the monk, by becoming a fool for the sake of the Lord (*cf.* 1 Cor. 4:10), and sacrificing his natural and corrupted mind, his natural and distorted will, receives the knowledge of the good and perfect divine will, through his father in the Spirit – to begin with. And this is only to begin with, because after he is initiated, God becomes his guide and his teacher directly. We must not forget that the Lord said, "one is your Master, even Christ" (Matt. 23:8, 10). Our fathers dare to give us birth, and we become their sons. Then we, in our turn, in due time, become fathers as well. God has not created masters and servants; He has created fathers and sons in a relationship of love: the fathers give birth to sons, and the sons, in their turn, become fathers. This is the good pleasure of God. *End of aside.*

By the free exercise of obedience the monk makes himself a servant after the example of the Son of God (*cf.* Phil. 2:5–7),[4] and for this voluntary enslavement he is given the freedom of the children of God. The schooling of obedience aims at introducing man into the life-giving and saving will of God.[5] This initiation makes him like Christ,[6] and leads him to the perfection of the Christian life, to the acquisition of the Holy Spirit.[7] *Aside:* To that enlargement about which we spoke earlier, which makes him a universal person, in the image and likeness of the New Adam. *End of aside.*

When the monk accepts the word or the decision of his spiritual father, he learns to accept within him the life and the will, firstly of God, and then of his brethren. By these means, the shell of his isolated individuality is shattered, broken, and his being is expanded. He is perfected in love, and finds harmony and perfection in his relationships both towards God and his brothers. At first, he has to struggle to bear within himself the will of his confessor and his fellow monks. However, as he progresses in the knowledge of the divine will, his hypostasis – his person – becomes enlarged, and contains in himself the life of the entire world, which he embraces in his prayer.[8] His small, individual will is denied. He sets aside his broken earthly reasoning, and receives as a gift the wisdom and the divine universality of Christ. From this point of view, obedience is a sacrament of the Church which creates true persons in the image of the truly personal God, hypostases having true universality. The spiritual father becomes a "labourer together with God" (*cf.* 1 Cor. 3:9), a co-worker of God, in the sacred and everlasting creation of gods "for eternity in the uncreated Light".[9] *Aside:* It is a wonderful service, brimming with inspiration. *End of aside.*

By the practice of obedience, the monk crucifies his intellect and his will, and thus removes from his life the supports and the security by means of which previously he had hoped to oppose death. *Aside:* Do not forget that it is because we are afraid of death that we are sinful. Sin reigns in the world because of the fear of death. The fear of death makes us selfish, and we would do anything to survive; and because of that we remain selfishly in our own "closed circuit", and all we succeed in doing is to increase death and sin. Therefore, the fear of death made sin reign in the world, and when we try to survive at all costs, we create false supports in order to resist death, but we become more and more entangled in its teeth. *End of aside.*

By obedience accomplished in God's name, the monk concentrates his spirit on the advice or commandment given him, and thus, freed from every care over transient matters, he directs his mind uninterruptedly to prayer. Because he does not rely on himself, but places all his trust in God "who raises the dead", as St. Paul says (2 Cor. 1:9), he is freed from bondage to all created things, and attains to purity of intellect. *Aside:* This is the goal of obedience: to help us become free from cares and thus acquire purity of mind, which is the necessary precondition for pure prayer. *End of aside.* Purity of intellect is the most precious fruit of obedience. This purity is also an essential precondition for pure prayer, which will re-establish the primordial communion of the creature with the Creator, bringing his person face to face with the unoriginate God.

It becomes very clear from the above that obedience is radically different from discipline, surpassing it as heaven surpasses earth. Discipline means submission to a superior human will, for the sake of earthly benefit. Discipline subjects man to an impersonal "Rule", to the "Law", the "Typikon", the "Institution", the "Administration". Discipline favours the general over the particular, or the majority over the individual. In complete contrast to this, obedience is a free act of faith in God and is always accomplished in His name. *Aside:* Strictly speaking, full obedience is only possible in a monastery, because only in a monastery are all things organized in such a way as to

function for the glory of God (*cf.* 1 Cor. 10:31), and to contribute
to the performance of the Liturgy. *End of aside.*

The most perfect form of obedience, which bestows on man
the fullness of the hypostatic principle, making him truly an image
of God, is shown, as Fr. Sophrony observes, when his spirit is led
by the "greater love" of Christ (John 15:13). Then man attains to
the grace of theology as a spiritual state, and becomes a receiver of
revelations. *Aside:* Fr. Sophrony saw monasticism as "a gift of God",
and as an "urgency" of the spirit of man to respond to the "greater
love" of Christ that had touched him. Monasticism is also an act of
thanksgiving. *End of aside.* This obedience fulfils all the commandments, and becomes the means by which the living Tradition of
Christianity is assimilated.[10] *Aside:* Without obedience, the thread
of Tradition is broken, as it is precisely through obedience that we
imbibe the spirit of Tradition. *End of aside.*

By cutting off his own will and denying his own reasoning
the monk does not lose his personality, nor does he come to
self-annihilation, as it may seem to people in the world. On the
contrary, he rises above the limits of his created nature, and
becomes manifestly a true person–hypostasis. He becomes the
bearer of divine life and of all humanity.

So we see how the first alienation is healed through obedience,
by denying our own reasoning and corrupted individual will, and
also how, as a consequence, we receive freedom from cares, purity
of mind, and then the enlargement of Christ.

The Vow of Virginity or Chastity

Aside: I say the vow of virginity or chastity (Gk. *parthenía* or
sôphrosynê), because it sometimes happens that people who are
married and living in the world, after a mutual agreement, decide
to separate in order to become monks and nuns. They do not
comprise a large proportion of monastics, but there are not a few,
especially in Greece. I say virginity or chastity because, strictly
speaking, what matters before God is not celibacy or married life
but the fulfilment of the commandments. Monastic life is created
"artificially", in such a way as to give the greatest possibility of

fulfilling the commandments of God. And again, I say virginity or chastity, because what Christ desires is more especially the virginity of the heart. He says in the Gospel that what counts before Him is what the heart does. There is "adultery in the heart" (*cf.* Matt. 5:28), when we give our heart over to a passionate, carnal thought; there is also virginity of the heart, when the heart is totally given to Christ. That is why I am talking about virginity or chastity, because what we target is the virginity of the heart. *End of aside.*

Virginity or chastity constitutes the second vow of monasticism. *Aside:* Of course, if one already has virginity of heart, then he is protected from every fall of that kind of passion. *End of aside.* The dogmatic basis for virginity is the life of Christ. Christ is indeed the prototype for the monk's ascetic effort. *Aside:* Virginity is an imitation of Christ's life. *End of aside.* In its highest form, virginity is spiritual. This virginity requires the fullest possible following of the first commandment of love for God, and purity of intellect. For this reason, the state of spiritual virginity presupposes obedience, and it is unattainable without it. *Aside:* We know that monks who are obedient are always rich with prayer and dead to sin. Their mind is always illumined and possessed by the word of God. *End of aside.*

Christ was born of the Holy Spirit and the Virgin Mary. His birth did not involved sensual pleasure which, according to the ancient law of life after the Fall, is followed by the just sentence of death. Neither did Christ ever base His conduct on kinship "according to the flesh", but was consumed by zeal for His Father's House (*cf.* John 2:17). He offered the bonds of physical kinship as a sacrifice for the sake of His heavenly patrimony. *Aside:* Remember when Christ was at the wedding in Cana, and the Holy Virgin came to Him and said, "They have no wine". Despite the love He had for His Mother, He told her, "Woman, what have I to do with thee?" That is to say, he was not there to fulfil the will of His Mother but the will of His Heavenly Father. The Holy Virgin humbly accepted His wish, denying her own will; and Christ accepted this sacrifice of His Mother, and "His hour" came immediately, although He had said, "Mine hour is not yet come" (John 2:3–5). So the obedience of the Mother of God, cutting off her will when Christ was sharp with her, accelerated the coming of His hour; and He performed the first miracle at the wedding of Cana. *End of aside.*

The monk, following Christ's example in unwavering obedience, attains to humility and attracts the grace of God, which purifies the intellect. *Aside:* Because God gives grace to the humble and resists the proud (*cf.* Prov. 3:34 Lxx, Jas. 4:6, 1 Pet. 5:5). *End of aside.* This purification is a necessary precondition for spiritual virginity, as indicated by Christ's word mentioned above (John 2:3–5). Furthermore, grace brings the sweetness of love for Christ. These two effects of grace: the purification of the intellect and the sweetness of love for Christ instil in the monk's spirit the exigency to strive for spiritual virginity.

In no sense do these sweetening effects of grace descend to the level of fleshly satisfactions or pleasures. *Aside:* That is to say, he who finds the grace of God has more than pleasure, he has "ineffable joy";[11] and so, having found such a treasure of life, he will not look down to earth for substitutes. *End of aside.* These sweetening effects inspire unmitigated temperance, and they distance the monk's soul as if instinctively from every thought or act that does not conform to the divine love. They bring forth an unrestrained attraction towards God, and an unquenchable thirst for Him. In such a state, the monk desires to respond to the Lord's love by gratitude. *Aside:* That is why the monastery becomes a place of thanksgiving. *End of aside.* Just as He lived His earthly life in virginity, so does the monk follow His example, and imitates Him (*cf.* John 13:15). He breaks every natural bond, and freed from every care, seeks only the presence of the loving and living God.

According to the great Apostle Paul, our only concern in this life is to please the Lord perfectly, either by death or by life. *Aside:* He says that it is not important whether we are in the body or are apart from the body; what is important is to be pleasing to Him (*cf.* 2 Cor. 5:9). Or in another place, he says that whether we live or die is not important, what is important is that we are the Lord's (*cf.* Rom. 14:8). *End of aside.* This goal is feasible for the monk who is without earthly cares, and has "presented his body as a living sacrifice, holy, acceptable to God" (*cf.* Rom. 12:1). Living in this way the monk is not reconciled to the law of corruption and death, which came into the world through the pleasure originating in disobedience. He transforms every energy into a spiritual force, so as to keep his spirit unceasingly abiding with the Spirit of God. *Aside:* He transforms psychological energy into spiritual energy in order to keep his spirit unceasingly united to the Spirit of God, that is to say, in prayer. *End of aside.* A life of spiritual virginity is an exalted art and culture, whose fundamental value lies in the "guarding of the mind". The most important rule of this contest is not to surrender one's mind to passionate images and thoughts. *Aside:* Our Father Founder, Fr. Sophrony, used to give us a slogan from time to time: "Do not surrender the mind", that is to say, do not give the mind up to any thought, to any kind of passion. "Do not surrender the mind." In this is the beginning of everything. *End of aside.*

The living presence of God gradually dissolves the "garments of skin" and vouchsafes the monk to be born anew in the "kingdom which cannot be moved" (Heb. 12:28), where dwell "the spirits of just men made perfect" (Heb. 12:23), the spirits that have become "hypostatic". The divine presence destroys the fraudulent security of fleshly kinship, and brings death to an end in the monk's person. *Aside:* Death is destroyed in the person of the monk. In ordinary life, death is prolonged, but in the person of the monk death is destroyed. *End of aside.* The monk remains in the presence of God and thus crosses over into eternal life, becoming a temple of the Godhead.

The Vow of Poverty

The vow of poverty (Gk. *aktemosynē*) heals the madness of idolatry, the frenzy of the desire for possessions. This third condition of monastic life – non-acquisitiveness – is a natural consequence of observing obedience and chastity. *Aside:* You can see the links: obedience helps chastity; now obedience and chastity help non-acquisition. *End of aside.* The observance of these three vows has as its aim the attainment of pure prayer and the perfect likeness to Christ, the Son of God. During his earthly life, Christ denied himself any security from material things. He had "not where to lay his head" (Matt. 8:20, Luke 9:58). He taught people by deeds and words to "seek first the kingdom of God" (Matt. 6:33, Luke 12:31), and to "have no anxiety for the morrow" (Matt. 6:34). He pointed out to us that where our treasure is, there our heart is also (Matt. 6:21). *Aside:* Always we look at the Person of Christ and at the life of Christ on earth in order to find our bearings. *End of aside.*

Monastic poverty derives its power from obedience. By practising obedience, the monk is trained to disregard, for the sake of pleasing God, both his own soul and body and anything else in this life that is precious to him. His spirit is liberated in this way from the very desire for material possessions.[12] He attains spiritual poverty, that is, he is freed from making any "provision for the flesh" (Rom. 13:14), and the kingdom of heaven becomes his sole desire. He is thus healed of the alienation brought about by greed for possessions, and vanquishes the temptation of its sham security. He becomes "rich toward God" (Luke 12:21), and keeps his soul "unto life eternal" (John 12:25). He becomes one who, "having nothing, yet possesses all things", as St. Paul says (*cf.* 2 Cor. 6:10).

Thus, monasticism offers man the possibility of imitating Christ in humility, in crucifixion, *without being destroyed.* The more deeply he goes downward by the practice of obedience and repentance – and we have already explained at length how important and how precious it is to learn to go downwards – the higher he ascends, by the grace of Christ who exemplified this path.

All Christ's disciples, led by the Spirit of God, make their way downwards, towards the apex of the inverted pyramid, in order to be united with Him.[13] Monastic life has its aim precisely in this downward progress and union with Christ. The monk submits to "every ordinance of man for the Lord's sake" (1 Pet. 2:13), and united with the Head of the inverted pyramid, he receives as a gift the same state as that of Christ Himself, that is to say, he takes within himself the whole human race, and prays for it. This grace, the gift of man's "dilation" to the point of infinity, is the prize of the monastic vocation for those who fulfil it with exactitude. It transforms man into a true hypostasis, like the hypostasis of the new Adam, Christ.

This path could seem self-centred and, in a certain sense, such a claim is justified because, at first, man is in need of healing. Furthermore, being in a fallen state, he cannot have Christ with him, because Christ is not a "minister of sin" (Gal. 2:17). Whereas, when man struggles legitimately and persuades God that he is not a "dog" (*cf.* Matt. 7:6), God then accepts him as His son, and entrusts him with His "holy things", that is, with all the riches of His eternal life.

In man, Christ condescends and becomes a minister to the world, in the work of salvation. This is the most precious service offered by the monk to the world. The monk does not have a specific liturgical priesthood, but through his humble life of repentance he becomes the priest of his own salvation, and through his prayer for the world, he becomes a partaker in the royal priesthood of Christ, the Saviour of the whole Adam. He becomes a "royal priesthood" (1 Pet. 2:9).

The alienations or pseudo-supports created by the Fall of Adam became laws which determine how people relate to one another. They are recognized in terms of morality, and even considered valuable in people's eyes. Even so, it is obvious that they do not witness to anything except love for this world and for the flesh. Scripture says that this love is "enmity against God" (Rom. 8:7, *cf.* Jas. 4:4), and its tenets are an "abomination in the sight of God" (*cf.* Luke 16:15).

Aside: Often we see people suffering terrible persecutions from their own family when they decide to become monks and nuns. It is easy to understand why, if the Fall of man created universal laws, you have to become super-universal, supra-cosmic, in order to overcome these laws, like Christ who said, "Be of good cheer; I have overcome the world" (John 16:33). *End of aside.* It is also easy to understand why the foundations of the world are shaken when someone shows monastic leanings. He collides with laws, states and ideologies of cosmic dimensions. But when, with the grace of God, he makes the leap of faith – taking the decision to become a monk – and follows the Lord on the road of monasticism, he too, like Christ, overcomes the world. The unutterable gifts of the Holy Spirit make him supra-cosmic, and proclaim him an immortal hypostasis in the bosom of the Trinity: the Father, the Son, and the Holy Spirit.

Questions & Answers

Question 1: You had said that there are three types of thoughts: thoughts from God, natural thoughts, and thoughts from the devil. How do we learn to discern these thoughts in our daily life?

Answer 1: We said that there are three kinds of thoughts: from God, from the enemy, and natural thoughts. St. John of the Ladder, in order to give us an example of a thought coming from God, takes the thought of becoming a monk. Indirectly, of course, this means that the thought of becoming a monk is always from God. However, a person with such a thought has to sit down and calculate his forces: if he is able to go into war against the king with twenty thousand troops, when he only has ten thousand; or whether he has the means to build a tower without enough money. The thought is from God, but then we have also to evaluate our strength. As for thoughts coming from the enemy, we are all familiar with such thoughts, because we all have bad thoughts, and it is not necessary to talk about them. A natural thought would be, for example: I am thirsty, so I drink a glass of water; I am sleepy, so I sleep. That is why we do not have any commandment to do natural things. We have no commandment to eat, or to drink or to sleep, because these are natural activities. But we do have commandments for super-natural things, for super-natural activities, such as to love, to humble ourselves, to make sacrifices.

Now, the problem is how to discern the thoughts in our life, because the struggle against thoughts is a very difficult struggle, and it is the labour of monks, day and night. In the beginning, of course, we learn by going to confession once, twice, ten times, a hundred times – the struggle is explained to us, and so on. But slowly, slowly we acquire an inner perception that discerns the thoughts, and this inner perception is installed in us through the pain of the heart. That is why the monk is happy when his heart is painful. And the heart experiences pain from the prayer of repentance, from fasting, from vigil, and from bearing shame in confession. All these things make the heart painful, and when the heart is painful, assuredly, man is able to discern the thoughts. St. Barsanuphius the Great assures us that without contrition of heart we cannot discern the thoughts. Therefore, with contrition of heart we are able to discern the thoughts because, as we said, contrition leads to humility, humility attracts grace, and grace does the work for us. St. Paul says, "I laboured more abundantly than they all: yet not I, but the grace of God which was with me" (1 Cor. 15:10). So it is very precious for the monk always to have even a little pain in his heart. Woe unto him, if he ceases to feel his heart! He would be exposed to danger, and to falling. But when the heart is "circumcised" with the pain of repentance, then he can stand against all the wiles of the enemy. That is the "circumcision of the heart" that St. Paul was preaching to the first Christians (Rom. 2:29), encouraging them to know *only* Christ, and Him crucified (*cf.* 1 Cor. 2:2), that is to say, His way of going down.

Question 2: How can we cut off the passions?

Answer 2: This is what I have just said. Fr. Sophrony was always of the same mind as St. Barsanuphius. I remember the first year I went to the monastery, he said to me, "If you want to cut off the passions, if you want to uproot the passions, learn to weep before God." Spiritual weeping is the most efficacious prayer; it immediately "crushes" the heart, not in a destructive way, but in a healing way: it brings spiritual pain to the heart. I remember when I first went to the monastery, Fr. Sophrony kept repeating this to me, "If you want to uproot the passions, learn to weep". I tried, but I could not. I thought to myself, "How is this done?" I would keep trying, forcing myself. But that was not the way. Then I happened to read the *Catechism* of St. Symeon the New Theologian, and when I read *Catechesis* XXX, "On Penitence",[14] having also in mind all that Fr. Sophrony had told me, I began to grasp how this is done.

Monks are encouraged to weep in their cells in order to bear in their hearts always the "mark of Christ", which is spiritual pain – contrition – and therefore to be unassailable. Perhaps "unassailable" is not the appropriate word, because we are always assailable; but not to be easily taken into captivity by the enemy. That is why monks are encouraged to weep in their cells. But this is not a morbid, psychological weeping. Fr. Sophrony used to tell us that when he was on the Holy Mountain, if the fathers saw a young monk, or any monk, being sad in his conduct with his brethren, they would say, "Ah, that monk did not weep during the night. If he had wept in the night, he would be happy and pleasant in his conduct with his brethren." Do not forget that St. Paul exhorts the brethren to be pleasant to each other (*cf.* Rom. 12:10, Eph. 4:32).[15] So spiritual weeping is achieved by the grace of God. And grace, already present in spiritual weeping, brings such great comfort and consolation that we become like those that dream. We are comforted by the comfort of the Comforter just like those that dream, as the Psalmist says (*cf.* Ps. 126:1).

And it is the same with the downward way. From the moment we put our hand to the plough of repentance – repentance being the fruit of the Cross and Resurrection of Christ – there is great joy, *which is inseparable from true repentance.* We cannot separate the Cross from the Resurrection or the Resurrection from the Cross – they inseparable, they go together. And when we give ourselves over to repentance, the Spirit of God *immediately* consoles us, otherwise it would be impossible to follow the Way of Christ. "Blessed are they that mourn: for they shall be comforted" (Matt. 5:4). This is the second step of the ladder to spiritual accomplishment, which the Lord Himself gave us. The Beatitudes, which we sing in every Liturgy, are a ladder of ascent to divine perfection. We begin with the first step, by seeing our spiritual poverty: "Blessed are the poor in spirit: for theirs is the kingdom of heaven" (Matt. 5:3). When we see our spiritual poverty, we become possessed of such a strong desire to be clothed with the spotless holiness of God that we begin to mourn. And so we come to the second step of the Beatitudes, that of spiritual mourning, and so on. In the Sermon on the Mount, we see that the first and sure foundation of divine ascent is the recognition of our spiritual poverty in and through the perception of the spotless and blameless holiness of God, and that the last and highest step is when we are persecuted for the sake of God, "for righteousness' sake" (*cf.* Matt. 5:10). Now, in practising the way of "going down" – as we explained earlier – the monk in effect becomes his own persecutor, and in fact persecutes himself more than anybody else could persecute him. We must not forget that persecution is also involved in the Way of the Lord: "If they have persecuted me, they will also persecute you", said the Lord (John 15:20). So, if persecution is the Way of the Lord, we must not forget that if the Lord was persecuted, we too shall be persecuted. And St. Paul says that all those who desire to live a godly life shall be persecuted (*cf.* 2 Tim. 3:12). But here, in America, we are not persecuted; we are even praised and exalted if we show even the slightest piety. And so here it is even more necessary to become the persecutors of our own pride, of our own arrogance, of our own fallen state.

Question 3: Father, if I understood you correctly, you said that the fear of death can encourage sin, whereas, as Christians, we are to have the fear of God. Would you elaborate a little further on this, please?

Answer 3: Yes. I was unable to expand on this question earlier, because it is based on a tremendous theory. The entire theory of redemption is contained in St. Maximus the Confessor's *Letter LXI to Thalassius,* an epistle of no more than six to eight pages.[16] You see, the sentence of sin is death. When man fell into sin death followed. And he fell into sin because he satisfied the pleasure of His eyes, the pleasure of the desire of the fruit of the tree. So there is pleasure, there is sin, and the sentence of sin, which is death. When that happened, and he saw himself in the state of death, man became afraid. He lost the ineffable enjoyment of the presence of God in Paradise, he realized that he was devastated, and he began to look for something to hold on to. And when he perceived all of this, he became selfish.

In the primordial state before the Fall, God fed the spirit of man, and the spirit of man fed his soul, and the soul passed the energy of God even to the body. When man was separated from the spirit of God, the soul was no longer fed from Above, and the soul became a parasite to the body. The soul was being nourished by the body instead of the body being nourished by the soul, and man became poor, devastated. And when man saw this, he became selfish, he began to fear death, and sought to devise ways to survive. But this was not possible without God, and the more he invented pleasures in order to survive the threat of death, and to prolong his life, the more entangled he found himself in death. The more pleasures he invented, the more death increased. And that went on through the whirlsome flow of the ages, until God in His humility, in His wisdom and in His omnipotence found a way to abolish this law of pleasure, sin and death, which was introduced by the Fall.

Now, a new beginning was needed, a beginning that should not have pleasure as its starting point, so that sin would be out of the way and therefore death out of place. And this the Lord did by becoming man from the Holy Virgin, through the Holy Spirit. We all have been conceived in sin, in accordance with that ancient law: "In sin did my mother conceive me", says the Psalmist (Ps. 51:5). And therefore we are all subject to death. The Lord found another way of making a new beginning, a new human root – the new Adam. He was incarnate of the Holy Virgin, fully man, but not through the conception of the will of man and of the flesh. St. John refers to this, when he talks about those who are born of the Holy Spirit, by saying: "As many as received him, to them gave he power to become the sons of God, even to them that believe on his name: Which were born, not of blood, nor of the will of the flesh, nor of the will of man, but of God" (John 1:13). He says this concerning our spiritual birth, the birth of the faithful in Him; but this is what He first did Himself in an absolute way. He began with the Holy Virgin: He took human flesh from the Holy Virgin, without the involvement of pleasure, and therefore without sin. And so death was alien to the Lord. That is why in the garden of Gethsemane it was not because of the fear of death that He prayed thus to the Father, "Let this cup pass from me" (Matt. 26:39). He wanted to show us that death was *unnatural* for Him, for He had neither been conceived by sin, nor had He ever committed sin in His life. Death was therefore unnatural to Him, and yet He consents to drink the Cup of the Father, to die an unjust death in our place (cf. 1 Pet. 3:18). And because the death He suffered was unjust, death suffered punishment in His Person – it was abolished (cf. 2 Tim. 1:10). What He has done is for all of us; it is a free gift. We only have to follow Him, and to clothe ourselves with Him, through baptism (cf. Gal. 3:27), to place ourselves in His Body, which is the Church, and in which Body dwells all the fullness of the divinity (cf. Eph. 1:22–23).

So, by making a new start, where there is no sin, no pleasure and therefore no death, and by voluntarily accepting to die an unjust death for us, Christ destroyed death (cf. 1 Cor. 15:26). That is why when we believe in Him, we make death unjust for us, because, through the gift of His grace, we cause sin to cease in ourselves. Therefore, strictly speaking, those who have accepted baptism, and kept the grace of baptism, should not die even a physical death: they die "by economy", by a special dispensation, says St. Maximus the Confessor, the greatest theologian of our Church. They die by a special dispensation, so that the same judgment of Christ might be repeated in them, that death also be put to shame in them – as unjust. This is the case with the martyrs: no one has ever doubted that a martyr is a saint. Through their faith and love for God, because of the unjust death suffered by them, death has no power or dominion over them. That is why martyrs, as we see in the case of St. Stephen the first martyr, go straight to heaven. In the Acts of the Apostles, we read that even before he died, St. Stephen saw "the heavens opened" (Acts 7:56). And in those faithful, who keep the grace of baptism and are continually fed by the Body and Blood of Christ, the same judgment takes place that occurred in the Person of our Lord Jesus Christ. Every time we perform a commandment, every time we participate worthily in the Body and Blood of Christ, we abolish death in us, we make death unjust. "O death, where is thy sting?", says St. Paul (1 Cor. 15:55), and St. John Chrysostom repeats his words in his sermon for Easter night.[17] Through Christ a new law of existence was inaugurated. What begins with an unjust death, or even with unjust suffering that leads to death, has glory, says St. Peter (cf. 1 Pet. 4:13), and leads to life. But what begins with pleasure and sin leads to eternal death. And what begins with unjust suffering, innocent suffering for the sake of God's commandment, leads to condemnation of death and life eternal. This is the new law, which the Lord established by His voluntary Passion, Cross and Resurrection.

Question 4: When speaking of obedience, you had said that this kind of obedience can only exist in monasteries. Why is this so?

Answer 4: Obedience, as a specific and total sacrifice, is found only in monasteries. *But to a certain measure,* it can also be found in people living in the world, because (we must not forget) in the final analysis, obedience means the keeping of the commandment of Christ. And it is the commandment that leads to eternal life; it is the commandment of Christ which matters. As I have already indicated, there is not much difference between monasticism and Christian life in general. The difference lies in the intensity in which we live the mystery of our faith. Oftentimes, though, we find Christians in the world who have an admirable spiritual tension, and who receive many gifts of the Holy Spirit. The Gospel of Christ has the power to change the lives of people anywhere and everywhere, not only in monasteries – otherwise it would be useless. Monastic obedience, however, because it is such a voluntary act, becomes a total sacrifice, and so abolishes the alienation which occurred through the Fall.

Of course, there is obedience even in the family. And when you go to your bishop or your priest and ask for advice about something which is important – we must not go for every little thing, because then it becomes a distortion or a monstrous way of life, but only when we are faced with a real dilemma – and you do what he says, then the sacrament of obedience is at work. I like to speak two or three times with young couples before they marry, in order to give them some principles to have in mind, as a foundation, because they do not receive any good thoughts in the world. When for example they have a minor disagreement, and, because they do not know how to see themselves correctly, they go to some friend or stranger even to talk about their problem, and receive such destructive advice that, if in the beginning there was a "little crack" in their home, now there is a complete demolition of it. But the goal of marriage is selfless love. Through marriage, we are taught selfless love, which is an image of the Love of God. Not to care for ourselves, but for the other – that is selfless love. Of course there must be obedience, and a competition: who will do the will of the other more? Then, truly, even marriage becomes a paradise, when there is this competition: "What does she want? That is what I will do!" "What does he want? That is what I will do!" In the end it will turn out that the will of both of them is done. It is essential not to keep any secrets from one another, to be transparent before one another. When one does something, the other should know about it as well. This protects them. Just as in the monastery, we refer everything to our spiritual father, in order to be protected, so also in marriage, if we refer our life to one another, as a couple, we are protected. And we must learn to see our own fault, when we fall into some argument, for example. I remember that a couple came to Fr. Sophrony – they were in strife – and it was obvious that the one was more at fault than the other. And Fr. Sophrony asked the wife, "What percentage do you think you are at fault?" She replied, "Only five percent, and my husband is ninety-five percent at fault". And Fr. Sophrony said to her, "Then correct that five percent, and let us see if the ninety-five percent remains!" This is what so often makes the work of a spiritual father a thankless task: time and again he has to point out the negative aspect, the wrong, of someone, in order to bring that person to an understanding of the wrong, so that he is able to take the blame upon himself. Because only then will there be healing. Unless we take the blame upon ourselves, we shall find no rest, as the monks of the fourth century say.

Question 5: What is the status of a person who becomes a monk, and then for some reason goes back into the world?

Answer 5: You are living a natural life now, a life "according to nature" (*kata physin*). When you become a monk, you try to live a "supernatural life" (*hyper physin*). When you fall, and go back into the world, you live a life that is against nature, an "unnatural life" (*para physin*), because the covenant made with the Lord at one's monastic profession has been broken, and therefore one remains bereft of grace. Of course, there is always repentance. But you know, when we sin voluntarily we may seek for repentance and not find it. We must not take it easy, and say, "Ah, I will sin and repent later", because if we sin voluntarily, we may not find repentance afterwards. Like Esau, we may seek repentance "with tears", and yet not find the "place of repentance", as St. Paul says (*cf.* Heb. 12:17).

You see, that is why the Lord said that we enter the kingdom through the "strait gate", through the "narrow way" (Matt. 7:14). Monasticism tries to create this "narrow way" for us to go through, and to leave behind the "old skin", like the snake. The snake goes through a narrow hole in order to leave behind its old skin, and it comes out with a new one. Monasticism tries to organize life in a way that will give the monk opportunities to endure certain hardships, so that he may thereby leave behind the "old skin". But this does not apply only to monasticism. St. Paul says to Timothy, "endure hardness, as a good soldier of Jesus Christ" (2 Tim. 2:3). That is to say, every soldier of Christ, all Christians, should endure hardship in order to overcome the old man.

NOTES

* First published in English as "Fidelity to the Monastic Vows Heals the Estrangement Brought About by Original Sin", in *Christ, Our Way and Our Life, op. cit.,* pp. 132–141.

1. *Cf. Principles of Orthodox Asceticism,* trans. Rosmary Edmonds, published in *The Orthodox Ethos: Studies in Orthodoxy,* Vol. 1, edited by A. J. Philippou (Oxford: Holywell Press, 1964), p. 271.

2. *Cf. ibid.* p. 270.

3. *Cf. On Prayer, op. cit.,* p. 155.

4. "Let this mind be in you, which was also in Christ Jesus: Who, being in the form of God, thought it not robbery to be equal with God: But made himself of no reputation, and took upon him the form of a servant, and was made in the likeness of men."

5. *Cf. Principles, op. cit.,* p. 272. "Life is in his will", Ps. 30:5 Lxx, and *cf.* Rom. 12:2.

6. *Cf. We Shall See Him, op. cit.,* p. 41.

7. *Cf. Principles, op. cit.,* pp. 271–272.

8. *Cf. We Shall See Him, op. cit.,* p. 225.

9. *On Prayer, op. cit.,* p. 88; *Principles, op. cit.,* pp. 272, 275.

10. *Cf. Saint Silouan, op. cit.,* p. 85.

11. First Prayer, in the *Prayers of Thanksgiving to be used after partaking of the Holy Communion.*

12. *Cf. Principles, op. cit.,* pp. 271, 273.

13. *Cf. Saint Silouan, op. cit.,* pp. 237–239.

14. See *Discourses (Catecheses)* XXX, in *Symeon the New Theologian: The Discourses, op. cit.,* pp. 318–328.

15. "Be kindly affectioned one to another with brotherly love; in honour preferring one another" (Eph. 4:32); "And be ye kind one to another, tender-hearted, forgiving one another, even as God for Christ's sake hath forgiven you" (Rom. 12:10).

16. *Letter LXI to Thalassius* (PG 90:628–641). The heading to *Letter LXI* runs as follows: *"For the time is come that judgment must begin at the house of God: and if it first begin at us, what shall the end be of them that obey not the gospel of God? And if the righteous scarcely be saved, where shall the ungodly and the sinner appear?"* (1 Pet. 4:17–18). *On the Meaning of "The time is come that judgment must begin at the house of God", and "If the righteous scarcely be saved".*

17. In his famous *Paschal Homily.*

THE END

AND TO THE ONE GOD IN TRINITY
THE FATHER, THE SON, AND THE HOLY SPIRIT
BE GLORY